AF553938

TEACHING LANGUAGE ARTS SUCCESSFULLY

ENCYCLOPAEDIA OF TEACHING - VI

TEACHING LANGUAGE ARTS SUCCESSFULLY

By

Dr. Marlow Ediger
M.S. Education, Ph.D.
Professor Emeritus in Education
Truman State University
Box 417, 201 W, 22nd St
North Newton KS 67117
United States of America

&

Dr. Digumarti Bhaskara Rao
M.Sc., M.A., M.A., M.Ed., Ph.D.
Reader & Research Director
R.V.R. College of Education
Srinivasa Nagar Colony
Guntur–522 006
(India)

DISCOVERY PUBLISHING HOUSE PVT. LTD.
NEW DELHI-110 002

Reprinted – 2019
First Published - 2007

ISBN: 978-93-5056-516-2 (Set)

ISBN: 978-81-7141-678-3

Teaching Language Arts Successfully

Published by:
DISCOVERY PUBLISHING HOUSE PVT. LTD.
4383/4B, Ansari Road, Darya Ganj
New Delhi-110 002 (India)
Phone: +91-11-23279245, 23253475; 43596065
E-mail: discoverybooksindia@gmail.com
discoverypublishinghouse@gmail.com
web: www.discoverypublishinggroup.com

Printed at:
Infinity Imaging Systems
Delhi

To

a Great Teacher

Mr. Gadde Mangaiah

Preface

Teaching language effectively is a major concern to many teachers throughout the world. Several practices are in use and efforts are under-way to enhance the status of language teaching and learning. As there are so many languages across the globe, it is better to understand the ways and means of successful teaching of language arts.

This book on successful teaching of language arts is written for teachers teaching presently as well as for prospective teachers. As a result of comprehending the contents, hopefully pre-service prospective teachers and in-service professional teachers will benefit well in class setting. Surely, this book will enlighten every language teacher to help each learner achieve optimally in the language arts.

Marlow Ediger
Bhaskara Rao

Contents

1

The Language Arts Curriculum

Teachers, principals, and supervisors must think of relevant ways of organising the language arts curriculum. One can perceive of different patterns of curriculum organisation being represented on a continuum. Thus, the separate subjects curriculum would be represented by a point on a line toward one end of the continuum. Toward the other end of the continuum, a point on this same line would be represented by the integrated curriculum. Somewhat in between these two points on a line the correlated and fused approaches in developing the language arts curriculum would be inherent.

The Separate Subjects Language Arts Curriculum

In the separate subjects language arts curriculum, the following basic principles would be emphasised in teaching-learning situations:

1. Reading, writing, listening, and speaking should be emphasised in teaching-learning situations as being separate facets of vocabulary development. Each of these vocabularies would be developed in isolation in the class setting;
2. In learning activities involving writing, each of the language arts areas of grammar, handwriting, spelling, capitalisations, punctuation, and content might be stressed in isolation in teaching-learning situations;

3. Reading instruction may be divided into the following categories: phonics instruction and other word recognition techniques, comprehension of content, and oral reading. Diverse purposes in reading may also be stressed in isolation from other curriculum areas in the elementary school. These purposes would include:

(a) reading to acquire facts;

(b) gaining a sequence of ideas;

(c) reading to follow directions;

(d) reading critically and creatively;

(e) acquiring main ideas and generalisations.

There are selected advantages in emphasising the separate subjects language arts curriculum.

1. Pupils who experience difficulty at a particular time in a specific facet of the language arts, such as punctuation may receive needed help and guidance;
2. There is a tendency to emphasise each specific facet of the language arts in teaching-learning situations, such as capitalisation, punctuation, usage, grammar, spelling and handwriting.

Disadvantages in relying too heavily upon the separate subjects language arts curriculum may be the following:

1. Each facet of the language arts becomes too fragmented such as separating phonics instruction from the actual act of reading, or discussing criteria for effective oral communication of content without emphasizing these standards in ongoing learning experiences involving speaking;
2. There may be very little transfer of learning from one situation to another if, for example, pupils are taught skills pertaining to oral communication of content and yet do not use these skills in various kinds of speaking activities within different curriculum areas in the elementary school. Thus, the separate subjects approach in organising the language arts

curriculum would not be a relevant trend unless the teacher diagnoses a specific difficulty pupils may have, such as formation of letters in handwriting, for example, and works in the direction of remediation.

The Correlated Curriculum

In the correlated curriculum, the teacher could stress the relationship of two or more areas of the language arts curriculum. Examples of the correlated curriculum in the language arts are the following:

1. the teacher stressing quality handwriting in the area of spelling;
2. improved proficiency in speaking emphasized in time devoted to oral reading;
3. minimal learning in punctuation stressed at the time that experience charts are developed by pupils with teacher guidance;
4. proper capitalisation emphasized as being important while learners are writing business or friendly letters.

Advantages given for the correlated language arts curriculum are the following:

1. Pupils perceive that content is related such as standards pertaining to speaking and to oral reading;
2. Learners have opportunities to transfer learning from one facet of the language arts to a different facet;
3. Fewer separate learnings are needed in the correlated language arts curriculum as compared to the separate subjects approach.

Disadvantages of the correlated language arts curriculum may be the following:

1. It does not relate enough of the different language arts areas;
2. There are times when a specific area of the language curriculum needs emphasising such as the correct spelling of a word within a selected context.

The Fused Curriculum

The fused language-arts curriculum relates its component parts into a broader whole as compared to the correlated approach. Thus, in developing an experience chart by pupils with teacher leadership in a reading readiness programme, the following language arts skills will be emphasized:

1. speaking by involved learners;
2. perceiving content being written on the chalkboard by the teacher;
3. seeing the teacher write punctuation marks in sentences containing experiences given by the pupils;
4. listening to the content presented by learners in the class setting;
5. reading the completed content by involved learners.

Thus, the listening, speaking, reading, and writing vocabularies are brought in and developed in the above language arts learning activities involving the fused curriculum.

Advantages in utilising the fused curriculum in the language arts involve the following:

1. Pupils perceive diverse facets of the language arts to be interrelated;
2. Learning becomes more meaningful to pupils as facets of the language arts are brought in as the need arises;
3. Artificial barriers pertaining to separating diverse facets of the language arts are no longer in evidence;
4. Less drill is in evidence when the fused language arts curriculum is used as compared to the separate subjects approach;
5. Learnings appear to become more to become more realistic when content is taught as being related as compared to isolating diverse facets of the language arts.

Disadvantages of the fused approach in developing the language arts curriculum may pertain to the following:

1. A specific facet of the language arts curriculum such as capitalisation may be overlooked when content is perceived as being related in terms of usage;
2. It may be more difficult to determine sequence in diverse facets of the language arts, such as sequence or order in the teaching of spelling.

The Integrated Curriculum

The integrated curriculum in the language arts would go a step further as compared to the fused approach in having pupils perceive content as being related. Thus, the integrated language arts curriculum would stress the following:

1. Subject matter loses its boundaries and borders;
2. Understandings, skills, and attitudes in the language arts are developed as needed;
3. Diverse curriculum areas such as mathematics, social studies, science, health, physical education, art, and music are brought into the language arts as needed;
4. The integrated curriculum may be called the functional curriculum since content may be utilised in problem-solving situations.

Grouping Pupils for Instruction

There certainly is a close relationship between the methods used in grouping pupils for instruction and approaches utilised in organising the curriculum, e.g., separate subjects, correlated, fused, or integrated language arts learnings. Teachers, principals, and supervisors must think of the best approaches in grouping and guiding learners to achieve optimum development. Professional educators need to be highly knowledgeable pertaining to the philosophy behind each method utilised in grouping pupils for instruction. A specific plan or plans adopted in grouping pupils for instruction in selected schools should be based on sound criteria with which educators agree.

Open Space Education

Open space education has become rather popular in the United States. Basic generalisations pertaining to open space education would be the following:

1. Pupils in small groups work at learning centers in the class setting;
2. Learners may select which center to work at as well as select the task to pursue from a selected learning center;
3. Pupils are to learn to respect each other at the different centers of learning;
4. Humaneness in the learning environment is stressed as being very important;
5. Pupils order their own achievement in selecting activities;
6. The teacher structures the learning environment from which learners may choose ongoing experiences.

The following are selected examples of learning centers in the language arts:

1. a reading center in which pupils individually may select a book to read of their own choosing;
2. a writing center wherein pupils may select a picture about which to write;
3. a speaking center containing suggested topics to speak on. A cassette recorder may give a learner feedback pertaining to his own achievement;
4. a listening center in which learners listen to selected tapes of their own choosing. A task card at this center may help learners assess their own achievement in listening;
5. a spelling center in which pupils may select a list of words to master in spelling and use in functional writing situations;
6. a dramatisation center wherein pupils look at possibilities listed on a task card for dramatising and proceed with their choice;
7. other possible learning centers may include a phonics center, a poetry center and a construction or art center relating to ongoing experiences in the language arts.

Non-graded Schools

All public schools in the United States should deemphasise grade levels in teaching-learning situations. For example, selected third graders read better than certain sixth graders. Or, a specific group of fourth grade pupils achieve at a higher level in spelling as compared to a selected set of sixth graders. Thus, grade levels in many cases may mean very little in terms of learner achievement. What is important is that new learnings are being achieved by each learner and success is inherent in learning. Also, each individual pupil needs to achieve to his or her own unique optimal rate of achievement.

All public schools need to work in the direction of being ungraded. Each learner then would achieve relevant objectives in different facets of the language arts regardless of age level. Continuous progress should be in evidence for each learner.

Advantages of the non-graded school may be the following:

1. Grade levels are not considered when determining a child's present level of achievement. If, for example, a pupil is eleven years of age and achieves to his/her optimum by reading content written on what is normally the third or fourth grade level, these materials must then be used in ongoing learning experiences;
2. Ideally, pupils individually should experience continuous progress in teaching-learning situations. Feelings of success on the part of individual learners are then an inherent part of ongoing learning activities.

Disadvantages in utilising the nongraded concept in grouping pupils for instruction may be the following:

1. Parents and the lay public tend to think of grade levels and graded text books in the school setting. (There are implications here for educating the lay public in terms of changing concepts pertaining to education.)

2. Teachers must keep relevant records pertaining to each child's achievement. Thus, new learning experiences should not duplicate nor be too far removed from previous learnings obtained by individual learners. Keeping adequate records for each learner at each step along the way in achievement can add to the heavy work load of professional teachers;
3. Learners tend to think they need, for example, to study from sixth grade commercially prepared textbooks if they are in the sixth grade. Many learners feel this way if these textbooks do or do not meet their personal needs. (Thus, learner attitudes also need to be changed in terms of interacting with learning activities or diverse achievement levels.)

Team Teaching and the Pupil

Team teaching has been a valuable asset in improving the public school curriculum. To be called a teaching team, the following criteria must be adhered to:

1. Two or more teachers must plan together the objectives, learning experiences, and assessment procedures for a given set of pupils;
2. Pupils are taught, generally, in large group sessions committee work, and individual study.

Advantages given for team teaching include the following:

1. More than one mind is involved in determining what to teach (goals of instruction), as well as the means used to have pupils achieve desired ends (learning experiences) and how learners are to be assessed (evaluation);
2. Teachers may learn from each other in a democratic planning session (in-service education is then in-evidence);
3. Selected teachers may do better in teaching when other professionals on the team assist in planning for instruction as well as help in evaluating teaching performance in the class setting.

Disadvantages of team teaching include the following:

1. There are teachers who would prefer not being members of a teaching team;
2. Selected teachers may feel uncomfortable teaching in the presence of other adults;
3. Planning sessions may be undemocratic and the thinking of one team member alone is then implemented in teaching-learning situations.

The Self-Contained Classroom

The self-contained classroom has much to offer in teaching-learning situations. Thus, a given teacher may teach a set of pupils in most of the curriculum areas, except perhaps music and art. The teacher in the self-contained classroom can:

1. get to know each pupil well and use this data to do a better job of providing for individual differences,
2. help pupils perceive that diverse curriculum areas in the elementary school are related;
3. keep the amount of time devoted to teaching each curriculum area flexible, thus using time flexibility for each curriculum area in providing for individual differences.

Disadvantages given for the self-contained classroom concept in teaching may be the following:

1. A specific teacher cannot teach all curriculum areas in the elementary school well. Thus, a teacher may not be interested in or have the skills to teach a specific curriculum area as compared to other areas;
2. Teachers need to specialise more in the teaching of a specific curriculum area. Adequate course work in content and methods should be taken by a teacher on the college or university level to qualify for a teaching position in a specific curriculum area such as the language arts.

Departmentalised Teaching

On the intermediate grade levels, there are educators who emphasise more of departmentalisation in terms of grouping pupils for instruction. Thus, in a departmentalised setup the teacher may:

1. become proficient in teaching one curriculum area only, such as the language areas;
2. obtain preservice training on the undergraduate level qualifying the future teacher to specialise in teaching a specific curriculum area only. This individual would take the necessary professional education sequence as well as have adequate background training in such areas as semantics, linguistics, literature, speech correction, language development, public speaking, and diagnosing and remediation of problem areas in the language arts;
3. make fewer preparations for each day of teaching since language arts only or a different curriculum area will be taught.

Disadvantages of the departmentalised plan in grouping pupils for instruction may be the following:

1. The teacher does not get to know each pupil well enough to do a good job of teaching. There are, for example, too many learners that are taught in a given school day;
2. Content pertaining to the language arts may become too isolated from other curriculum areas such as social studies, mathematics, health, and science. Pupils should have ample opportunities to notice that diverse curriculum areas may be perceived as being interrelated;
3. Time devoted to each curriculum area is rigid. Pupils, for example, may spend forty to fifty minutes on the intermediate grade level where language arts is taught. After this amount of time has elasped, pupils must move to a different classroom for learning activities pertaining to another curriculum area.

Homogeneous Grouping and the Language Arts

Selected teachers of language arts prefer homogeneous grouping of pupils as compared to heterogeneous grouping. Thus, learners in a classroom will be more uniform in language arts achievement in homogeneous as compared to grouping pupils heterogeneously. The following, among others, may be advantages of homogeneous grouping:

1. It may be easier to teach a given set of learners where the range of achievement is not, as great as compared to other plans for grouping learners for instructional purposes;
2. Learners individually may not look down upon others as much whose capability and/or achievement is not extremely different;
3. Pupils may be challenged more in learning where achievement is more uniform in the class setting as compared to heterogeneous grouping;
4. The class as a whole may be taught more frequently as compared to heterogeneous grouping.

Disadvantages pertaining to homogeneous grouping may be the following:

1. The class setting may be more democratic if mixed achievement levels are in evidence;
2. There still are marked differences in achievement of a given set of learners even if homogeneous grouping is being tried;
3. Pupils must become accustomed to being with others regardless of capacity and/or achievement levels. In society individuals tend to interact with others regardless of factors pertaining to language arts achievement;
4. The teacher may teach learners as if they are uniform in achievement.

Heterogeneous Grouping and the Language Arts

Selected educators recommend that pupils be grouped heterogeneously. Thus, a greater range of achievement in the class setting will be true in the language arts as compared to using homogeneous grouping. Advantages given for heterogeneous grouping may be the following:

1. Pupils can learn from each other regardless of capacity and/or achievement levels. These learnings may include getting along with others in a atmosphere of respect involving individuals who may be greatly different from others in many ways;
2. Teachers need to provide for individual differences regardless of the method used to group pupils for instruction;
3. Provision can be made for individual differences by using open space education, individualised reading, programmed learning, and other innovations in individualised instruction regardless of the plan used in grouping pupils for instruction.

Disadvantages which may be listed for heterogeneous grouping include the following:

1. It may be difficult to teach the class as whole at selected intervals due to an extreme range of pupil achievement in the class setting;
2. Gifted and talented pupils may not achieve to their optimum when slow learners take up much of the teacher's time in teaching-learning situations;
3. Fast learners may not appreciate the contributions of slow learners in the class setting.

Schools Without Walls

The alternative school movement was rather popular in the United States. One type or kind of alternative school is the school without walls. Basically, all public schools have used the "schools without walls" concept in teaching-learning situations. Thus, purposeful excursions of field trips have become an important part of the curriculum. The use of field trips or excursions in teaching-learning situations may be represented on a continuum using a line. On this continuum, selected schools may strongly believe in and implement the use of many excursions in the curriculum. Toward the other end of this continuum, a public school may not implement any field trips related to units of study during a given school year. Most of the learnings gained by pupils in a school without walls take place in the community. These would be purposeful learnings that are planned in class setting. Learning obtained in the community may be assessed in the class setting. Listening, speaking, reading, and writing vocabularies can be emphasised thoroughly in the school without walls. Advantages given for schools without walls may be the following:

1. Realistic learnings are definitely in evidence with the use of excursions and field trips into the community;
2. Purpose is inherent in learning if pupils with teacher guidance have planned excursions;
3. School is not separated from society in that realistic learnings in the community can be obtained by pupils;
4. Students sequence their own learnings through teacher-pupil planning involving objectives, learning experiences, and evaluation procedures;
5. Interest in learning should be high on the part of students since they are in involved in planning the curriculum;
6. Students must be responsible individuals since their concerns are important in terms of what is to be studied.

Disadvantages inherent in the school without walls concept in teaching learners may be the following:

1. This method of teaching may not harmonize with the learning styles of selected pupils. This would be true of any approach in grouping pupils for instruction as well as methods used in teaching;

2. Selected learners may not be responsible enough to participate in planning the curriculum;
3. Pupils may lose out on the basic in each of the curriculum areas.

The Dual Progress Plan

The dual progress plan in grouping pupils for instruction has much to recommend itself. On the intermediate grade levels social studies and the language arts may be taught as being related by one teacher. These two curriculum areas, as well as health, and physical education are taught on a graded or grade level basis. Science, mathematics, music, art, and foreign languages are taught using a departmentalised system in grouping pupils for instruction and are taught on a non-graded level of instruction. Intermediate grade pupils may experience both the self-contained concept as well departmentalisation in grouping practices.

Advantages for the dual progress plan in grouping pupils for instruction may be the following:

1. It is a more gradual way to introduce pupils to departmentalised teaching which is typical on the junior high school level. The change from the elementary to the junior high years may be abrupt if the self-contained room is emphasised from kindergarten through grade six and departmentalisation is stressed in grades seven through twelve;
2. Teacher who like to teach a specific curriculum area such as science or mathematics may do so;
3. Pupils may experience teaching-learning situations from more teachers as compared to the self-contained classroom.

In Summary

Teachers, principals, and supervisors must become very knowledgeable and conversant about different approaches utilised in organising the curriculum. Thus, the separate subjects, the correlated, the fused, and the integrated curriculum represent diverse ways of organising each of the curriculum areas in the elementary school. There are advantages as well as disadvantages in using any one of these approaches in organising the language arts as well as other curriculum areas in the school.

Related to the problem of how each curriculum area should be organised in the school is the question pertaining to ways of grouping pupils for instructional purposes. Thus, teachers, principals, and supervisors must assess each of the following approaches in grouping pupils for instruction before any single plan is adopted:

1. open space education and learning centers;
2. the nongraded school;
3. team teaching;
4. the self-contained classroom;
5. departmentalised grouping of learners;
6. homogeneous grouping;
7. heterogenous grouping;
8. schools without walls;
9. the dual progress plan.

REFERENCES

Anderson, Paul S. *Linguistics in the Elementary School Classroom*. New York: The Macmillan Company, 1971.

Anderson, Paul S. *Language Skills in Elementary Education*. Third Edition. New York: The Macmillan Company, 1979.

Beane, James A., Conrad F. Toepfer, Jr., and Samuel J. Alessi, Jr. *Curriculum Planning and Development*. Boston: Allyn and Bacon, Inc., 1986.

Berman, Louise M. *New Priorities in the Curriculum*. Columbus, Ohio: Charles E Merrill Publishing Company, 1968. Chapter Eleven.

Ediger, Marlow and Digumarti Bhaskara Rao (2002), *Language Arts Curriculum*, New Delhi, India: Discovery Publishing House, 2002.

Frost, Joe L., and G. Thomas Rowlan. (Eds.). *The Elementary School, Principles of Problems. Boston: Houghton Mifflin Company, 1969.* Chapter Thirteen.

Oliva, Pete. F. *Developing the Curriculum.* Boston: Little Brown and Company, 1982.

Saylor, J. Galen, and William M. Alexander. *Planning Curriculum for Schools.* New York: Holt, Rinehart, and Winston, Inc., 1974. Chapters Five, Six, and Seven.

Taba, Hilda. *Curriculum Development, Theory and Practice.* New York: Harcourt Brace, & World, Inc., 1962. Chapters One and Twenty-one.

Walter, Dick and Lou Carey. *The Systematic Design of Instruction.* Second Edition Glenview, Ilinois: Scott, Foresman, and Company, 1985.

Wilson, L. Craig. *The Open Access Curriculum.* Boston: Allyn and Bacon, Inc., 1971. Part II.

2

Issues in the Language Arts Curriculum

There are selected issues in the language arts which have not been resolved. Students of education must be avid readers of trends and issues in the language arts with the intent of adopting new ideas in the public (government) schools using rational criteria as evaluation techniques to assess these innovative ideas.

Handwriting as an Issue

Pupils do need to develop legible handwriting so that content may be effectively communicated to others. The methods or approaches used in teaching handwriting certainly are an issue.

1. Should handwriting textbooks be used to develop pupil proficiency for all learners? Or, can teachers guide learners in handwriting achievement without the use of textbooks in this language arts area?
2. If a handwriting textbook is used in teaching-learning situations, shouid each child be guided in developing sequential learnings pertaining to every page in order as it exists within the book? Or, should each learner complete those exercises in a handwriting book where a need exists pertaining to achieving selected objectives?

3. Does the use of handwriting textbooks guide learners in experiencing continuous progress in the area of handwriting? Could pupils achieve continuous progress in this facet of the language arts without the use of handwriting textbooks?

Thus, as an important issue in the language arts curriculum, one can ask relevant questions pertaining to the use of handwriting textbooks in guiding learners to achieve to their optimal level when communicating written content to others.

Phonics Instruction as an Issue

A frequent question raised pertaining to the teaching of reading relates to phonics instruction in the elementary school.

1. How much phonics should be taught in order to be able to identify new words in the reading curriculum?
2. Should phonics be taught to each learner? Are there better ways to help selected learners become proficient in using word recognition techniques other than through phonics instruction?
3. How can balance be maintained in teaching-learning situations among diverse techniques to identify and recognise new words, e.g., phonetic analysis, configuration clues, picture clues, context clues, syllabication, and structural analysis?

Rubins wrote:

"Teachers should not present initial consonants in isolation from words. Since letters do not have sounds, but are merely representations of them, it is not correct to refer to the sound of B or G. Teachers may state a number of words beginning with the initial consonant. They may ask the children to listen to the words ball, book, and bee. They should write the words on the board. Then they should ask how ball, book, and bee are similar. They all have the same beginning letter b. They all start with the same sound. Teachers can then give a list of words that begin with b and ask students to state some others like big, book, and balloon."

Use of Spelling Textbooks as an Issue

Many schools in the United States use spelling textbooks to develop pupil proficiency in the correct spelling of words. Questions that might be raised about this approach in teaching-learning situations may be in the following:

1. Are the words contained in weekly lists of words in spelling functional in the lives of pupils?
2. Are learners able to spell these words correctly in functional writing situation after they have been mastered as revealed in a test?
3. Can pupils perceive purpose in learning to spell a list of words which they have not identified as being relevant?
4. Are teachers able to provide for individual differences in terms of the number of words mastered per week when spelling textbooks provide major learnings for pupils in this facet of the language arts curriculum?
5. Do spelling textbooks contain learning experiences which pupils find meaningful and interesting?

Direct Instruction in Listening as an Issue

It is important for pupils to become proficient listeners as a method of obtaining new information as well as in showing respect toward others in situations involving oral communication of content. There are selected issues which may be discussed pertaining to teaching listening in the elementary school.

1. Can skills in listening be taught directly to pupils, or good listening occur only within a stimulating environment in which interesting content is being presented?
2. Does direct teaching of skills in listening have transfer value in that there is a carry-over of these skills to different curriculum areas in the school setting?

Using Textbooks and Workbooks as an Issue

Certainly, language arts textbooks and workbooks can provide valuable learning experiences for pupils. No teacher, basically, would be able to creatively develop objectives, learning experiences, and evaluation procedures for each curriculum area taught in a self-contained classroom without the use of the selected basal textbooks providing a framework for pupil learning. The issue centers itself more around the methods used when language arts textbooks and workbooks provide major learnings for pupils.

1. If textbooks and workbooks are followed Sequentially, as written by the authors in providing learning activities, does this aid pupils perceiving proper sequence in learning?
2. Could teachers creatively develop a better language arts curriculum than that presented in textbooks and workbooks?
3. Which criteria would writers of elementary school language arts materials need to follow when developing content for learners which is interesting, meaningful, purposeful, and makes provision for individual differences?

Specific Plans of Reading Instruction as an Issue

There certainly are many methods available in teaching reading in the elementary school. Each plan of instruction has its strengths and weaknesses.

1. Do pupils actually select library books on their own individual unique reading levels in individualized reading, or are books selected for reading based on those which can be completed with little or no effort?
2. Do all pupils actually read a library book during time set aside for individualised reading?
3. Is it good teaching procedure for pupils in beginning reading instruction to use Initial Teaching Alphabet symbols when traditional symbols need to be understood and used at a later time?

4. Do schools have an ample supply of library books which have ITA symbols when supplementing basal readers which utilise these symbols in teaching-learning situations?
5. Is it realistic to have pupils in beginning reading instruction learn to read words which follow a specific pattern? Attempt to build meaningful sentences using the following pattern or structure of words: bat, cat, fat, hat, mat, nat, rat, sat, and vat.
6. Does the use of basal readers provide for unique interests and rates of learning that individual pupils have?
7. What kind of reading programme would be in evidence if experience charts alone would be used in teaching-learning situations involving reading instruction?

Grammar in the Language Arts Curriculum

Pupils in the school, especially in the intermediate grades, have spent a considerable amount of time in the study of grammar. Thus, pupils have attempted to learn to classify words within sentences in terms of specific parts of speech such as nouns, verbs, adverbs, adjectives, pronouns, prepositions, conjunctions, and interjections. They have also learned to tell how words are used within a sentence such as a word or words being used as:

(a) the subject of the sentence;

(b) the direct object;

(c) the object of the preposition;

(d) an indirect object;

(e) a predicate adjective or predicate noun;

(f) an adverb or adverb phrase;

(g) an adjective or adjective phrase;

(h) gerunds, infinitives, and participles;

(i) independent or dependent clauses.

Pupils in the study of grammar also learn to classify sentences in terms of the following types:

(a) declarative (states a fact or opinion and ends with a period).

(b) interrogative (asks a question and ends with a question mark).

(c) exclamatory (reveals strong feeling and ends with an exclamation mark).

(d) imperative (issues a command or request and ends with a period).

Thus, pupils spend much time in the study of grammar in the elementary school. There are selected issues which may be identified pertaining to the study of grammar.

1. Does a study of grammar aid pupils in achievement in the areas of speaking and writing?
2. Can learner interest be developed in the study of grammar?
3. Do teachers use a variety of learning activities in the teaching of grammar so that memorisation of content and rote learning are minimised?
4. Is there a transfer of learning from content learned in grammar to other curriculum areas in the elementary school?

Standard and Non-standard English

Much has been written about the issue of changing pupil's speaking behaviour from nonstandard to standard English. In American society a premium is placed upon individuals being able to speak and write using standard English. One can, no doubt, express content equally clearly using nonstandard English. The following are examples of standard and non-standard English:

1. He is going to walk to school. (standard English)

   He goin to walk to school. (nonstandard English)

2. He is not ready yet. (standard English)

   He ain't ready yet. (nonstandard English)

3. The dog and the cat are scrapping. (standard English)

   Da dog and da cat are scrappin. (nonstandard English)

Thus, in speaking either standard or nonstandard English, content may be clearly presented. Middle and upper class individuals socio-economically prefer and stress the importance of standard English in functional speaking and writing situations.

Issues that arise in these two value systems are the following:

1. Should pupils be guided in switching from non-standard to standard English?
2. What approaches should be utilised in helping pupils change from non-standard to standard English?
3. How can pupils who speak nonstandard English continually respect themselves and their heritage when learning to speak standard English?
4. Can pupils learn to speak and write standard English in the school setting and still communicate content with feelings of respect using nonstandard English in the home setting?
5. Should teachers "correct" learners in the school setting who use nonstandard English?

Norton[2] wrote:

"Traditional grammar is considered prescriptive, because it provides a series of rules for constructing sentences and classifying parts of speech. In contrast, structural grammar is referred to as descriptive grammar, because it describes words according to form classes, and describes sentence patterns or positions of words in sentences. Transformational grammar is built on the work of the structuralists, but extends grammar into the meaning of language. Whereas structural grammar is concerned primarily with syntax, transformational grammar is concerned more with semantics and the generating of sentences. The term transformation refers to the division of sentences into kernal sentences and the transforms or variations that can be developed from these basic sentences."

Evaluating Pupil Progress in the Language Arts

There are numerous ways to assess pupils achievement in the language arts. Frequently, much emphasis has been placed upon the use of standardised tests in the evaluation process, These tests have the following advantages:

1. An individual pupil's achievement in school may be measured against the norms of the test;
2. These tests are generally highly reliable in that consistency of results is in evidence on the part of learners;

Disadvantages given in using standardized tests are the following:

1. Selected items are not valid in measuring learner achievement;
2. Not all facets of pupil development can be measured using standardised tests, e.g. skills in speaking, creative writing, and achievement in listening.

Thus, numerous approaches must be utilised in assessing learner progress in the language arts.

Manuscript versus Cursive Writing

There is a relevant issue pertaining to the teaching of manuscript versus cursive writing. In most elementary schools, pupils on the early primary grade levels begin with manuscript writing. This is due to the following reasons:

1. The content in textbooks and library books is printed in manuscript writing. Thus, there is a relationship between writing in manuscript letters and printed content that pupils read;
2. Manuscript letters are easier to form as compared to cursive letters;
3. Pupils have better control over their finer muscles when engaging in manuscript writing as compared to cursive writing.

Pupils, however, ultimately need to switch from manuscript to cursive writing. Cursive writing generally, is expected of adults, although manuscript writing is being accepted more and more in terms of adult usage. There are selected elementary schools in which pupils begin their own writing experiences using cursive letters. The following problems arise pertaining to the teaching of handwriting using manuscript or cursive letters:

1. When should pupils begin using either manuscript or cursive symbols in writing experiences?
2. If pupils begin with manuscript symbols, when should the change-over be made to cursive writing?
3. Which methods are best to use in the teaching of handwriting when either manuscript or cursive letters are to be in evidence?

In Summary

There are numerous issues which have not been resolved in the language arts curriculum. Teachers, supervisors, and principals should certainly become highly knowledgeable about these issues and take a position based on understanding and thought. Issues which need to be resolved in teaching the language arts include the following:

1. the use of handwriting textbooks for pupils;
2. the teaching of phonics in the reading curriculum;
3. the utilisation of spelling textbooks for learners in teaching-learning situations;
4. direct instruction in developing pupil proficiency in listening;
5. diverse plans and programmes of instruction in the curriculum area of reading;
6. the teaching of grammar in guiding pupils to communicate ideas more effectively in speaking and writing;

7. the use of standard versus non-standard English in oral communication;
8. how pupil achievement should be assessed in the language arts;
9. manuscript versus cursive writing in the language arts curriculum.

REFERENCES

Burns, Paul C., et. al. *The Language Arts in Childhood Education.* Second Edition. Chicago: Rand McNally and Company, 1971.

Knight, Lester N. *Language Arts for the Exceptional: The Gifted and Linguistically Different.* Itasca, Illinois: F.E. Peacock Publishers, Inc., 1974.

Lamb, Pose. *Guiding Children's Language Learning.* Second Edition. Dubuque, Iowa: William C. Brown Company Publishers, 1971.

Norton, Donna E., *The Effective Teaching of Language Arts. Columbus,* Ohio: Charles E. Merrill Publishing Company 1985.

Rubin, Dorothy, *Diagnosis and Correction in Reading Instruction.* New York, New York: Holt Rinehart, and Winston. 1982.

Petty, Walter T. (Ed.). *Issues and Problems in the Elementary Language Arts.* Boston: Allyn and Bacon Inc., 1968.

Schell, Robert E. and Elizabeth Hall. *Development Psychology Today.* New York: Random House, 1983.

Silberman, Melvin L., et. al. *The Psychology of Open Teaching and Learning.* Boston: Little, Brown, and Company, 1972.

Smith, James A. *Creative Teaching of the Language Arts in the Elementary School.* Second Edition. Boston: Allyn and Bacon Inc., 1973.

Stewing, John Warren. *Exploring Language Arts in the Elementary Classroom.* New York: Holt, Rinehart, and Winston, 1983.

3

Objectives and the Language Arts

It is important for teachers, principals, and supervisors to study and evaluate relevant objectives for pupils to achieve. The following sources may be utilised in gaining information pertaining to relevant educational objectives:

1. reading content from recent textbooks written for undergraduate and graduate students in teacher education programmes on the college and university level;
2. studying ideas written in recent periodical articles in professional education journals;
3. attending professional meetings relating to teacher education and improving the curriculum;
4. visiting progressive schools and talking with professionals pertaining to ways of improving the curriculum;
5. reading research studies relating to determining and selecting educational objectives.

Educational objectives should be categorised so that rational balance may exist among the diverse kinds which pupils may achieve. One category scheme that can be used pertains to understandings, skills, and attitudinal general objectives. Understandings objectives comprise important facts, concepts, and generalisations which learners are to achieve as a result of teaching. Understanding objectives to achieve in the language arts could be the following:

1. various techniques to utilise in reading to identify new words;
2. diverse purposes involved in comprehending written content such as skimming and scanning, reading for factual information and gaining a sequence of ideas;
3. appropriate methods to use in the spelling of words;
4. guidelines to follow in giving an effective oral presentation within a group setting;
5. the importance to communicate ideas effectively to others;
6. different purposes involved in communicating ideas orally such as in conversing, discussing, interviewing, introducing, and solving of problems;
7. the need to reveal legibile handwriting exhibited through proper letter formation, spacing of letters and words, alignment of words, proportion of letters within words, and slant of individual letters.
8. the need for unity of content within a paragraph and the necessity of having appropriate sequence of paragraphs;
9. the need to listen for a variety of purposes, such as listening for facts, main ideas, generalisations, sequence of ideas, as well as engage in listening critically and creatively;
10. differences in meaning between the concepts of standard and non-standard English;
11. generalisations pertaining to how the English language operates.

Relevant skills objectives for pupils to achieve could be the following:

1. reading for a variety of purposes such as reading to acquire facts, generalisations, main ideas, sequence of ideas, evaluate content, engage in divergent thinking, and solve problems;

2. identifying new words through the use of phonetic analysis, syllabication, context clues, picture clues, structural analysis, and configuration clues;
3. developing increased proficiency in the correct spelling of words;
4. writing for a variety of purposes such as in business letters, friendly letters, poems, stories, plays, announcements, thank you notes, and congratulatory messages;
5. developing increased skill in utilizing oral communication for a variety of purposes, such as in conversation, discussions, dialogues, panel presentations, creative dramatics, buzz groups, and oral reports;
6. working cooperatively with the teacher and other learners in developing recommended guidelines to be used in evaluating learning experiences in oral communication;
7. developing increased skills in writing legibly to communicate written content effectively;
8. developing skills pertaining to the mechanics of writing such as in proper capitalization and punctuation;
9. using the concepts of stress, pitch, and juncture when communicating oral content to others;
10. utilizing diverse sentence patterns in writing such as the subject-predicate pattern; subject-predicate-direct object pattern; subject-linking verb-predicate adjective pattern; subject-linking verb-predicate noun pattern; and the subject-predicate-indirect object-direct object pattern;
11. developing proficiency in suing various types of sentences such as interrogative, imperative, declarative, and exclamatory sentences.
12. developing increased skill in expanding sentences through compounding, modifying, subordinating, and using appositives;

13. being able to write diverse kinds of poetry such as couplets, triplets, free verse, quatrains, limericks, tankas, and others;
14. putting more of the child's own thoughts and feelings into creative writing;
15. developing adequate reading, writing, speaking, and listening vocabularies.

Attitudinal Objectives in the Language Arts

It is of utmost importance for pupils to achieve relevant attitudinal objectives. Achieving attitudinal objectives will also aid pupils in attaining important understandings and skills objectives. Positive attitudes toward learning aid in achieving understandings and skills objectives. The following may be vital attitudinal objectives for learners to achieve:

1. an attitude of appreciation in desiring to know how the English language can be described;
2. an appreciation for contributions of linguists in improving the language arts curriculum;
3. an attitude of interest in the history and development of the English language;
4. a desire to develop increased proficiency in listening, speaking, reading and writing;
5. an attitude of respect toward the contributions of classmates in listening, speaking, reading, and writing;
6. wanting to read as an appropriate leisure time activity;
7. desiring to be more creative in speaking and in writing;
8. wanting to evaluate one's own achievement in the language arts in terms of appropriate standards;
9. desiring to participate in teacher-pupil planning pertaining to selecting objectives, learning activities, and evaluation procedures;

10. wanting to improve in the mechanics of writing when communicating content to others.

Specific Objectives in the Language Arts

Selected educators are recommending that precise, specific objectives be utilized in teaching-learning situations. This has many advantages providing that creative thinking, critical thinking, and problem solving are emphasized adequately in teaching-learning situations. Specific objectives should emphasize the following criteria:

1. The objective should state what learners are to achieve as a result of teaching;
2. Learning activities selected by the teacher should guide students in achieving desired objectives;
3. It can be measured if the stated objective(s) have been achieved.

The writer recommends the following additional criteria ˙ting specific objectives:

An adequate number of objectives comes from pupils in ongoing learning experiences;

2. Teacher-pupil planning is utilized to determine educational objectives, learning activities to achieve objectives, and assessment procedures in evaluating learner achievement.

The following are examples of specific objectives in the language arts:

1. The pupil will write a haiku poem;
2. The learner will identify a problem area and write a related solution;
3. The pupil will write a story of at least three hundred words using a title of his/her own choosing.

Advocates of sp‹ ific objectives recommend that goals be stated prior to teach..g so that the direction of learning may be determined beiore pupils engage in ongoing learning activities.

Outcomes Within Learning Experiences

There are selected educators who state that objectives for learners to achieve cannot be determined prior to teaching. These educators would say that from selected learning experiences, pupils achieve ends of their own choosing. Activities for pupils then should achieve the following outcomes;

1. obtain pupil's interests;
2. help pupils perceive purpose in learning;
3. provide for diverse achievement and capacity levels;
4. aid pupils in identifying problems and questions;
5. increase teacher-pupil planning;
6. involve learners in evaluating their own achievement;
7. learners being involved more in the decision-making process;
8. pupils respecting other individuals;
9. improved sequence in learning;
10. intrinsic motivation being present on the part of the learner, rather than extrinsic motivation.

Learning Centers and Open Space Education

Advocates of open space education have made many important contributions in improving the curriculum. The teacher in open space education plays a different role in teaching-learning situations as compared to more traditional practices in education. The following guidelines should be followed by teachers who are actively involved in open space education:

1. Pupils are involved in determining what to learn and the media to be used in learning;
2. Pupils engage in decision-making practices pertaining to which learning center to participate in;
3. The teacher guides and stimulates pupils in learning; lecturing, assigning, reprimanding, forcing, and dictating are concepts not associated with open space education;

4. Pupils with teacher guidance are involved in determining content of diverse learning centres;
5. Learners have ample opportunities to work in small groups at different learning centers in the class setting;
6. Good human relations are emphasized very strongly in open space education;
7. Sharing of ideas gained at a specific learning center and also with the class as a whole is significant in open space education;
8. Pupils sequence their own learnings when making selections as to which goals to achieve as well as learning activities selected;
9. Self-evaluation by learners is vital;
10. The integrated curriculum is advocated rather than the separate subjects approach.

To implement the above listed statements involving open space education, the following are given as examples pertaining to possible learning centers in the language arts curriculum:

1. ***Reading Center:*** At this center each pupil would have ample opportunities to select a library book written on his/her achievement level. The library books at this center should pertain to various topics and titles, thus providing for the interests of each child in the class setting. After having completed the reading of a library book, the child may have a conference with the teacher to reveal comprehension of what has been read. The child may also indicate comprehension in reading library books through the following ways:

(a) sharing ideas with other learners;

(b) developing a related diorama;

(c) completing a mural with other learners who have read the same library book;

(d) dramatizing what has been read (this would involve creative dramatics and pantomiming);

(e) presenting an oral report to the class related pictures and other audio-visual materials.

2. ***Listening Center:*** Here, pupils individually or in committees may select tape recordings to listen to. The teacher may wish to prepare task cards for this learning center. From the task, card, the child may select which task to work on. The tasks will vary in levels of complexity in order to provide for individual differences in the class setting. The child may reveal comprehension as a result of answering questions from a task card. Or, he/she may select a task which pertains to a problem solving activity whereby needed information is obtained from recorded voices.
3. ***Speaking Center:*** Pupils working at this center may practice using the concepts of stress, pitch, and juncture when communicating content orally to others. Cassette recorders may be used by learners to record the spoken voice and notice changes in meanings of selected sentences when emphasizing the concepts of stress, pitch, and juncture. For example, pupils can notice changes in meanings of a sentence when commas are left out in writing or when pauses are not clear between words when communicating content orally:

Jim Allen Ralph Henry Bob Martin and Linn went to the picnic. (There, of course, is a lack of clarity as to the number of people who attended the picnic.)

4. ***Spelling Center:*** Spelling textbooks may provide learning experiences for pupils at this center. It is good to pretest pupils to determine present individual achievement levels. Thus, each learner can be working at a different achievement level as compared to other children in the class setting. Once a child has acquired the correct spelling of a given set of words, the teacher, aide, or another child can test the individual child's mastery of these spelling words. Each child can work at his/her own optimum rate of speed in mastering the spelling of selected sets of words within the adopted spelling textbook.

Each pupil with teacher guidance may also select a specific set of words to master in spelling. The individualized set of spelling words could come from units of study in social studies, science, mathematics, and the general area of language arts, including reading. Once a child feels he has learned to spell a selected set of agreed upon words, he may be tested to insure mastery.

The teacher should guide pupils in using these spelling words in a variety of functional writing situations such as in writing business letters, friendly letters, announcements, plays, poems, and stories.

5. ***Writing Center:*** Ample opportunities need to be given learners to put ideas in writing. Pupils individually may select a picture, from among several, to write about. Pupils should be encouraged and rewarded to write creatively. Originality and uniqueness of content are to be encouraged.

Pictures as well as objects should be present in the classroom setting to encourage pupils in writing diverse kinds of poetry such as free verse, triplets, couplets, quatrains, tankas, and limericks. These pictures and objects may also stimulate learners in writing creative stories. Within these stories, at the proper stage of development, pupils may be guided in thinking and writing about the setting, characterization, and the plot of the story.

6. ***Vocabulary Center:*** At the vocabulary center, pupils may be guided in at teaching new meanings to words as well as learning to use in a meaningful way new concepts and content. Thus, pupils may view and discuss selected pictures and objects with the ultimate goal of developing a richer listening, speaking, reading, or writing vocabulary.

Pupils in the class setting may also discuss new terms read about in library books. They may also discuss vocabulary terms heard from viewing television programmes or listening to radio broadcasts.

Learners may also be guided in attaching meaning to new words encountered in reading through the use of context clues. For example, a child reading a sentence such as the following may not know and understand the meaning of the italicized word:

The boy rode his *bicycle* to town.

Numerous words would make sense to take the place of the unknown new word which in this case happens to be 'bicycle.' Other words that would be meaningful within that sentence would include 'horse,' 'donkey,' and 'tricycle.' With the use of phonetic analysis, the child would associate the beginning letter 'b' which has a consistent sound with words that begin like 'bed,' 'boy,' 'bay,' and 'bail.' A bicycle, of course, is something to ride on and is used much more frequently in riding to town as compared to the use of a horse, donkey, or tricycle. Pupils then need many experiences in reading to use context clues in determining the meaning of new words.

7. ***Audio-visual Centers:*** Pupils should have ample opportunities to view filmstrips, slides, and films of their own choosing. These presentations could provide background information in setting the stage for creative writing. Audio-visual presentations may provide background information for pupils in a quality reading readiness programme. Later on, in a more formal programme of reading, pupils generally have an easier time in learning to read, since familiarity of content is in evidence due to having developed adequate background information within a reading readiness programme.

The audio-visual center may also provide background information for pupils to use in diverse kinds of speaking activities, such as conversing, discussing, and interviewing.

8. ***Puzzle Center:*** The teacher and/or pupils at the appropriate stage of development may make crossword puzzles. By filling in the blank spaces on the crossword puzzles, learners may be guided in developing to an optimum level in vocabulary development. Pupils individually or in committees

may work on these crossword puzzles. The puzzle center could be increased in scope to include the playing of games pertaining to the language arts curriculum. Games may be made or purchased commercially pertaining to helping pupils in spelling, word recognition, and vocabulary development. These games should be on the understanding level of pupils. New learnings would be developed by pupils and at the same time success can be in evidence for pupils.

9. ***Dramatization Center:*** After selected pupils have completed reading a library book, they may wish to dramatise its contents to others. Formal dramatisation may be used whereby play parts are written by a committee of learners. Cooperatively, these learners decide upon and designate who is to play the role of each person in the play. Scenery may be developed by committee members to go along with the formal dramatisation. The final presentation may be given to other learners in the class setting or to other classrooms of pupils.

Creative dramatics may also be used to present content to listeners in the class setting. The content may come from having listened to a story or library book read by the teacher. Content for the creative dramatisation may also have come from the telling of a story by teacher. Pupils in creative dramatics spontaneously develop speaking parts as the need arises. Pantomiming may also be used to convey the contents of a story or library book to viewers. The spoken voice is not used in pantomiming.

Summary Statements on Open Space Education

Within a structured environment determined by the teacher, pupils have much leeway in determining what to learn in open space education. Thus, pupils are involved in decision making. It is important for pupils to learn to work together harmoniously in open space education. Humaneness is an important concept to emphasize in this method of providing learning activities for pupils.

In Summary

Objectives should be selected carefully which pupils are to achieve. There should be rational balance among understandings, skills, and attitudinal objectives in teaching-learning situations involving the language arts. Attempts should be made by teachers, supervisors, and administrators to state objectives precisely (specific objectives) when writing goals for learners to achieve. These objectives, however, must contain relevant learnings for pupils to achieve such as critical thinking, creative thinking, and problem solving. Ample opportunities must be given learners in determining objectives, learning experiences, and evaluation procedures.

REFERENCES

Corcoran, Gertrude B. *Language Arts in the Elementary School. A Modern Linguistic Approach*. New York: Ronald Press Company, 1970. Chapters One, Two and Fifteen.

Dallmann, Martha. *Teaching Language Arts in the Elementary School.* Second Edition. Dubuque, Iowa: William C. Brown Company Publishers, 1971. Chapters One, Two, and Three.

Ediger, Marlow and Digumarti Bhaskara Rao (2002). *Elementary Curriculum*. New Delhi, India: Discovery Publishing House, 2002.

Ediger, Marlow and Digumarti Bhaskara Rao (1996). *Science Curriculum*. New Delhi, India: Discovery Publishing House.

Funk, Hal D., and DeWayne Triplett (Eds.). *Language Arts in the Elementary School: Readings,* Philadelphia: J.B.. Lippincott Company, 1972.

Hatchett, Ethel L., and Donald H. Hughes. *Teaching Language Arts in Elementary Schools*. New York: Ronald Press Company, 1956. Chapters Five-Thirteen.

Keith, Lowell, *et. al. Contemporary Curriculum in the Elementary School*. New York: Harper and Row, Publishers, 1968, Chapters Three and Four.

Reisman, Fredricka and Payne, Beverly. *Elementary Education*. Columbus, Ohio: Merrill Publishing Company, 1987.

Saylor, J. Galen,and William M. Alexander. *Curriculum Planning for Better Schools*, 1974. Chapters One, Two, and Three.

Stewig, John Warren. *Exploring Language Arts in the Classroom*. New York: Holt, Rinchart and Winston, 1983

Tiedt, Iris M. *The Language Arts Handbook*. Englewood Cliffs, New Jersey: Prentice-Hall, 1983, Chapters One and Two

4

Theories of Learning and the Language Arts

It is important for teachers of language arts to develop recommended guiding principles when selecting objectives, learning activities, and evaluation procedures in the language arts curriculum. All teachers possess something that guides them in teaching-learning situations if this can be verbalized or not. Thus, a teacher may believe strongly that textbook writers in the language arts have relevant learnings that all pupils need to develop sequentially. A different teacher believes that much rote learning and memorization are methods to use in acquiring complex knowledge, skills, and attitudes. This same teacher then has a selected theory of learning which is a guide in implementing the curriculum. It may well be that a teacher of this description cannot describe orally or in writing which theory of learning is adhered to. The theory of mental discipline, emphasized in the United States prior to the 1900's, may then be in evidence. Basic principles back of the theory of mental discipline would be the following:

1. Difficult content must be learned by pupils to exercise the muscles in the mind;
2. Memorization of content is important to exercise the muscles in the mind;

3. A formal classroom setting is needed so that pupils may learn much content;
4. Content objectives become important to the exclusion of skills and attitudinal objectives.

Stimulus-Response Theory of Learning

Stimulus-response school of thought in terms of how pupils learn is very important for all educators to be knowledgeable about. This theory emphasizes the following criteria:

1. Programmers may determine what pupils are to learn, using microcomputers or textbooks;
2. Pupils progress forward very slowly at each sequential step of learning;
3. Learners know immediately if their response to an item is correct or incorrect;
4. Reinforcement is inherent in programmed learning. Thus, pupils basically are correct in each sequential step in learning.

The use of behaviourally stated objectives also stresses stimulus-response psychology in teaching-learning situations. Behaviourally stated objectives generally follow the following criteria:

1. Specificity is important in the writing of stated objectives;
2. It must be possible to measure pupil achievement after instruction, to determine if the desired ends have been achieved;
3. Learning activities are selected in terms of having pupils achieve the desired objectives;
4. The objectives are stated in terms of what pupils will be learning.

The following are examples of behaviourally stated objectives in the language arts:

1. Each pupil will spell correctly nine out of ten words;

2. The pupil will write a haiku poem;
3. The pupil will write a two hundred word paper on a topic of his own choosing;
4. Pupils will write a sentence following each of these sentence patterns:
   (a) Noun-verb or subject-predicate;
   (b) Noun-verb-noun or subject-predicate-direct object;
   (c) Noun-verb-noun-noun or subject-predicate-indirect object-direct object;
   (d) Noun-linking verb-predicate adjective or subject-predicate adjective;
   (e) Noun-linking verb-predicate noun or subject-predicate-predicate nominative.
5. The pupil will write a paragraph of forty words using a topic sentence;
6. Given a paragraph of fifty words, the pupil will find five errors in spelling.

In each of these objectives, the teacher can determine if pupils have or have not achieved the desired end or ends.

Behaviourally stated objectives written by the teacher for teaching-learning situations differ from programmed learning in the following ways:

1. Behaviourally stated objectives may be achieved by pupils in more than one class session. Pupils need to follow learnings sequentially determined by the programmer in programmed learning;
2. Sequential steps in learning using behaviourally stated objectives are not as specific as compared to programmed learning. In programmed learning, the pupil moves forward very gradually from one sequential step to the next;
3. The teacher will need to do much of the evaluating when assessing pupil achievement in terms of behaviourally stated objectives, whereas in

programmed learning, the pupil generally knows immediately if he is right or wrong after making a response by noting the answer given by the programmer;

4. The classroom teacher writes behaviourally stated objectives for teaching-learning situations whereas the programmer determines what pupils are to learn in programmed learning.

The following would be an example of programmed learning in the language arts:

1. Which word has a different beginning letter as compared to the other two words? (bat)

   bat cake cat

2. Which two words of the following have the same beginning letter?

   (bat, ban)

   apple bat ban

3. Which words in the following set have the same beginning letter?

   (bat, ban, banana)

   bat ban cat banana dad

4. Which of the following words have two beginning letters which are alike?

   (bin, bit)

   bin cat bit saw

Sequential steps for pupils to achieve are smaller in programmed learning as compared to the use of behaviourally stated objectives written by the teacher. In programmed learning as well as in using behaviourally stated objectives, the following criteria must be followed:

1. It definitely can be measured if pupils have been successful in achieving desired objectives;
2. Pupils are to be successful in each sequential step of learning;

3. The child does not sequence his or her own learning; the teacher or programmer determines correct order of experiences in learning for pupils.

Criticisms given of stimulus-response school of thought in terms of how pupils learn include the following:

1. It is mechanistic and emphasizes lower levels of cognition on the part of learners;
2. Attitudinal objectives may be slighted in teaching-learning situations;
3. Sequence and content in learning should be determined more by children as compared to programmers and/or teachers;
4. Selected pupils may find that this approach in teaching does not harmonize with their own individual learning styles;
5. A single method used extensively in teaching may not aid in developing and maintaining pupil interest in learning.

Gestalt Theory of Learning

Gestaltists emphasize the importance of wholistic learning. Thus, individuals have a tendency to perceive content in terms of the wholeness of the situation. After perceiving the wholeness of an object, scene, or situation, specific facets or parts of the whole are then noticed. In reading and spelling, a pupil will view a complete word and then notice the parts that make up this word. In the teaching of reading then, the teacher may utilize the following teaching procedures in the gestalt approach:

1. The teacher would guide learners in getting an overview of an entire story before discussing relevant parts. Thus, in developing background information within learners prior to reading, related ideas would be stressed-emphasizing content covering the wholeness of the situation;

2. In introducing new words which pupils would encounter in reading, learners see these words in sentences on the chalkboard prior to engaging in the act of reading. The words may then be analyzed phonetically to aid learners in gaining important learnings pertaining to word recognition and identification;
3. Pupils attach necessary meanings pertaining to the new words within context. Thus, meanings to words are not learned in isolation but within a wholistic situation such as in a sentence;
4. From these experiences above (numbers 1, 2, and 3), pupils are encouraged to ask questions for which related content can be obtained through reading.

Following the reading of content on an individual basis, content may be discussed answering previously identified questions or purposes. Further learning experiences emphasizing wholistic approaches in teaching and learning emphasize the following:

1. pupils in a committee developing a mural pertaining to ideas gained from reading;
2. selected learners cooperatively dramatising content taken from the completed reading activity;
3. individual pupils summarising major generalizations achieved.

The gestalt school of thought in terms of stressing how pupils learn emphasizes wholistic learnings initially. These initial wholistic learnigs then may be followed by analyzing facets or parts of the whole.

Structure of the Disciplines

Selected leading educators in the United States emphasize that pupils inductively develop key main ideas of a discipline. Thus, for example, college and university professors cooperatively would identify structural ideas pertaining to the academic discipline in which they specialize. Linguistics then may identify structural ideas such as the following which pupils would achieve inductively:

1. diverse sentence patterns such as the subject-predicate pattern; the subject-predicate-direct object pattern; the subject-linking verb-predicate adjective pattern; the subject-linking verb-predicate noun pattern; and the subject-predicate-indirect object-direct object pattern;
2. ways of expanding sentences through the use of modifiers, appositives, subordinate clauses, and compounding parts within a sentence;
3. word patterns such as those which represent consistency between symbol and sound, e.g. cat, hat, mat, fat, and bat, as well as understand word families where consistency is not in evidence between symbol and sound, e.g., box and fox, or weight and neigh;
4. difference in meaning of grammar as compared to usage in developing major concepts pertaining to the study of the English language;
5. the changing English language in terms of new vocabulary terms being added as well as meanings changing of selected words. Other changes are also identifiable such as spelling of words and word order in sentences.

In Summary

It is important for teachers, principals, and supervisors to study and develop a theory or theories of learning pertaining to the selection of objectives, learning experiences, and assessment procedures. Faculty members in schools must be guided by relevant and agreed upon principles and theories of learning.

REFERENCES

Ausubel, D.P. *Educational Psychology, a Cognitive View.* New York: Holt, Rinehart, and Winston, 1968.

Bhaskara Rao, Digumarti (2001). *Educational Psychology.* Guntur, India: Nagarjuna Publishers. (in Telugu language)

Becker, Wesley C. (Ed.). *An Empirical Basis for Change in Education.* Chicago: Science Research Associates, Inc., 1971.

Ediger, Marlow and Digumarti Bhaskara Rao. *Elementary Curriculum.* New Delhi, India: Discovery Publishing House, 2002.

Eliot, John (Ed.) *Human Development and Cognitive Processes. New York: Holt , Rinehart and Winston, Inc., 1971.*

Finn, Patrick. *Helping Children Learn to Read.* New York: Random House, 1985.

Gagne, Robert M. *The Conditions of Learning.* Second Edition, New York: Holt, Rinehart and Winston, 1985.

Hilgard, Ernest R. *Theories of Learning.* New York: Appleton-Century-Crofts, Inc., 1948.

Hyman, Ronald T. *Ways of Teaching.* Second Edition. Philadelphia: J.B. Lippincott.

Kim, Eugene C., and Richard D. Kellough, *A Resource Guide for Secondary School Teaching.* Fourth Edition. New York: Macmillan Publishing Company, 1987.

Kourilsky, Marilyn, and Lory Quaranta. *Effective Teaching.* Glenview, Illinois: Scott, Foresman and Company, 1987.

Looft, William R. (Ed.) *Development Psychology: A Book of Readings, Hinsdale,* Illinois: The Dryden Press, Inc., 1987.

Schell, Robert E. and Elizabath Hall. *Developmental Psychology.* Fourth Edition. New York Random House, 1983.

Torrance, E. Paul, and R.E. Myers. *Creative Learning and Teaching,* New York: Dodd, Mead & Company, 1970.

Walcutt, Charles Child, et. al. *Teaching Reading, A Phonic/Linguistic Approach to Developmental Reading.* New York: Macmillan Publishing Company, Inc., 1964.

5

Learning Activities and the Language Arts

Learning activities must be carefully selected which guide pupils in achieving relevant objectives. Criteria should be utilized by those involved in the selection of learning experiences. These criteria should include the following:

1. The interest of learners are important to consider when selecting learning activities;
2. Learning activities must relate to the diverse learning styles that individual pupils have;
3. Learnings should be perceived as being sequential from the pupil's point of view;
4. Pupils must be guided in perceiving reasons for learning;
5. Diverse kinds of thinking should emphasized in ongoing learning activities, particularly higher levels of thinking in the cognitive domain;
6. Pupils should attach meaning to what is being learned;
7. Learners must ample opportunities to engage in problem-solving activities;
8. Decision making by pupils should be stressed in teaching-learning situations.

9. Pupils should be actively involved in learning and not behave as passive individuals;
10. Each pupil must be respected for present levels of achievement in understandings, skills, and attitudinal objectives and be guided in achieving continuous progress.

Teachers, supervisors, and principals must continually seek learning activities which guide learners in creative writing. Developing pupil proficiency in creative thinking and creative writing is a major goal in the language arts curriculum. Learning activities pertaining to creative writing will now be discussed:

1. From a library book or story that has been read, the pupil could write additional happenings. The pupil may also write a different ending to the completed library book or story;
2. The teacher could read a new story to pupils and stop at a given point. Pupils individually write an ending to the story. Voluntarily, pupils compare content that has been written. Ultimately, the teacher could read the rest of the story to pupils;
3. Pupils at a learning center select a picture to write about. Learners may write what happened prior to or after the scene in the picture. Pupils individually may write how the person or persons, animal or animals feel in the picture. They could also write how an inanimate object in the selected picture feels;
4. The teacher could give a brief beginning to a continued story. A committee of three or four pupils add one or two paragraphs to this story. Other committees in sequence may also add to the continued story;
5. From the object center in the class setting a pupil may write about three of these objects in developing a creative story. Unique, novel content is desired from pupils in final products pertaining to creative writing;

6. One child may write a beginning sentence for a creative story. A second pupil can add a sentence in sequence relating to the first sentence. Each learner in sequence adds additional sentences to the creative writing activity;
7. Pupils select and event from an ongoing social studies unit involving history and write weekly diary entries pertaining to that event. For example in the adventures of Marquette and Joliet sailing down the Mississippi River, what experiences did these explorers have specially on a day-to-day basis;
8. A committee of pupils could write about what the United States would be like today is a selected event, such as World War I, had not occurred;
9. A child may be stimulated to draw an interesting set of lines using a variety of crayons on a sheet of paper. Learners exchange papers and write a paragraph or several paragraphs pertaining to these designs containing lines of diverse colours.

Writing Poetry

Pupils should have ample opportunities to listen to and write poetry. The teachers must think of ways to stimulate learners to write poems. The following methods should be considered by teachers as means to stimulate pupils to write poems:

1. The teacher reads carefully selected poems to pupils on their appropriate developmental level. The poems must be read with enthusiasm and interest on the part of the teacher. Hopefully, pupils will wish to write the same kinds of poems. For example, a teacher may read limericks to pupils whereby the latter may wish to write limericks;
2. Commercially prepared or teacher prepared tapes can be played to learners in stimulating interest to write poetry. In the tape a stimulating voice could read and tell about haiku, thus developing interest within learners in writing haiku poetry.

3. The teacher may present orally two rhyming words to pupils; pupils in groups of two can develop a couplet whereby these rhyming words are used at the end of each of these two lines;
4. Pupils in small groups may think of three words which rhyme and cooperatively develop a poem of three lines (a triplet). The rhyming words come at the end of each of the three lines;
5. Pupils in a committee may suggest four words which rhyme to another committee of learners with the intent of writing a quatrain. As and end result, each committee of pupils would ultimately develop a poem containing four lines of rhymed verse;
6. Using objects in a learning center, each pupil in the class setting may be stimulated in writing free verse. In writing free verse, rhyming of words is not necessary, and there is no requirement as to the length of each line. Thus, from the object center, a pupil may write about a model farm tractor in the following manner:

   A farm tractor can be big and powerful.
   is used to pull implements.
   looks beautiful when new.
   is as powerful as a giant.
   winds its way through the fields.
   pupils a plow and tears the earth apart.

Spelling in the Language Arts

It is important for pupils to develop increased proficiency in spelling to communicate content more effectively to others. There are selected guidelines which teachers should utilize in the teaching of spelling:

1. Pupils should understand the meaning of and be able to correctly identify words prior to mastering these words in the area of spelling;
2. Learners should be able to use these new spelling words in sentences;

3. A variety of interesting learning experiences should be provided for pupils in learning to spell selected words;

4. A specific methodology should be used by individual pupils which will aid them to develop increased power in the correct spelling of words. This methodology includes (a) careful perception of the new word; (b) correct pronunciation of the new word and listening to sounds that each letter or letters make; (c) the pupil writing the word once and then checking with the correct spelling of that word; and (d) once the word has been spelled correctly, the pupil practices the spelling of that word in functional writing situations;

5. It is important for pupils to perceive purpose in learning to spell words;

6. Pupils should practice spelling words correctly within diverse writing activities such as writing business letters, friendly letters, stories, poems, announcements, and thank you notes;

7. The number of words that a pupil is to learn to spell correctly per week depends upon his/her present achievement level;

8. An individualized spelling programme is recommendable. Each child's list of spelling words may be planned with teacher guidance utilizing words that come from units of study in social studies, science, mathematics, and other curriculum areas. A recommended series of spelling textbooks may also be used in individualising spelling programmes for learners. Each pupil in the class setting will be achieving at a different rate of speed as compared to others in mastering the spelling of a set of words;

9. Creative teaching methods should be used in helping learners to spell words. From a list of spelling words, learners may write a creative story, poem, or engage in other kinds of creative writing activities;

10. Pupils should be rewarded for volunteering to learn to spell additional new words. Praising pupils for improved performance in spelling can spur learners on to greater efforts.

Handwriting in the Language Arts

Legible handwriting on the part of pupils is important in effectively communicating content to others. Legibility in handwriting is the major objective for pupils to achieve in this facet of the language arts.

General guidelines that teachers may follow in the teaching of handwriting include the following:

1. The handwriting curriculum must make provision for individual differences among pupils in the class setting;
2. Specific and general objectives in handwriting should be attainable by pupils;
3. The teacher may group pupils for instruction in handwriting. Desks can be moved quickly by learners in order that pupils who need the most assistance in handwriting instruction are sitting within a group as compared to learners who may need very little guidance;
4. Each pupil may evaluate his/her own achievement in handwriting by (a) comparing his own individual product with a model contained in a handwriting textbook, (b) comparing his own product with that of a reputable commercially prepared handwriting scale, and (c) comparing his present achievement in handwriting with earlier accomplishments in this area.
5. The teacher must give specific guidance to learners after diagnosing weaknesses such as the following in the area of handwriting:
   (a) formation of specific letters;
   (b) space between words and letters;
   (c) alignment of letters and words;
   (d) proper proportion of letters;
   (e) neatness in the final product;
   (f) proper slant of letters and words.

6. pupils should be able to see models of good handwriting in the classroom. These models may be provided by the teacher and other learners;
7. A model of upper and lower case letters of the alphabet may be purchased from a reputable publisher in the area of handwriting and placed where it can be referred to by pupils as the need arises;
8. Reputable handwriting textbooks may provide excellent learning activities for pupils if the sequence of learning activities followed is based on student need;
9. Pupils should have ample opportunities to practice quality handwriting in functional writing situations such as in writing business and friendly letters, poems, stories, plays, announcements, and notes of sympathy;
10. Each pupil should be evaluated in terms of improvement over past performance and not compared unfairly against others;
11. Pupils should be encouraged to voluntarily display finished products in handwriting on the classroom bulletin board.

The teacher must follow recommended procedures in teaching so that each pupil may achieve to the highest development possible in legible handwriting.

Speaking Activities and the Pupil

Each child must develop optimal achievement in the area of oral communication. This is necessary so that effective communication of content is possible. There are many kinds or types of speaking activities. The following, among others, are important kinds of speaking activities for pupils:

1. telling of stories;
2. making of announcements;
3. taking part in discussions;
4. interviewing others;
5. introducing visitors and guests;
6. conversing with others;

7. participating in panel discussions and debates;
8. reading content orally;
9. conveying ideas in creative dramatics;
10. being a member of a buzz group;
11. presenting oral reports;
12. leading a small or large group discussion;
13. responding to questions raised by other individuals.

It is important for teachers to provide an adequate number of learning activities to help pupils develop proficiency in each of the above named types of speaking activities. Guidelines that a classroom teacher must follow to assist each pupil to achieve well in the area of speaking are the following:

1. A relaxed classroom environment should be in evidence. Difficulties in oral communication of content may come about due to a tense, anxious learning environment;
2. Pupils individually should be treated with respect by other learners and by the teacher;
3. Each child should be guided in feeling that he/she is an important human being and has status;
4. The teacher should guide pupils to become active participants in the class setting. Thus, the child feels that he belongs to the group in the class setting;
5. Models for good speaking can come from the teacher, pupils tapes, records, resource persons, and content contained in library books;
6. Pupils are not forced to make changes in speaking; an inward desire to improve in oral communication should be an ultimate goal;
7. The teacher may give guidance in helping pupils overcome deficiencies in speaking; however, the teacher must realize his/her area of responsibility here and be aware of difficulties in speaking which involve the help of specialists;
8. Definite goals in oral communication must be in evidence for each pupil. These objectives must be attainable;

9. Pupils should have ample opportunities to evaluate their own achievement in speaking in terms of stated realistic objectives. The learner may assess his own achievement in speaking in terms of stated realistic objectives. The learner may assess personal achievement in speaking by listening to his/her recorded voice pertaining to a specific learning activity involving oral communication;
10. Learners must perceive purpose in ongoing learning activities involving speaking;
11. Realistic situations in speaking should be inherent as learning experiences.

Thus, for example, the pupil may engage in discussing solutions to problems which are real and life-like.

Listening and the Pupil

Pupils should become good listeners so that ideas, knowledge, and skills may be obtained. Courtesy in also involved when individuals listen carefully to the thinking of others. The teacher guides pupils in developing skills pertaining to improved listening. Selected criteria must be followed when helping each learner achieve optimum development in listening:

1. Standards for listening should be developed cooperatively between pupils and the teacher as guidelines for the former to achieve in listening. Periodically, pupil achievement in listening should be assessed in terms of these standards. This could involve self-evaluation by learners, or pupils with teacher guidance may evaluate learner progress in achieving the objectives;
2. Interesting learning activities should be inherent in the classroom setting involving listening. This will aid learners in becoming better listeners. Tape and cassette recordings, discussions, reports, films, filmstrips, and slides should contain content which is interesting to pupils;

3. Pupils should perceive reasons for listening to ongoing learning activities. Prior to the time that pupils are to become involved in a learning activity involving listening, purposes or reasons should be established for listening. Learners may then sense a necessity to listen to content carefully so that information may be obtained pertaining to the stated purposes or reasons for listening. It is important to stimulate pupils in raising questions prior to the learning activity involving listening so that an inward desire to listen carefully will be in evidence;
4. Special time must be set aside in the class schedule to provide specific learning activities pertaining to listening. For example, pupils could rest their heads on their desks, and with eyes closed, identify sounds the teacher is making. Individual pupils may also take turns presenting specific sounds to other learners under the same conditions. Sound that could be made may include the crushing of paper, tapping of a pencil, snapping of fingers, and pouring of water;
5. During story hour, the teacher may ask interesting questions of pupils pertaining to content read. These questions should stimulate pupil interest in wishing to listen to content being read orally. Pupil listening may then be evaluated during story hour;
6. Task cards at listening centers, can aid in evaluating pupil comprehension pertaining to listening to tape and cassette recordings. These task guide pupils in developing and inward desire to learn. Intrinsic motivation is important on the part of learners;
7. Reputable elementary school language arts textbooks have selected learning experiences which aid learner achievement in listening. The teacher can select experiences from these textbooks which assist learners to achieve to an optimal level;

8. The teacher must evaluate his/her own teaching to determine if explanations are repetitious. If content presented by the teacher is repetitious, pupils may come to depend upon statements being repeated. Poor listening may be encouraged through excessive repeating of ideas;
9. Learning activities need to be varied in the classroom setting in order to prevent boredom on the part of learners when listening to ideas being expressed. Boring routine, dull learning activities hinder in developing optimal achievement;
10. The teacher must present a model to pupils in the area of listening. When conversing and discussing content with children, the teacher must be a good listener;
11. Unnecessary noises can hinder pupils in the area of listening. It is important to have a learning environment which is conducive to good listening;
12. The teacher must accept each pupil as a human being having worth. Each child's progress in listening must be evaluated in terms of present levels of achievement. There are, of course, pupils who have grave personal and social problems. Situations such as these do not aid pupils in listening to content to the fullest of their ability. Each child must be treated with respect regardless of race, creed, and socio-economic level;
13. The teacher must emphasize good listening in all curriculum areas. In special class sessions devoted to the teaching of listening, hopefully learners will transfer these attained skills to different curriculum areas in the elementary school.

Reading and the Child

Developing proficiency in reading is a very important objective for pupils to achieve. A person who reads poorly is greatly hindered in most cases in getting a good position, job, or vocation in life. It is difficult to experience and enriched life unless one has developed proficiency in reading.

It is important for early primary grade pupils to have and experience a good reading readiness programme. Learning activities such as the following in a reading readiness programme should guide pupils to do better in a more formal reading programme later:

1. ***Developing an experience chart with the teacher:*** Pupils, first of all, would have a learning activity such as viewing a filmstrip or film, set of slides, scenes during an excursion, or a set of pictures. Following this experience, pupils with teacher guidance would present related content for the latter to record on the chalkboard or on a chart in neat manuscript letters. After the ideas have been recorded, pupils read the abstract words with the teacher pointing to the content as it is being read;
2. ***Having an object center:*** Here pupils discuss content pertaining to these objects. This learning activity guides learners in getting needed background information necessary for understanding related content in a formal reading programme. The objects on the learning center may pertain to units on the farm, city, neighbourhood, and transportation. Later on, in a formal reading programme, pupils read content related to these objects;
3. ***Labeling selected objects in the classroom:*** Pupils with teacher leadership select important items in the classroom and attach related labels written in neat manuscript style. Objects such as 'chair,' 'Door,' and 'window' may have labels attached;
4. ***Discriminating between words and letters:*** The teacher prepares exercises for pupils to work in helping the latter notice likeness and differences between and among letters and words. In beginning lessons pertaining to visual discrimination, the child may, for example, tell which picture is different from two other pictures. Two pictures, of course, would

need to be identical in content. Later, in sequence, pupils could identify gross differences in printed words such as word is different from two other words within a set: man boy man; girl girl machine; dog owl dog. Pupils may also cross out a letter that is different from two other letters in a set; 1 m 1; b b a; y d y. in sequence, pupils should pick out a word or letter which is different from two other words or letters in a set; however, the discriminations are becoming more complex such as the following: l b l; o o a; c m m;

5. ***Using audio-visual aids:*** The use of video tapes, slides, filmstrips, films, pictures, and tapes can give pupils much background information pertaining to what pupils will be reading later in a more formalized reading programme. In utilizing these audio-visual materials, pupils gain much needed content relating to pets, the zoo, the circus, children at play, the home, and the school. Major concepts and generalizations are acquired by learners when interacting with these learning activities;

6. ***Developing skills in hearing likenesses and differences in sounds:*** Pupils must develop proficiency in the area of phonetic analysis. Learners should make continuous progress in associating sounds with abstract symbols represented by letters and words. In a reading readiness programme, pupils may listen to poetry containing rhyme read by the teacher.. Pupils at the appropriate stage of development give words which rhyme with each of the following: cat; ball; tin; and cold. In proper sequence in learning, pupils give words which begin with the same beginning sound as the following words: call; baby; same; and game. It is good to use pictures and objects pertaining to the abstract words whenever possible. Learnings acquired by pupils should become meaningful. Pupils need to understand what is being taught. Pictures are good to use in teaching. The

pictures aid pupils in getting needed background information. They also assist pupils in using picture clues in the act of reading. If a pupil, for example, cannot identify the word 'Cat' in a sentence, the picture on the printed page may show a cat, thus helping pupils to select appropriate unknown words in reading. Context clues are also important to use in reading whereby a new unknown word makes sense within a sentence. In a sentence, "I see a . . . . . .," there are many words that made sense in context. The following words, as examples, would make sense: boy, girl, dog, man, tiger, woman, map, cat, and cow. There may be, as was stated previously, a picture of a cat on the printed page. However, other animals or people may also be in the same picture such as a dog, a man, and a woman. The learner needs another approach to use in recognizing new words such as phonetic analysis. The first grapheme of the unknown word 'cat' is the letter 'c'. The words 'cat' and 'cow' would now fit in as appropriate words within the sentence, since they have the same beginning sounds. However, the word 'cat' has a different ending sound as compared to the word 'cow'. 'I see a cat' would pertain to reading the intended sentence correctly as written by the author;

7. There are patterns of sentences with which pupils should become familiar. These include the subject-predicate pattern (Jack runs); the subject-predicate-direct object pattern (Michael threw the ball); The subject-linking verb-predicate adjective pattern (The dog was tall); the subject-predicate-indirect object-direct object-pattern (Jim gave Ivan some candy); subject-linking verb-predicate noun pattern (Miss Smith is a singer). Pupils should also become familiar with approaches used in expanding sentences such as in using modifiers and appositives within each of the above listed patterns of sentences. Equally important ways of expanding sentences pertain to

compounding verbs, nouns, adjectives, independent clauses, and adverbs in sentences as well as in using dependent clauses;

8. Pupils should understand word patterns such as ban, can, dan, fan, man, pan, ran, tan, and van. By changing the initial consonant in each of these words, a new word is in evidence. These words follow a pattern or structure. Linguists strongly emphasize patterns as far as recognizing words and sentences is concerned;

9. In beginning reading experiences, young pupils encounter words where there is consistency between symbol and sound such as in the following words: hat, cat, mat, fat, rat, and bat. In later reading experiences pupils read words where irregularity in spelling is in evidence.

Advantages which may be given for linguistic approaches in the teaching of reading are the following:

1. Young readers obtain security in reading when words are consistent in terms of sound-symbol relationship;
2. Pupils may perceive order or structure of sentences and words in the English language.

Disadvantages inherent in a linguistic approach to the teaching of reading are the following:

1. Meaningful content cannot be written where a family or a pattern of words is used only, in written content for beginning readers. Written sentences for all age levels of pupils in the elementary school contain words where there is consistency as well as a lack of consistency between symbols and sounds;
2. Meaningful words in reading are those which are perceived to be relevant in the lives of the learners.

The language experience approach in teaching reading may be valuable to many learners in realizing optimal achievement:

1. Content for reading comes from the learner. Pupils present ideas based on personal experiences to the teacher. The teacher records these ideas for learners on the chalkboard;
2. The ideas expressed and the abstract words used in the experience chart are meaningful to pupils when reading the recorded content;
3. Pupils experience security in reading since they presented content for the experience chart.

Disadvantages of the language experience approach in reading are the following:

1. Pupils' achievement in reading may indicate the need to use more complex words than those given on an experience chart;
2. When content for a single experience chart comes from several or many learners, the needs of a single individual may not be met. Experiences are unique to an individual pupil.

The Initial Teaching Alphabet (ITA) has been used in selected elementary schools in the United States. There are basal reading series using ITA symbols. There are forty-four symbols representing forty-four sounds. Pupils are to experience consistency when relating a sound to a symbol. Irregular spelling of words is not a problem when using ITA symbols in reading and writing activities. Silent letters are omitted in reading and writing words using ITA. No differentiation is made between upper and lower case letters using ITA except that a capital letter is taller than a lower case letter.

Advantages given when using ITA symbols in reading instruction are the following:

1. There is consistency basically between each symbol and its related sound in ITA;
2. Pupils experience security in reading and writing when this consistency is in evidence.

Disadvantages which may be given in using ITA are the following:

1. There is not set of letters or symbols whereby perfect consistency is in evidence between each symbol and its related sound;
2. Pupils must always made the transfer after having used ITA symbols to traditional ways of spelling and reading words. Selected ITA symbols vary greatly in appearance from those used in traditional writing.

In Summary

It is important to help each pupil develop optimal proficiency in understandings, skills, and attitudes in listening, speaking, reading, and writing vocabularies. Content may be presented meaningfully to others when speaking and writing. Relevant ideas may be obtained through the language arts skills of reading and listening. Recommended criteria must be followed in teaching-learning situations pertaining to guiding each pupil in achieving to the optimum in different facets of the language arts curriculum.

REFERENCES

Arnstein, Flora J. *Poetry in the Elementary Classroom*. New York: Appleton-Century-Crofts, 1962.

Burns, Paul C., and Leo M. Schell. (Eds.) *Elementary School Language Arts*, Selected Readings, Chicago: Rand McNally & Company, 1973.

Burrows, Alvina T., et. al. *New Horizons in the Language Arts*. New York: Harper and Row, Publisher, 1972.

Chenfield, Mimi Brodsky. *Teaching Language Arts Creatively*. Second Edition. New York: Harcourt Brace Jovanovich, Publishers, 1987.

De Stefano, Johanna S., and Sharon Fox. (Eds.) *Language and the Language Arts*. Minneapolis: Burgess Publishing Company, 1966.

Donoghue, Mildred R. *The Child and English Language Arts*. William C. Brown Publishers, 1971.

Ediger, Marlow and Digumarti Bhaskara Rao. *Teaching Reading Successfully*. New Delhi. India: Discovery Publishing House, 2001.

Norton, Donna E. *The Effective Teaching of Language Arts*, Second Editon. Columbus, Ohio: Charles E. Merrill Publishing Company, 1985.

Smith, James A. *Setting Conditions for Creative Teaching in the Elementary School*. Boston: Allyn and Bacon, Inc., 1966.

Sutherland, Zena,/and May Hill Arbuthnot. *Children and Books*. Seventh Edition. Glenview, Illinois: Scott, Foresman Co., 1986.

6

Linguistics and the Language Arts

The contributions of linguists in the language arts curriculum have been numerous. Through these contributions, a modified curriculum has resulted. Teachers of language arts need to be thoroughly versed in content and methodology recommendations made by linguists. The language arts has changed much due to input from linguists in the curriculum. Petty, Petty, and Becking write the following pertaining to structural grammar, a linguistic means of studying language:

"Structural grammar is the product of linguists' scientific study of the way we speak. Structural grammar does not prescribe what is 'correct' but simply reports the language as it exists, including its growth and changes. In structural grammar the ways words are put together into utterances have been categorized, and from this categorization certain principles and patterns of the language system have emerged. One difficulty with this grammar is the problem of determining how people actually do speak, a matter that is basic to the categorization that produces the patterns. Not everyone speaks the same way; that is, there are social and regional differences in usage and pronunciation. Then there is the problem of completeness. How large a sample of language must be examined to determine whether or not all possible patterns and principles of the system have been discovered? Of course both of these weaknesses are of

no greater importance to structural grammar than to any other, except that since the basis of this grammar is its scientific determination, they introduce some limitations to generalizing about the completeness of its patterns as a description of the language system."

Structural Grammar

Selected pupils enter the school setting speaking the English language rather proficiently. They generally have little or no knowledge of sentence patterns and yet effective communication on their developmental level is definitely in evidence. A rich learning environment must continually be provided so that learners may enrich their speaking and listening vocabularies to develop further skills in the oral use of language.

Pupils in the school setting need to understand and appreciate how the English language operates. As learners progress through sequential school years, they should experience continuous success in achieving relevant objectives in the language arts curriculum.

The teacher on the present achievement level of each pupil must provide stimulating learning activities to motivate learners in understanding structure and patterns in the English language. The easiest sentence pattern for most learners to understand generally is the noun-verb or subject-predicate pattern. The teacher can select a subject-predicate sentence pattern from an experience chart developed by pupils with teacher guidance. The teacher may also ask pupils to give a sentence of two words pertaining to a picture on the bulletin board or objects at a learning center. Contributions made by pupils must be respected. As an additional approach to use in having pupils understand sentence patterns, the teacher could write two words on the chalkboard resulting in a subject-predicate sentence.

Tiedt and Tiedt write the following involving pupils studying sentence patterns:

"The sentence merits considerable attention in the study of language and in developing composition skills. It is through study of the sentence that students can be made aware of grammar, for there is little justification in teaching grammar as an isolated subject. Grammar is not just a set of terms and rules to be learned; it is a study of the relationships of words and groups of words in the context of a sentence. These ideas should be taught, therefore, as students learn to write, to manipulate words and phrases, to create interesting, varied sentences. Structural linguistics introduced the concept of the sentence pattern, of which there are many. In the elementary school, however, we might concentrate on working with five basic patterns. After introducing one pattern– for example, the simplest of all, Noun-Verb—let the students play with the pattern as they modify in in many ways. At any time, of course, they can still identify the basic patterns. Challenge class members to create a long sentence beginning with only two words, perhaps: Horses run. Compare the results."

The following illustrates the noun-verb or subject-predicate sentence pattern.

1. Lions roar.
2. Birds fly.
3. Boys walk
4. Girls swim.
5. Babies cry.

In each of these sentences pupils may provide words which replace the verb or predicate. Learners need to be actively involved in presenting these words. Thus, the teacher might ask, "What else do lions do?" Pupils may respond with the following: 'walk,' 'run,' 'jump,' 'eat' and 'sleep.' Pupils may then be guided to notice that the sentence pattern stays the same; however, other words have been utilized in place of the original verb or predicate.

In sequence, the teacher could have pupils think of words to replace the noun or subject of the sentence. In the sentence 'Lions roar,' what other animals might take the place of the word 'lions'? Pupils may respond with words such as 'tigers,' 'giraffes,' 'dogs,' and 'wildcats.' Pupils must have ample concrete and semi-concrete experiences when participating in ongoing learning activities, such as in viewing models and pictures of animals.

A second sentence pattern, not necessarily in sequence taught to pupils, might pertain to pupils developing understandings of the noun-verb-noun or subject-predicate direct object pattern.

1. John threw the baseball.
2. Ralph held the bat.
3. Sally met her friends.
4. Nancy bought a doll.

In each of these sentences, pupils may present a word which takes the place of the subject, the predicate, or the direct object. The concepts of 'subject,' 'predicate,' and 'direct object' may be used by the teacher when referring to specific words in a sentence; however, pupils definitely should not be forced to use these terms when oral or written communication is being utilized. Generally, pupils will attach meaning to and use these concepts in speaking and writing at the appropriate developmental level.

A third sentence pattern to be studied by pupils would pertain to the noun-linking verb-adjective or subject-linking verb-predicate adjective pattern.

1. The house looked beautiful.
2. The vase was decorative.
3. The owl was brown.
4. The candy was delicious.

Each of these sentences has a subject, such as the word 'house' in sentence on and 'vase' in sentence two. The words 'house' and 'vase' in sentences one and two are nouns. Why are these words nouns? They can be changed from singular to plural or plural to singular in context. 'House' is singular, while 'houses' is plural. 'Vase' is singular, while 'vases' is plural. The word 'looked' in sentence one and the word 'was' in sentence two are linking verbs. Why are these words verbs? Verbs are words which can be changed from past tense to present tense and present tense to past tense, in context. Thus, the word 'looked' pertains to a completed action and indicates past tense; however, the word 'look' indicates present tense. The word 'was' is in past tense; however, the word 'is' is in present tense.

Interesting learning experiences can be provided whereby understandings may be developed by pupils in a meaningful way pertaining to be following concepts: 'singular' and 'plural,' 'present tense' and 'past tense.' For example, the teacher might have one boy walk across the front of the room. Other pupils could give a sentence such as the following pertaining to the dramatization: The boy walks. Next the teacher may call for a second boy to come to the front of the room and join in the same act. The resulting sentence to describe the dramatization reads as follows: The boys walk. In learning experiences such as these, pupils may realize in a concrete, meaningful way the concepts of 'singular' and 'plural.'

Again, the boy (or boys) could walk across the room and viewers give the following sentence: The boy walks (present tense). Once the act has been completed, the resulting sentence might be the following: They boy walked (past tense). Thus, with a variety of concrete learning experiences, pupils may develop understandings pertaining to 'present tense' and 'past tense.' The sentence patterns used in illustrating concepts pertaining to nouns and verbs pertain to the subject-predicate or noun-verb pattern.

A fourth sentence pattern for pupils to attach meaning is the noun-linking verb-noun or subject-predicate-predicate nominative pattern.

1. John was a coach.
2. Bill is an umpire
3. The man is a grocer.
4. Sally is a singer

In each of these sentences, the predicate nominative equals the subject of the sentence joined by a linking verb. In sentence one, John equals coach. In sentence two, Bill equals umpire while man equals grocer in sentence three. Sally equals singer in sentence four. Notice that a linking verb joins the predicative nominative to the subject of the sentence.

A fifth pattern of sentence involves pupils inductively developing understandings of the subject-predicate-indirect object-direct object or noun-verb-noun pattern. The following would be examples of this sentence pattern:

1. John gave Jerry a gift
2. George presented Alice a present
3. Mark wrote Jim a note.

Pupils at Christmas time and at the time birthdays are celebrated frequently use the subject-predicate-indirect object-direct object sentence pattern. For example, at Christmas time, a child may say the following: "Daddy gave me a bicycle." Or, when a child's birthday is being celebrated, the involved pupil may say, "Mother gave me a basketball."

Sentence patterns that pupils acquire should meet the following criteria:

1. Responses should come from pupils;
2. Learning by discovery is to be encouraged;
3. Pupils need to relate sentence patterns to their own unique background of experiences;
4. Learners must attach meaning to sentence patterns;
5. A variety of methods should be utilized in helping learners attach meaning to diverse patterns of sentences;
6. Learning activities should be interesting to pupils;
7. Provision must be made for individual differences; not all learners in a class achieve at the same level of achievement. In which facets of instruction might a teacher provide for individual differences? Disick writes:

"Briefly, individualized instruction is an approach to teaching and learning that offers choices in four areas: objectives of learning, rate of learning, method (or style) of learning, and content of learning. The extent to which choices are offered determines the degree of individualization in a particular programme. If a wide variety of choices exists in all four dimensions, then the programme may be considered fully realized. Programmes that provide fewer areas open to choice may be called uni- or multidimensional. Within this broad category, the type of individualization carried on may be further specified. Programmes featuring selection of course objectives are known as 'independent study'; those emphasizing variations in learning rates are known as 'continuous progress' or 'flexibly paced'; those stressing a variety of learning methods or styles are considered 'multimedia'; and those offering mainly a choice of content are labeled 'mini-courses.' Naturally, two or more dimensions may be combined in one programme of instruction. One such combination would be continuous progress-multimedia, for example."

Expanding Sentences

Sentences are short, choppy, and lack thorough description if the concept of expansion is not utilized in writing situations. The following structural patterns lack expansion:

1. Boys run. (Subject-predicate or noun-verb pattern.)
2. Abe caught the ball. (Subject-predicate-direct object or noun-verb-noun pattern).
3. The orange was delicious. (Subject-linking verb-predicate adjective or noun-linking verb-predicate adjective pattern).
4. Curt is an auctioneer. (Subject-linking verb-predicate nominative or noun-linking verb-noun pattern).
5. Bill gave John a top. (Subject-predicate-indirect object-direct object or noun-verb-noun-noun pattern.)

Each of the above sentences is complete and recommendable in speaking and writing. However, clarity in writing in many situations indicates the need for expanding each of the sentences. In the first sentence above (Boys run), pupils might be asked to tell more about the boys. For example, what kind of boys were these? The following examples are given as possible learner responses:

1. *Tall* boys run.
2. *Small* boys run.
3. *Tall* boys with *blue coats* run.
4. *Small* boys *in the yard* run.

Next, pupils may expand the predicate part of the sentence. For example, how did the boys run?

1. Boys run *slowly*.
2. Boys run *very rapidly*.
3. Boys run *with great speed.*

A further question can be asked of pupils pertaining to where boys run. Pupils may give responses such as the following:

1. Boys run *in the yard.*
2. Boys run *her*.
3. Boys run *around the building.*

In the sentences above, pupils might think of their own personal experiences in terms of where they have run. Learners may also think of 'when' boys run. Examples include the following:

1. Boys run *today*.
2. Boys run *in the morning.*
3. Boys run *at noon.*

Pupils with teacher guidance should have numerous opportunities to expand sentences using modifiers for the subject and/or predicate parts of sentences:

Learners inductively may also expand sentences through the use of appositives. Compare the first sentence with the second sentence.

1 Mr. Jones lives on Line Street.

2 Mr. Jones, our teacher, lives on Line Street.

In the first sentence, the subject-predicate pattern is in evidence. 'Mr. Jones' is the subject while 'lives' is the predicate. The words 'on Line Street' involve the use of a prepositional phrase used as an adverb. These words tell where Mr. Jones lives. In the second sentence, the words, 'our teacher,' are another name for Mr. Jones. Thus, an appositive has been added.

Dependent clauses may also be utilized to expand sentences. Notice the following two sentences:

1. John likes to swim.
2. John sleeps much.

These two sentences may be written as one sentence, thus eliminating short, choppy statements in writing:

Although John sleeps much, he likes to swim.

In this sentence the dependent clause is 'Although John sleeps much.' 'John' is the subject and 'sleeps' is the predicate. The dependent clause does not stand by itself but makes sense when it is related to the independent clause. The independent clause is 'he likes to swim.' The word 'he' is the subject and 'likes' is the predicate. Thus, sentences can be expanded through the use of dependent clauses. The dependent clauses are italicized in the following sentences.

1. *If Jim can earn enough money,* he will buy a new basketball.
2. The boy *who works in the grocery store* is our neighbour.
3. The dog *that wore a new collar* is my pet.

Pupils will realize that dependent clauses generally do not make sense by themselves. The dependent clauses add meaning to an independent clause. Pupils should have ample experience in expanding any sentence pattern through the use of dependent clauses.

Pupils also need to have ample experience when readiness for learning is in evidence pertaining to expanding sentences through compounding. Notice the following sentences.

1. Sally sings.
2. Sally dances.

These sentences follow the subject-predicate pattern. Monotonous writing is in evidence if all written work consisted of short sentences. The two sentences may be rewritten by compounding the predicate parts: Sally *sings and dances.* Two sentences may also be rewritten by compounding the subject.

1. Jim played baseball.
2. Owen played baseball.
3. Jim and Owen played baseball.

Sentence numbers one and two above pertain to the subject-predicate-direct object pattern. Sentence number three compounds the subjects of sentences one and two.

Hennings writes the following involving structural linguistics:

> *"The historical and comparative linguists by relying on analytical techniques were paving the way for the structural linguists of the twentieth century. Using systematic analysis, these linguists have been able to explain the structures through which speakers communicate meaning in English. They have described how meaning is communicated through*
>
> *1. intonation—pitch, stress, juncture, or pause;*
>
> *2. sentence patterns—the order of words in sentences;*
>
> *3. function words—words like noun markers, verb markers, phrase makers clause markers, question markers that communicate relationships among the four major word classes, the nouns, verbs, adjectives, and adverbs.*
>
> ***4. inflectional endings like the s through which we form a plural noun and affixes through which we change words from one class to another. For example, govern, a verb becomes government, a noun, with the addition of the affix ment while courage, a noun, becomes courageous, an adjective, with the addition of the affix -ous."***

Stress, Pitch, and Juncture

Pupils need to become thoroughly familiar with meanings and applications of the concepts *stress, pitch*, and *Juncture*.

When words are pronounced within a sentence, differences in stress occur. Study of following sentence: "Hand me the toys."

If the word 'hand' is stressed more than the other words in the sentence, this means that the toys should be handed rather than thrown or tossed. Stressing the word 'me' more than the other words in the same sentence indicates that the toys should go to the person who is speaking rather than to any other individual. If the word 'toys' is stressed more than any other word in the sentence, the emphasis is upon 'toys' rather than a book, pamphlet, or other object.

Pupils should practice speaking using the same sentence in meaningful ways and stress a different selected word each time more than any other word in the same sentence. A tape recorder might be utilized in this learning activity. Pupils may also perceive how a specific sentence changes in meaning when a selected word is stressed more than other words within the sentence. Linguists recognize four degrees of stress. Pupils with teacher guidance should practice using different degrees of stress when communicating ideas orally in speaking experiences.

Pupils should also have ample opportunities to practice using pitch in oral communication of ideas. Linguists recognize four degrees of pitch. Selected words in a sentence may be pitched higher or lower and thus change the meaning of a sentence. In some cases, words will be pitched higher at the end of a sentence when questions are asked. However, not all words are pitched higher at the end of a sentence when questions are asked. Consider the following sentences:

1. Did you do and reading today?
2. Bill has moved?

In the second sentence, the ending word is pitched higher as compared to the ending word of the first sentence. Pupils with the use of a cassette recorder should practice oral communication involving interrogative sentences. Learners may notice the degree of pitch of ending words in a sentence. Pupils may also notice how other words are pitched within these sentences as well as in imperative, declarative, and exclamatory types of sentences. Attempts should be made in identifying different degrees of pitch of words within sentences.

Much misinterpretation of sentence meaning occurs when juncture is not utilized properly in speaking and writing. Consider the following incorrectly punctuated sentence; At the picnic jello salad ham sandwiches and milk were served. It is difficult to determine how many different kinds of food were served.

The following might be possibilities depending upon pauses in oral communication or commas in written communication within each sentence:

1. At the picnic jello, salad, ham, sandwiches, and milk were served.
2. At the picnic jello salad, ham, sandwiches, and milk were served.
3. At the picnic jello salad, ham sandwiches, and milk were served.

Pupils should practice reading and speaking different sentences where proper placement of commas (or pausing adequately between words) is important. The meaning of a sentence can certainly change depending upon emphasized pauses, within a specific sentence. As a further example, pertaining to juncture, consider the following sentences:

1. Leon, my cousin, works in a factory.
2. Leon, my cousin works in a factory.

In the first sentence, the speaker is stating a fact about Leon. In the second sentence, the speaker is speaking directly to Leon. Using the same words in a sentence, meanings can change depending upon printed commas or orally emphasized pauses within a sentence.

Ragan and Shepherd write the following involving language development:

"Just as the language of a child is developed through experiencing, so is the language arts programme. The symbols and patterns of language are abstractions applied to the realities of the objects, events and values experienced by a culture and an individual. Without these applications, the mastery of the skills and tools of language is somewhat like practising a violin in a vacuum: even if a skill is mastered in abstract, it is inert and valueless until it is activated in a social experience. For example, the skill of diagramming a sentence (for the elementary child) does not conduct into significant changes in the oral or even written language patterns of the child. On the other hand, learning to perceive differences in sounds and patterns does seem to significantly influence the child's oral and written language. Listening and voicing imitations are concrete experiences; diagramming is an abstract experience.

Instruction in language arts must therefore begin with the social maturation and experiences which are already encoded by the learner. From this beginning, additional social maturation and experiencing must be provided as the foundation for the new symbols and patterns to be learned."

Generating New Sentences

Pupils should have meaningful experiences pertaining to how a declarative sentence, for example, can be changed to other kinds of sentences such as an interrogative sentence. First of all, pupils on the appropriate developmental level need to understand and attach meaning to a kernal sentence. A kernal sentence is simple and declarative. A declarative sentence states a fact. The subject of the kernal sentence is the actor, not the receiver of the action. The following are examples of kernal sentences:

1. John plays baseball.
2. Paul works in a store.
3. Josephine eats in the cafeteria.

In each of the above sentences, a fact is stated. Thus, a declarative sentence is in evidence. Also, in each of the sentences, the subject performs the action. That is, in sentence number one, John does the playing. In sentence two, Paul does the working, while in sentence three Josephine does the eating. Each of these sentences may be transformed or changed to a different kind of sentence other than the declarative sentence. In sentence number one which reads, "John plays baseball," the pitch of the ending word may be raised resulting in an interrogative sentence: "John plays baseball?" A few changes may also be made in the original sentence and result in the question: "Does John play baseball?" To change the original declarative sentence to a negative, the following sentence can result: "John does not play baseball." The original declarative sentence might also be rewritten to state a request: "John, please play baseball." A command may result when making the following selected changes: "John, play baseball." Imperative sentences result when requests or commands are in evidence. Very few changes need to be made when changing declarative sentences to the following:

1. Sentences which ask questions.
2. Sentences which issue commands or requests.
3. Sentences which show strong feeling.

In the declarative sentence reading, "John plays baseball," the statement can be transformed to read, "John plays baseball!" The latter sentence reveals strong feeling and states an exclamatory sentence. The same words were used for the declarative and exclamatory sentences. The only difference was in the end punctuation marks. Declarative sentences end with periods while exclamatory sentences with exclamation points.

Usage and Communication of Ideas

The words a speaker uses when communicating ideas orally or in writing are a matter of choice. Middle class individuals in society, in most cases, demand that standard English be spoken. However, effective communication also takes place with the use of non-standard English. Contrast the following pairs of sentences.

1. They have completed their work.
   They done their work
2. I haven't any money.
   I ain't got no money.

3. I ran in a race
   I ranned in a race.

4. He is going to town
   He goin to town.

No doubt, effective communication can take place when using either standard or non-standard English. In selected environments, non-standard English is accepted as good and sounds right to its users. In other environments, standard English only, is acceptable. An important item to remember is that the teacher accept all pupils has having much worth if standard or non-standard English is spoken. Each person is important in a democracy. Respect for others is the heart of democratic thinking. Each pupil must be guided in achieving optimum development.

Teachers in the past felt that pupils using non-standard English should be corrected on the scene so that standard English alone might be an important end result. Linguists have stated the following for not using this approach:

1. The pupil may come to feel that this/her home environment is inferior since non-standard English is unacceptable in school;
2. Pupils cannot make rapid changes when switching from non-standard to standard English in the school and class setting;
3. Negative attitudes are developed toward speaking and writing when teachers criticize the speaking efforts of those who speak non-standard English;
4. Basically, it does not help most pupils in making desired forced changes to speaking standard English.

Anderson and Lapp write the following on usage in the language arts:

> *"Correct public usage is concerned with proper form. The agreement of verb and subject in number and tense, the form of the pronoun in various positions in the sentence, and the word order in sentences are some of the situations that present learning problems of proper form. The child who says, "I done my work" is using the wrong verb form. Another who says, "Him and me are friends" is using the wrong form of the pronoun. Children use these forms because they here them at home, on television and on the playground.*

First of all, the teacher will encourage the child to enjoy his private language. He will be accepted, no mater what he says or how he says it. His language is a verbal expression of his thoughts and feelings. If we reject it, we reject him. Furthermore, we reject by implication the family who has taught him to speak and with whom he has strong emotional ties that he needs as he develops as a human being."

Pupils who speak non-standard English can learn to speak standard English in the following ways:

1. by listening to the teacher who may serve as a model in speaking standard English;
2. by reading library books which utilize standard English in their content;
3. by listening to pupils speak where standard English is used;
4. by listening to tapes and records pertaining to content in relevant units of study where meaningful standard English is used by the speaker;
5. by viewing and listening to content in slides, films, and filmstrips where standard English is used;
6. by listening to presentations by resource personnel who utilize standard English in communicating ideas.

Pupils can learn to speak standard English in school and yet respect, as well as use, nonstandard English in the home environment. Thus, usage in speaking and writing pertains to choices if words and word order that are made in communicating ideas.

Anderson and Lapp write about the following forms that teachers might provide needed assistance to learners involving standard English:

1. A transition from all 'baby-talk' and 'cute' expressions;
2. The acceptable uses in speech and writing of *I, me, him, her, she, they and them.* (Accepted: It's me.");
3. The appropriate uses of *is, are was, were* with respect to number and tense;
4. Standard past tenses of common irregular verbs, such as *saw, gave, took, brought, stuck;*

5. Elimination of the double negative: "We don't have no apples";
6. Elimination of analogical forms: *ain't, hisn, hern, ourn, hisself, theirselves,* and so on;
7. Appropriate use of possessive pronouns: *my, mine, his, hers, theirs, ours;*
8. Mastery of the distinction between *its* (possessive pronoun) and *it's* (it is, the contraction). (This applies only to written English.);
9. Elimination of *this here* and *that there;*
10. Approved use of personal pronouns in compound constructions: as subject (Mary and I), as object *(Mary and me)*, as object of preposition *(to Mary and me);*
11. Attention to number agreement with the phrases *there is, there are, there was, there were;*
12. Elimination of *he don't, she don't, it don't;*
13. Elimination of *learn* for *teach, leave* for *let;*
14. Avoidance of pleonastic subjects: *my brother he; my mother she; that fellow he;*
15. Sensing the distinction between *good* as adjective and *well* as adverb (for example, "He spoke well").

In Summary

It is important for pupils to ultimately understand patterns of sentences in the English language. These sentence patterns include subject-predicate, subject-predicate-direct object, subject-linking verb-predicate adjective, subject-linking verb-predicate nominative, and subject-predicate-indirect object-direct object pattern. Pupils should also attach meaning to the concept of expanding sentences. Sentences may be expanded through the use of modifiers, appositives, dependent clauses, and compounding. It is important for learners to attach meaning to concepts such as stress, pitch, and juncture. Meanings of sentences change when utilizing these concepts.

Learners should be able to change sentences in functional writing and speaking situations from kernal sentences to those involving the asking of questions, the stating of negatives, and the issuing of commands or requests. Pupils with teacher guidance need to understand the concept of usage as it relates to standard and nonstandard English in oral and written communication of content.

REFERENCES

Anderson, Paul S. (Ed.). *Linguistics in the Elementary School Classroom*. New York: The Macmillan Company, 1971. Part One.

Anderson, Paul S., et al. (Eds.). *Readings in the Language Arts*. Second Edition. New York: The Macmillan Company, 1968. Chapter Six.

Anderson, Paul S., and Diane Lapp *Language Skills in Elementary Education*. Third Ed. New York: Macmillan Publishing Company, Inc., 1979.

Beane, James A., et. al. *Curriculum Planning and Development*. Boston: Allyn and Bacon, Inc. 1986.

Corcoran, Gertrude, *Language Arts in the Elementary School. A Modern Linguistic Approach*. New York: The Ronald Press Company, 1970.

Disick, Renee S. *Individualizing Language Instruction*. New York: Harcourt Brace and Jovanovich, Inc., 1975.

Donoghue, Milderd R. *The child and the English Language Arts*. Dubuque, Iowa: Wm. C. Brown Company Publishers, 1971.Chapter Nine.

Hennings, Dorothy Grant, *Communication in Action*. Chicago: Rand McNally College Publishing Company, 1978.

Meras, Edmond A. *A Language Teacher's Guide*. Second Ed. New York: Harper and Row Publishers, 1962, Chapters One, Two, and Three.

Newman, Harold (Ed.). *Effective Language Arts Practices in the Elementary School: Selected Readings*. New York: John Wiley and Sons, 1972. Chapter One.

Orlich, Donald C. *Teaching Strategies*. Second Edition. Lexington, Massachusetts, D.C. Health and Company, 1985.

Petty, Walter T. *Issues and Problems in the Elementary Language Arts: A Book of Readings*. Boston: Allyn and Bacon, Inc., 1968. Part II.

Petty, Walter T., et al. *Experience in Language.* Second Ed. Boston: Allyn and Bacon, Inc., 1976.

Ragan, Williman B., and Gene D. Shepherd, *Modern Elementary Curriculum.* New York: Holt, Rinehart and Winston, 1977.

Roberts, Paul, *Modern Grammar.* New York: Harcourt, Brace & World,.Inc., 1968. Chapters One and Two.

Shuster, Albert H., and Milton E. Ploghoft. *The Emerging Elementary Curriculum Methods and Procedures.* Columbus, Ohio: Charles E. Merrill Publishing Company, 1970. Chapter Seven.

Tiedt, Iris M., and Sidney W. Tiedt. *Contemporary English in the Elementary School,* Second Ed. Englewood Cliffs, New Jersey: Prentice Hall, Inc., 1975.

7

Reading and the Language Arts

The pupils should learn to enjoy reading and realize that many benefits accrue from the act of reading. The teacher needs to communicate to pupils that he/she loves to read and communicates these feelings to learners. An attitude of reading is a good endeavour which needs to be communicated to pupils. Not only should reading be enjoyable to pupils but also useful in its many manifestations. There are numerous things that a teacher can do to stimulate young children in becoming lovers of library books.

Strommen and Mates (1997) conducted research into young children's ideas about the nature of reading and wrote the following:

Our observations confirm that learning to read is a developmental process but show that a young child's age, word and later-level decoding skills, are not necessarily reliable indicators of what he/she understands reading to be, and, therefore of what intervention may be useful.

It is important for teachers to realize that a child's growth in ideas about what readers do and his/her growth in reading itself are interdependent. A fundamental goal of beginning reading instruction should be to move each child toward the understanding that readers reconstruct texts by using multiple strategies to interpret the language encoded by print and at the same time, to make it possible for the child to do this by providing information that will enable construction of appropriate strategies. With this in mind we make the following recommendations regarding children early literacy instruction:

1. Teachers of young children should initially stress a child's ideas about the nature of reading, written language and the written code, as well as his/her reading strategies and tailor reading experiences to the child's ideas about what readers do;
2. Teaches should ask themselves what new formation could cause a child to rethink or interpret what he or she believes and challenge each child's non-conventional ideas through demonstrations that contradict his/her current thinking. For example, frequent re-readings of a particular text help to build's knowledge of written language, but may also promote the idea that reading is memorizing texts. If a child believes this is what readers do, then demonstrating that readers can and do read a variety of unfamiliar texts may contribute to a shift in the child's thinking;
3. Teachers should set expectations for a child's reading performance that always take into account the child's ideas about how readers read.

Developing a Love for Reading

The act of reading means that pupils are reading enjoyable and useful materials. Reading does not mean a study of phonics, nor lessons on syllabication. Rather, reading involves securing ideas, content and subject matter. Thus, reading stresses a form of holism in that concepts and generalizations are obtained from print materials. An immersed reader find few distractions and is actively engaged in what is being read. The interest factor in reading propels pupils to reach toward higher levels in reading subject matter. Thus, the pupil and the content to be read become one, not separate entities.

With active involvement in reading, the pupil should attach meaning to ongoing concepts and generalizations. Meaning is attached to what is being read. The abstract print then makes sense to the reader. Understanding of print materials assists pupils to like reading in its diverse purposes. Pupils learn to predict what comes sequentially in ongoing reading tasks. This helps the pupil to overcome difficulties in recognizing individual words when predicting in a contextual situation. Further reading will provide the pupil with clues as to the predictions being correct or incorrect. Holism is involved in reading ideas, not fragmented sounds or syllables. Learners need to feel they have control over what is being read. In other words, they are able to understand in a meaningful way that which is being read. Pupils have control over their own reading when they can break the code involving abstract symbols. Does this mean that phonics need to be taught in beginning reading? Good teachers have always brought in phonics instruction when stressing a holistic reading curriculum. The phonics is brought in contextually, not within isolated word analysis lessons.

Pupils need to develop a basic sight vocabulary of relevant words as they progress through the early primary grades. The sight vocabulary for reading needs to be developed within a viable context, not within isolated words presented by the teacher. A more meaningful procedure is then in evidence when contextually pupils achieve a vocabulary for reading whereby words are recognized at sight. In addition to a basic sight vocabulary, pupils need to attain basic learnings in phonics. Phonics has its many values when a pupil cannot determine an unknown word, but can identify this word through analysis such as in phonics. Thus, the pupil associates individual sounds with their related symbols. It does not take long before pupils can apply relevant phonics principles when unlocking unknown words in a contextual situation. Interest in reading should never be destroyed through the development of a basic sight vocabulary of words whereby these are known by immediately observation. Nor should phonics instruction in which pupils truly enjoy learning phonics within a contextual situation as the need arises. It have supervised many student teachers and cooperating teachers who have devised games to assist pupils to enjoy mastering new words which then are recognized at once through observation.

As the young child progresses in reading, he/she develops concepts pertaining to what a word is when seeing it in print.

Usually, pupils individually also learn the letters within a word and the related sounds inherent in the word. There are words which contain letters that have a one to one correspondence with the related sounds. Other sounds need two letters such as the 'th' sound in words such as 'the', 'this' and 'that'. Pupils need to do much reading with teacher guidance as well as by themselves so that increased skills in word recognition occur. The teacher also needs to read aloud to pupils so that the latter obtains concepts pertaining to content, sequence of ideas presented, punctuation, stress, pitch and structure of sentence patterns. Selections read aloud by the teacher should be interesting, understandable and purposeful. These reading selections might well serve as a basis for pupils liking or disliking reading instruction.

The Experience Chart

Experience charts are an excellent way for pupils to enjoy reading as well as extend their skills in this area. Here, the classroom of pupils or a smaller group has had an interesting experience such as looking outside the classroom window to notice the rain falling. After an ample period of time for observing the rain fall, pupils may dictate ideas to the teacher in developing the rain fall, pupils may dictate ideas to the teacher in developing an experience chart. These learners should understand the content presented to the teacher since a concrete situation was provided to children to think about. The teacher records subject matter on the chalkboard, when presented by pupils. As the ideas are given, pupils can see talk written down. A word processor may also be used to record pupil's ideas for the experience chart.

Once the ideas have been presented, the teacher guides pupils in reading the recorded ideas from the experience chart. Pupils read the content orally with the teacher as he/she points to each word or phrase. Here, pupils have opportunities to develop a basic sight vocabulary of words for reading. The contents of the experience chart may be read over again as pupils desire. With re-reading, pupils are aided in identifying more and more words by sight. Also, pupils notice that talk is written down. These can be considered as written experiences for young pupils when they see talk written down. Thus, there are individual letters, words, phrases and sentences. Whatever is said by pupils can be recorded on the chalk-board or by using the word processor. Learners usually begin to make statement such as the following pertaining to the recorded contents in the experience chart:

1. Here are two words that begin or end with the same letter;
2. These two words rhyme;
3. These are long words or these are short in length;
4. These are the same letters in the two words but they make different sounds;
5. This word has taller letters as compared to that word.

It is quite obvious that pupils are making discoveries within the experience chart and appear to be interested in this activity at the same time. We have personally observed much enthusiasm when pupils engage in making discoveries by examining words and sentences.

When making comparisons among different experience charts with content provided by young children and recorded by the teacher, it is quite obvious that more sophistication is involved on the learner's part when sequentially experiences of this nature are provided. Ediger (1988) list the following assumptions involving experience charts:

1. Pupils are actively involved in experiences which provide content for an experience chart;
2. Learners present ideas for the experience chart;
3. Pupils teacher help read content pertaining to their very own experiences;
4. Learners may notice how ideas are written down using abstract letters and words;
5. The content in the experience chart is familiar to learners since it relates to their own personal lives;
6. The experience chart method may assist pupils to develop interest in reading;

7. Individualization is inherent in using experience charts since each child has unique experiences. Each child may then present content for a group or individual experience chart.

Pupils soon select library books to read and practice reading those same words that were experienced on the experience chart. Pupils should experience many reading activities so that learing to read is pleasurable and progress is made sequentially. Fountas and Pinnell (1996) wrote the following objectives for guided reading which serve well in all reading programmes:

- It gives children the opportunity to develop as individual readers while participating in a socially supported activity;
- It gives teachers the opportunity to observe individuals as they process new texts;
- It gives individual readers the opportunity to develop strategies so that they can read increasingly difficult texts independently;
- It gives children enjoyable, successful experiences in reading for meaning;
- It develops the abilities needed for independent reading;
- It helps children learn how to introduce texts to themselves.

Young children need to achieve these broad objectives in reading sequentially. Success in each sequential step is important. Interesting and purposeful reading materials need to be in the offing. The reading teacher needs to know each pupil well so that a quality reading curriculum may be continuous and ongoing.

Guided Listening Thinking Activity

The Guided Listening Thinking Activity (GLTA) emphasizes the teacher choosing a library book which children would love to participate in. A large picture book for young children would suffice. The teacher asks the children to predict what the book would be about as the title and illustrations therein are viewed. The teacher then reads aloud to pupils a short section in which the height of action in the story is involved. Pupils then need to evaluate their original prediction or hypothesis. Each hypothesis must be respected and further hypothesizing encouraged for the rest of the story. Then the teacher may read to find out what did happen in the picture book. Higher levels of cognition need to be emphasized already on the early primary grade levels. Pupils should be encouraged to do critical and creative thinking as well as problem solving as early as possible in life. Higher levels of cognition are necessary in every day life with its many perplexities and difficulties.

After the reading of the picture book has been completed, the teacher may raise additional questions about the contents. It is salient to obtain pupil reaction to the contents. Pupils should be able to provide reasons for their answers given. Learners should also ask questions covering what was read from the picture book.

The GLTA is teacher directed. The teacher chooses the book to be read. He/she determines questions to be answered by pupils. The teacher stimulates pupils to make predictions, develop hypotheses, thin at higher levels of cognition, set the classroom climate for the activity and provide support for each pupil. This does not mean that pupils are left out of the reading curriculum when the GLTA is being stressed. Rather, the teacher encourages pupils responses and is the leader in setting the stage and implementing the reading lesson. It is also child centered in that pupils are encouraged to make predictions and hypothesize. Pupils have opportunities to raise questions, especially at the end of reading the selection from the picture book. We believe with a teacher directed reading lesson, the pupil needs to be as actively involved as possible in responding to the questions of the teacher as well as the child raise questions of his/her own. Listening carefully and well is an important goal to stress in GLTA.

The Shared Book Experience

The shared book experience emphasizes more pupil participation in the actual reading of content as compared to the Guided Listening Thinking Activity in which the teacher does the oral reading and pupils follow along in their own books to achieve in word recognition and other elements in reading. The shared books experiences stresses the use of a Big Book. With the Big Book, all pupils in the group can clearly see the illustrations and print from where they are seated. Examples of two Big Book are *When the King Rides By* (Mahy, 1986) and *The Greedy Goat* (Bolton, 1986).

Contents in Big Books should have predictable subject matter for pupils so that they can rather readily determine what will come next in the story in sequence. The teacher introduces the Big Book to pupils by looking together at the illustrations therein. These illustrations are discussed and provide pupils with background information in order to understand Big Book contents more effectively. The pupils with the background information will be better able to read along with the classroom teacher from the Big Book. Predictions may be made by pupils in terms of outcomes of the story. These predictions may be checked at an appropriate point when reading the Big Book cooperatively. Higher levels of cognition is definitely a goal here, including critical and creative thinking as well as problem solving. These higher cognitive goals are to be encouraged and based upon the present developmental level of each pupil. Respect for the learner and his/her abilities is always important. Good citizenship and democracy need to be practised continuously in the classroom.

When pupils read along together with the teacher from the Big Book, they learn to identify words which present problems in the teaching of reading. The experience chart approach made it so that pupils presented ideas for the chart with the teacher then reading together with the pupils the contents therein. The Big Book philosophy of reading instructions also emphasizes pupils learning to recognize words contextually while reading together with the teacher. At the end of the reading experience, the teacher may ask questions such as the following to provide interest in phonics:

1. Which words did you notice that started with the same letter or sound?
2. Which words end with the same letter and sound?
3. Which vowel letters in words make the same sound?
4. Which vowel letters makes a different sound when comparing two or more words?
5. Do you see words whereby two letters make a single sound?

Each of the above learning activities needs to be emphasized or adjusted to the present achievement level of pupils. Pupils should enjoy phonics activities. These experiences need to be positive for pupils and assist in developing word recognition skills. Phonics should not be taught for its own sake, but rather to assist learners to unlock unknown words. Phonics then has practical and utilitarian values and is not taught for its own sake.

When pupils and the teacher orally read together the contents from a Big Book, a type of choral reading is being emphasized. Learners may perceive sentence patterns which provide structure for the English language. Re-reading of a Big Book, especially if desired by pupils is to be encouraged. We think most of us had our favourite books a children which we re-read many times, in my case *The Little Red Hen* was read over and over again as a child! A major objective here is to guide pupils to want to read more literature and at a more complex level as optimal progress is being made by individual pupils. With re-reading, comprehension appears to increase, meaning that more complex questions may be discussed with pupils. Familiarity with words is important when assisting pupils in developing a basic sight vocabulary. Choral reading and re-reading assists pupils in achieving a core of functional words, necessary in becoming a good reader.

Word Banks and the Young Reader

One way to assist pupils to master words in reading is to stress the word bank concept. With the word bank, each pupil prints on a three by five inch card a word that has been mastered in reading. With the addition of new cards, each card having a word printed thereon, the pupil must alphabetize the set of words and rehearse the correct identification of each word. The reward to the pupil is to see the stack of cards get larger due to having mastered more words as sight words. The teacher could place an interesting sticker on each card as reinforcement.

There are pupils who enjoy making sentences from words in the word bank. Pupils could work in teams doing this. The point is to have pupils read words within context frequently and thus become better readers.

Peers may also work together by providing drill and practice experiences from the use of these word bank cards.

Word bank cards could also be grouped in terms of:

1. those having the same beginning sounds;
2. those having the same ending sounds;
3. those having the same vowel sounds;
4. those having grave irregularities in spelling between symbol and sound.

As many uses as possible should be made of word bank cards. Games may be devised, sentences expanded and stories written with the the use of these cards.

Story book Time with Children

The teacher needs to read orally to pupils each day. Why? Here, pupils learn about a story, about vocabulary terms, about sequential ideas in a story, abut sentence patterns, about characterization, about the setting of a story, about the plot about the theme and messages presented by the author. Pupils also may learn to enjoy good literature for their developmental level. Perhaps, an individual child desires to read the same book during spare time or at home. Background information for the child's time to read has then come from the teacher's oral reading. There should be familiarity when the pupil reads the same book as compared to not having heard the contents read by the teacher. The teacher needs to become very familiar with children's literature so that pupils perceive a model to emulate. A few years ago while supervising a student teacher and cooperating teacher, we noticed how knowledgeable the latter was about library books for pupils. This teacher related library books with the books being read to children. We believe young children here were fascinated with the knowledge the teacher had about library books when integrating different sources. Thus, a good characteristic of a teacher who reads orally to pupils is that he/she likes children's literature. The horizons of the primary grade teacher need to be expanded in knowing about recent books that have come out in children's literature as well as remaining informed about older books of high quality, the latter being important to Perennialists. Perennialism, as a philosophy of education, believes that the enduring ideas in time and space are important and not recently published books.

The primary grade teacher should also read enthusiastically to pupils. Learners are very attentive to these read aloud sessions if the teacher shows love and enjoyment of oral reading of library books. As the oral reading progresses, the teacher needs to show related illustrations in the book to pupils. There should be adequate time for pupil to comment abut the issustrations and content. If the comments from pupils seem endless, the teacher may politely say that we have time for one more pupil.Otherwise, it is wholesome and good for children to react to what is contained in a library book.

The teacher needs to observe pupils when reading aloud to notice the pace at which learners can understand the content. I have observed teachers read too rapidly whereby pupils seemingly cannot understand the contents. The opposite has been true also in which the content was read too slowly by the teacher. Remember, pupils can listen to and comprehend content more rapidly as compared to the reading that they do. Thus, pupils read more slowly as compared to comprehending content listened to. With practice and feedback from pupils being read to, the teacher can adjust the speed of reading aloud to what pupils can process in terms of subject matter listened to.

Voice inflection which includes stress, pitch and juncture is very important in oral reading to pupils. Certain words need to be stressed more than others so that proper interpretation is an end result. A monotone says all words with the same stress, but a dynamic speaker places more stress on specific words as compared to others so that meaning in interpretation is in evidence. Proper pitch is important also when reading aloud. Thus, selected words are pitched higher or lower than others. Why? Whatever is said involves interpretation by the speaker as well as by the listener. If all words are pitched on the same level, a monotone results. By pitching words properly, there are better chances for appropriate communication. It is much easier to secure the attention of others with proper pitch of words as compared to a monotone voice. And by pitching words appropriately, the reader of library books to pupils emphasizes what he/she wishes to communicate. Proper pauses or juncture needs to be in evidence in oral reading of children's literature. Juncture then indicates that the reader pause where commas, periods and other punctuation marks are located. By omitting or slighting punctuation marks, distortion in meaning of content read certainly can be an end result.

In our teacher education classes, we do emphasize university students reading well orally to peers, according to quality criteria and also that they received practice in the schools in reading orally to pupils at different age and achievement levels. This is vital for a good teacher.

The teacher should have good eye contact with each pupil as the read aloud continues. This indicates that a teacher is communicating with all pupils and watches the attention span of pupils. Pupils do need to be attentive and engaged when the teacher reads aloud content from sequential library books. Literature read to children needs to be carefully chosen by the teacher. Hopefully, the contents will be interesting and enjoyable to pupils whereby these learners will have an inward desire to achieve in reading skills and attitudes. The teacher needs to choose a variety of genres in literature so that the diverse interests of pupils is meet. Teachers usually tend to become knowledgeable about which library books would fascinate learners when being read aloud to pupils.

It is good teaching practice for a teacher to read privately the library book which will be read aloud to pupils later. A definite strategy should then be developed by the teacher as to how the library book should be introduced to pupils. Here, readiness factors enter in as to what to do to assist pupils to like the new book to be read aloud. Certainly, the teacher should discuss the illustrations at the beginning of the books with children, prior to reading so that there is more familiarity of learners with the content to be read aloud sequentially. By thinking of procedures as use when reading each library book, the teacher soon develops a repertoire of skills which assist in gaining the attention of pupils in desiring to read children's literature. I think it is good procedure too for a teacher a read aloud these library books he/she enjoys. After all, the positive attitudes should have their affects within listeners. A special time needs to be set aside each day for oral reading of children's literature so that pupils realize the importance of this activity. Primary teachers always set aside time after the one hour noon recess for oral reading of children's literature to pupils. The read aloud had a tendency to make for a relaxed feelings and we believe, provided readiness for studying in the next curriculum area.

Where should the teacher be when reading aloud to pupils? We have noticed teachers for read aloud at different places when supervising student teachers in the public school, such as:

1. being seated in front of the classroom;
2. being seated in a chair while pupils are nearby seated on the carpet;
3. being seated on the floor on an even level with the pupils;
4. being seated in the middle of the classroom;
5. being in a standing position and moving around the classroom while reading aloud to pupils.

Individualized Reading

Once children have developed and adequate number of basic sight words for reading, they may become involved in individualized reading. Here, there needs to be an appropriate number of library books for pupils to select from in choosing a book to read. The titles need to indicate different genres to provide for the interest needs of individual pupils. Also, the library books must be written on diverse achievement levels so that each pupil may chose a book which harmonizes with his/her present achievement level in reading. Content which is too complex to read frustrates the reader. Subject matter that is too easy might well become boring to the reader. Thus, there are library books which are on the reading level, not frustration nor boring level, of pupils to select from for individualized reading.

These library books should be displayed at a learning center in an interesting manner to capture pupil attention. A bulletin board with neatly displayed book jackets of new library books should also assist pupils to develop interest in individualized reading. The teacher should tell a few interesting things about a library books as it is held up for learner viewing. Hopefully, this will also assist in whetting the appetites of pupils for individualized reading. The primary grade teacher needs to think of different strategies in developing within pupils a desire to select and read sequential library books. The pupil is the chooser, not the teacher, as to which library book a pupil is to read. The teacher offers assistance if pupils are hesitant in choosing or if they do not find an appropriate library book to read.

The individual pupil then chooses a library book to read at the learning center. Usually, a learner will select a book that refers to a preferable genre and is on his/her reading level. Sometimes, a pupil needs to select a different library book to read due to the complexity of the original book selected. Once a pupil has settled down to read silently, the library book chosen, a good reader or teacher aide may assist pupils with word identification. Each pupil should be given adequate chances to determine an unknown word before assistance is given in word recognition. Primary age pupils need to become as independent in identifying words as possible. Sometimes, a few pupils become too dependent upon the teacher for word identification. Through the use of content clues and phonics, a pupil can identify many words which generally would be unknown to the reader (Ediger, 1997).

Following the completion of silent reading of a library book, the pupil should have a brief conference with the teacher. Here, the involved pupil reads a short selection to the teacher from the library book. The teacher may also choose the selection to be read orally by the pupil in conference. The primary grade teacher may then observe errors made by the pupil in oral reading and assist in remedying the problems areas. Which problems do pupils reveal on oral reading on the primary grade levels? Student teachers and cooperating teachers whom we supervised have enumerated the following:

1. ***Omitting Words:*** This can be a major problem if meaning is distorted when reading the selection. Sometimes when 'a', 'an', and 'the' are omitted by learners in reading in the conference setting, the meaning may not change any;
2. ***Adding Words:*** When the young child adds words that are not in the reading selection, the resulting meaning may or may not change. Pupils do add the article 'the' with no change in meaning of the sentence. Other words added may really distort the meaning of what is read;
3. ***Disregarding Punctuation Marks:*** If commas are omitted when words are in a series, the meaning will be greatly distorted. The same is true if a period is omitted and a run on sentence is an end result. Errors made by pupils provide a basis for determining objectives to stress in the reading curriculum;
4. ***Hesitating to Long Before Pronouncing Words:*** Frequent hesitations, lasting each five seconds or longer, do hinder pupils in reading with understanding. Generally, a library book is too complex for reading if hesitating before word pronunciation hinders pupils in attaching meaning to what is being read;
5. Repeating what has been read correctly.

Teachers of individualized reading need to record the types of errors made by pupils in reading aloud in a conference setting after the letter his completed the reading of a library book. These reading errors should be examined and then noticed if remediation instruction is necessary. As was indicated, some types of errors may not be important enough to stress in remediation work. Thus inserting or omitting articles, among other kinds of errors, might be quite minimal in a holistic approach of reading instruction whereby learners may become skillful in predicting what will flow in sequence in reading.

In the conference within the individualized reading programme, pupils and the teacher need to appraise comprehension of the learner. With would suggest that the teacher stress higher levels of cognition in individualized reading. Thus critical and creative thinking, and problem solving need adequate emphasis in the conference involving pupil and teacher. The teacher needs to have a good working knowledge of children's literature when an individualized reading programme is in evidence.

We would suggest that the teacher read children's literature. Keeping a file on each book read as to its contents as well as reading reviews of new library books for pupils to read. There are excellent reviews of children's literature in *The Language Arts* (See bibliography entry of the National Council Teacher of English) as well as in *The Reading Teacher* (See bibliography entry of the International Reading Association). The teacher should become very familiar with Caldecott and Newbery Award winning library books. The Caldecott Award is given to the author of the best illustrated library book written for children whereas the Newbery Award is given to the author, also annually, who wrote the best judged content. There are other awards given annually to the best judged content. There are other awards given annually to the best writer of the year in children's literature such as in Missouri the Mark Twain Award is given for writing the best judged children's library book.

Every year, a Children's Literature Festival is held on the Truman State University Campus. I (Ediger) have served as a member of the Children's Literature Festival Committee for several year. Live authors speak to children and show their written works. At this Festival, children are divided into small groups of ten so that there are ample opportunities for pupils to ask questions of the authors. Children make some very positive informal comments about the festival during its sessions. Some of these comments which I heard in passing were the following:

1. I didn't know good authors were living individuals. I thought they had to have died sometime ago to be called an author;
2. I am thrilled to see and listen to an author;
3. One author even signed his signature to a library book I now have;
4. I like to ask questions of five authors that I could never have asked before;
5. I have written letters to authors but never listened to one talk to us.

In a questionnaire provide pupils directly after the Children's Literature Festival, the following were rated high with a 4 to 5 average rating, as marked by pupils in the questionnaire.

1. The Festival was truly worth attending;
2. The pupils listened carefully to authors as they talked about writing their books;
3. I learned much about the children's books discussed.

The lowest rating was given to one author speaking in too quiet a manner when presenting his library book to children.

A Children's Literature Festival seemingly does much to interest pupils in the reading of library books. This observation was confirmed by teachers of pupils attending the Festival. Seemingly, pupils did more reading that previously. Motivation to read had increased. Many pupils read library books written by the authors who appeared at the Festival. Apparently, the authors had provided readiness or an introduction to reading the library books. It does help pupils in wanting to read a book if they have become familiar with in one way or another. Modelling by authors at the Festival is a powerful factor in encouraging pupil reading of books.

We have observed to how Sustained Silent Reading (SSR) can offer to children a positive model for reading. In one school I visited, everyone in the elementary school building read during a certain time of the day, usually twenty minutes in length. When the word 'everyone' is mentioned, this included the custodian and cafeteria workers. Pupils can then notice that people do read and there must be something enjoyable and valuable in doing so. One very important model for pupils in reading is the primary grade teacher. This teacher needs to be enthusiastic about reading and what has been read. One of us noticed a second grade teacher tell about Plato's *The Republic* she had read the previous summer in a university graduate class. She told pupils of how Plato had divided people into three class—the rulers of the nation, the military personnel and the artisans or workers. This teacher showed pictures of present day adults and asked pupils which of the three categories of Plato's Republic they would come under. Pupils were fascinated with the discussion and were actively engaged in the activity. We do believe pupils will remember sessions such as these and consume more literature now as well as when they progress through the different levels of schooling.

Conclusion

Primary grade reading teachers need to provide a variety of concrete, semi-concrete and abstract experiences for pupils so that a solid foundation is laid for successful reading. The instruction should be as holistic as possible so that pupils read content, not work on isolated sound/symbol relationship. The act of reading is holistic whereby learners need to perceive the whole of the selection read. This leaves room for the teaching of phonics as needed. Some children will need much less phonics as compared to others. How much phonics is to be taught depends upon the needs of individual pupils.

To identify unknown words, contexts clues are important for pupils to use. Further help for pupils in unlocking unknown words is to use phonics. Teachers and pupils need to realize the upper limits of phonics use. There are letters which are rather consistent between symbol and sound. However, there are many weaknesses or limits in phonics use, such as in the following words: phone, through, rough, flight, among others. Here, the relationships between individual sounds and symbols do not harmonize in most cases.

The primary grade reading teacher needs to have all pupils experience initial successes with continual optimal progress emphasized for each child. No child should be permitted to fall through the cracks to be a failure (Ediger, 1998).

REFERENCES

Bolton, F. (1986), *The Greedy Goat*. New York: Scholastic Book Services.

Ediger, Marlow (1988), *Language Arts Curriculum in the Elementary School*. Kirksville, Missouri: Simpson Publishing Company, 19.

Ediger, Marlow (1998), "Goals of Reading Instruction", *Experiments in Education*. 26(1), 11-18.

Edgier, Marlow (1997), "Reading and the Psychology of Teaching". *The Educational Review*. 103(3), 41-45.

Ediger, Marlow and Digumarti Bhaskara Rao (2001). *Teaching Reading Successfully*. New Delhi. India: Discovery Publishing House.

Fountas, Irene C. and Gay Su Pinnell (1996), *Guided Reading Good First Choice for all Children*. Portsmouth, New Hampshire: Heinemann, 1 and 2.

Interantional Reading Association, *The Reading Teacher*. 800 Barksdale Road, Newark, Dwlaware 19714.

Mahy, M. (1986), *When the King Rides By*. Bothel, Washington: The Wright Group.

National Council Teachers of English, *The Language Arts*, 1111 Kenyon Road, Urbana, Illinois 61801.

Strommen, Linda Teran, and Barbara Fowles Mates (1997), "What readers do: Young Children's Ideas about the nature of reading", *The Reading Teacher*. 51(2), 106.

8

Writing and the Language Arts

The reading and writing curriculum correlate well with each other Why? Very often, reading experiences provide the springboard for writing. Thus a variety of kinds of poetry may be written based on content acquired from reading. Diverse kinds of rhymed and unrhymed poems may then be written. Literary elements such as characterization, setting, plot, irony, theme and point of view may be rewritten or elaborated upon by pupils from having read a given story or selection. Creativity should be a major objective of pupil writing, Novelty, uniqueness and originality of content from pupil writing, should be wanted Written work should emphasize cutting across all academic disciplines. Written work then has no single academic discipline to stress but writing across the curriculum should be the objective of instruction (Ediger, 1997).

There are definite assumptions pertaining to writing. These assumptions are the following:

1. Pupils learn to write by writing;
2. Proficiency in oral language assists the learner to do a better job of writing;
3. Success in writing helps pupils to extend major goals to improve continuously in written work;
4. Writing seemingly is the most difficult of the four areas of vocabulary development—listening, speaking,

reading and writing, but each needs to be emphasized to assist pupils to achieve as optimally as possible;

5. Pupils individually learn to write, but each pupil may learn much through collaborative endeavours in writing. Pupils learn from each other in writing;
6. Writing needs to be taught as being interrelated with grammar, punctuation, spelling, vocabulary, syntax, semantics, structure in the English language, handwriting, whole language and phonics;
7. Written work cuts across all academic disciplines whenever print discourse is used;
8. Pupils need to write for a variety of audiences such as the teacher, parents, friends, brothers and sisters among others;
9. Sequence in writing improvement begins with the pre-school years, including scribbling and occurs throughout adulthood;
10. Written work should be useful whereby application is made of print discourse, as well as be creative for leisure type and utilitarian activities.

The teacher needs to focus upon the above named objectives in teaching writing and their inter-relationship with the other areas of the language arts. Writing must be related to all academic disciplines when written work is being stressed. These ideas are expressed further in basic goals that pupils need to acquire in on-going lessons and units of study. Pupils are to:

1. write frequently to record ideas in print discourse;
2. experience the relationships among listening, speaking, reading and writing;
3. expand literary experiences to incorporate written expressions;
4. use a variety of purposes to convey meanings in writing;
5. experiment with diverse genres and subject matter when engaged in writing;
6. attend to conventions in writing such as quality punctuation, capitalization and grammar;

7. edit personal work and the work of others in writing by using collaborative endeavours;
8. appreciate writing skills possessed and enjoy what has been written;
9. utilize reading and children's library books as spring-boards in writing in their diverse manifestations;
10. indicate pride in being successful in listening, speaking, reading and writing.

Leadership from the principal is vital. The principal and the teacher need to work together for the good of the child in attaining more optimally in the school setting (Ediger, 1998).

Creative Writing and Poetry

An important source for writing is to use content from basal texts and library books, among other print discourse sources, to engage pupils in written work. Through reading, viewing objects, items, illustrations and audio-visual materials directly related to what is/has been read, might well encourage creative poetry writing by learners. Discussions pertaining to what has been read might also impress pupils to apply what has been learned in poetry writing.

First of all, let's take a lông at writing poems which rhyme. Many pupils like to write poetry which contains rhyme. There are numerous patterns in rhyming poetry. Early primary grade pupils who can here rhyme may wish to write couplets, individually or in a small committee. A couplet contains two lines with ending words rhyming. These young learners may wish to dictate the couplet for the teacher to print in neat manuscript letters. Dictated poems may be saved for re-reading by pupils in class. Later on, and for all pupils, learners may wish to write triplets containing three lines. With a triplet, all ending words rhyme. A slightly more difficult poem to write is the quatrain. Here, with four lines of verse, all ending words need to rhyme or lines one and two as well a lines three and four should rhyme.

The limerick has five lines with lines one, two and five rhyming as well as lines three and four rhyming. Limericks generally being with "There once was.... The limerick may be written as follows:

There once was a man of great height
He always seemed to be up tight.
He swatted a bee
And landed in the sea
That wonderful man of great light.

There are pupils who cannot hear rhyme or may wish to write unrhymed poetry. The haiku is a favourite of many people to write. The haiku contains three lines with the following sequence: five syllables for the first line, seven for the second line and five syllables for the third line. The following haiku is an example:

Birds

Birds fly without rest
Where do they get the power?
I do not know why.

A tanka is a slight variation of the haiku and has a total of five lines with the following number of syllables for each line; five seven, five, seven, and seven. The following tanka present a model:

The Arctic in Winter

The blasts of cold air
Keep the polar bear on ice
Whither the young cubs?
Walking on the tall iceberg
Never mind the cold weather.

The haiku and the tanka above were written by elementary age pupils whom we observed when supervising student teachers and one of us cooperating teachers in the public schools. We find that pupils like to write poetry when background information has been experienced and motivation to write is there.

Free verse has no rhyme and no syllabication involved for writing. One pupil whom one of us observed in the classroom wrote the following free verse:

The horse

Gives us rides when wanted.
Is fed well in the barn.
exercises much during the day time.
loves to be petted.
wants to be noticed.
desire to be comfortable all year long.
hates flies and gnats in summer.
eats grass in summer and grain/hay in winter.
wants to please others.
may ever be grateful for good care.

In the writing of poetry, pupils need to use elements that poets apply in writing verse creatively. One element is onomato-poeia which stresses words written to make echoic sounds. The following emphasize words making their very own sounds: splish, splash, swoosh and slash. The relationship will not always be sound made in the environment. These words also bring in a second element poets use in writing and that is alliteration. With alliteration, two or more sequential words start with the same sound. In this case, the 's' sound is made. A third element is imagery. Imagery has two dimensions and these are similes and metaphors. Similes connect two phrases, in general, such as in the following example of a poem written by a pupil: The cloud of smoke looked like a billowing lion. Thus, the 'cloud of smoke' is compared with 'a billowing lion', The world *like* connects the two phrases. Another word used in similes to make these creative connections is the word as e.g.. "The crow caws as a coughing giant. Metaphors, as a second element of imagery, do not have the words 'like' or 'as' to make these novel connections. For example, the following imagery pertains to a metaphoric approach: "The egg in the pan bubbles tiger like in the water." There is no connector, such as *like* or as between, "The egg in the pan" with "bubbles tiger like in the water".

Writing in Journals

Journals writing is quite popular as an activity for children in the elementary school. There are numerous items that might be written in a journal. Here, many pupils record what they have experienced in a reading lesson such as summaries of content read and discussed in the classroom. Vocabulary terms learned in a lesson or unit of study, results discussed from a test taken, and/or impressions acquired from a study of characterization, setting, plot, theme, point of view and/or messages of the writer of stories and literature in general.

Some pupils write journal items each day. Others write once a week or biweekly. We suggest encouraging pupils to write each day, but a least once a week. Pupils need to do much writing in order to become proficient in written work. Practice makes for proficiency in writing. We do much writing of manuscripts for publication and at the beginning, our written work left much to be desired. With effort put forth, we have been quite successful in having our manuscripts published in educational journals. We are convinced that most pupils can communicate effectively in writing if there is adequate practice, assistance from the teacher and from parents in the home setting, encouragement from many, a stimulating environment to provide ideas for writing and a designated place for writing with the necessary materials.

Journal writing should have important purposes such as the following for the writer: to be more observant of happenings in every day life, to keep record of ideas and events, to use models that stress quality writing and to establish meaning in life's endeavours. It is important for the pupil to carry his/her journal and a pencil along, in order to record important things in life. What might go into journal writing?

1. Happenings in class that were of interest;
2. Content read from library books as well as the basal textbook;
3. A sketch of something that is difficult to write about;
4. Poems that were of personal interest;

5. Letters written and received;
6. Frustrations felt in writing;
7. Descriptions on items and objects that fascinate the writer;
8. A creative description of a modified setting, characterization, plot, theme, point of view and other elements of a story read;
9. Statements on what you would like to be or become in the future;
10. Play parts of a story in literature or unit in the social studies.

Writing a Personal Experience

Pupils tend to like telling incidence about their own life times. The personal experience involves a part of the person's life time. The learner needs to choose what is personally relevant and what might be important to the reader of the essay. Sometimes, pupils have so much to write about that the reader feels overewhelmed in its reading. At the opposite end of the continuum, selected pupils just cannot get started in writing a personal experience. Readers like to know which events truly shaped the history of the writer. The pupils also needs to write he/she fits into wider social roles in life.

A narrative account of events then needs to be shared with peers. The account actually involves a part of the history of the individual doing the writing. Some important pointers for the writer of the essay are the following:

1. Think of what is truly relevant to write about in your life and times;
2. Select an event that is clear and distinct. The event(s) should be written about in detail;
3. Describe each incidence carefully so that readers may role play selected characters in the story of life. There needs to a character, setting and plot in the historical account;
4. Sequence the order of events in the writing so that it makes sense to the reader;

5. Write details which assist the reader to be an inherent part of the story;
6. Use depth coverage in writing about the major events or characters in the writing;
7. Emphasize dialogue in the writing to breath life into the personnel experience;
8. Build the major events or incidences of a story up to a climax;
9. Write for a target audience and identify this audience;
10. Give each person in the essay should have a name.

Writing an Outline

Outlining salient subject matter may be a good way to learn about main ideas, subordinate ideas and details.When a person reads, he/she needs to sort out what is of major importance as compared to that which is less salient. To view each sentence as having the worth of others, robs the reader of securing important ideas. With the explosion of knowledge, it behooves the reader all the more to arrange content read in terms of major versus minor ideas. Otherwise, the reader is bombarded with ideas which do not lend themselves to remembering effectively what has been read. The teacher needs to model good outlining habits to pupils. Peers may also assist each other in outlining subject matter read.

When pupils outline content read or the spoken voice listened to, careful attention needs to be paid to major as compared to more minor ideas. Let us suppose we are reading/ listening to an essay on *Bears*. The first major division of the presentation is, "Looking for food" is a phrase. A subdivision may indicate the kinds of food being looked for. The pupil doing the outline may write the following kinds of foods—fish, rodents, seals and birds. The latter animals emphasize details. A second major division under the heading *Bears* might be, "Finding shelter". A subdivision here might be the kinds of shelter which are acceptable, such as caves, an old deserted building, the side of a mound of dirt and among intertwined branches.

Questions that might be raised pertaining to outlining include the following:

1. How long should the outline be? This depends upon the length of the reading selection being outlined. Or a teacher might assign the length of the outline;
2. How many main major division are there in an outline? This depends upon how many broad ideas there are in a selection that is being read and outlined. We would say that a reading selection of 250 words will generally have two major divisions. Rules in outlining say that there need to be two major divisions at least under one title or topic. There also need to be two subdivision, at least, under a major division. There also should be a least two details under a subdivision. What if *two of each* (such as main divisions, subdivisions and details) cannot be found? Then put the data within the statement preceding the two items of lesser value.
3. Should there be a sentence outline or a phrase outline? This depends upon the teacher and the pupils involved in writing the outline. We prefer the sentence outline since each sentence says something that is complete in meaning. In my thinking, phrases lack the clarity that sentences possess. The above examples emphasized a phrase rather than a sentence outline. We will now write a model sentence outline:

The Holy Land

A. A region that is sacred to Muslims, Jews and Christians.

   1. There are Five Pillars of the Muslim religion.

      (a) the Hajj at Mecca, Saudi Arabia is made at least once during the life time of a devout Muslim.

      (b) The Holy Book of the Muslims is *The Koran.*

   2. The Pentateuch, the first five books of the Old Testament, is holy to devout Jews.

   3. The Church of the Holy Sepulcher is a holy place to devout Christians inside the walled city of Jerusalem.

B. A religion made up of the Mediterranean climate has rainy weather from October to April.

The above outline contains two major divisions, such as in A and B. It has three subdivisions such as the numerals 1, 2 and 3. Two details are in evidence such as *a* and *b* under the first subdivision. As more content is read, additions may be made to this outline.

Writing an Opinion

A personal perspective of a writer contains a point of view or an opinion. Generally, the writer wants to be understood in terms of what is believed in the opinion. The writer may challenge his/her own point(s) of view in the writing. Sometimes, through writing, the writer wants to understand the premises better of his/her own ideas. By writing about personal beliefs the writer may also clarify and critically evaluate thoughts brought fourth. The following are selected pointers for the pupil in writing about his/her opinions:

1. Choose something that has been on your mind for a long time;
2. Assist readers to comprehend and understand your beliefs;
3. Be yourself in the written content... Do not write about someone else's opinion;
4. Use your own distinct style in writing;
5. Write in the first person;
6. Use examples and details in your writing to make meaningful the opinions expressed;
7. Write on what 'bugs' you;
8. Take a point of view which represents your thinking on an issue;
9. Give your thinking on capital punishment, the creation story or the evolution of the universe or the pros and cons of governmental spending on social projects;
10. Write about your favourite pet peeve.

Proofing your writings provides numerous opportunities for reading ideas and content. The final copy should be one that you are very proud of.

Writing on How Something Should be Done

There are numerous occasions when we are asked to provide information on how something is to be done. Directions need to be given frequently on assembling a mower, repairing a kitchen appliance, installing a door bell and building a deck, among other items. People tend to be curious on how something works as well as why something does not work. We believe children find it interesting and challenging to write about something within their area of readiness involving how to do something. The 'how to' essay may also involve providing explanations about an event or reasons for an occurrence or happening. There are a plethora of writings that stress how to do something. We would want pupils individually to be involved in determining content for developing the how to essay. Pupils do need to be ready in terms of subject matter acquired so that writing on how to do something is possible.

We have the following suggestions when pupils write the 'How To' paper. The pupil needs to choose a topic that he/she understands well and can explain it to pupils. It is truly frustrating when one is asked to do something that is not conceivable. Second, the content should relate to what others do not understand and need assistance in its doing. Third, the writer should have an audience that needs to have this information conveyed. This means that content needs to be written on the understanding level of the target audience. The writer needs to determine what it is that the reader might lack in understanding. There might be something in the how-to-essays that clarifies that which makes for confusion on the part of the reader. Proper sequence needs to be in offing when writing clearly and distinctly the order of steps involved in how to do something. The ordered steps should not be isolated from each other, but rather follow a related set of ideas. Thus, the sequential steps follow a relationship, not an isolation from each other. Step one is related to step two while step two is related to step three and so on.

The following additional pointers are salient in an How To Do It paper, as well as in all written work:

1. eliminate redundant ideas;
2. modify vague statements that are relevant otherwise, so that the reader may follow directions carefully and implement successfully what was given in the essay;
3. try the steps written in the 'How To' paper to see if they work;
4. proofread very carefully that which was written;
5. have a peer try out what is written in the essay.

Writing and Problem Solving

Developing problem solving skills is important for elementary age pupils presently as well as in the future at the work place. Seemingly, problems are with us continually. Selected problems may be solved rather quickly. Others are much more time consuming in solving. What is important is that pupils learn to identify and solve problems. The first flexible step is to identify the problem. Clarity is involved when identifying problem areas. Data is then gathered in order to offer solutions to the problem area. Information then is available for an hypothesis. The hypothesis is a tentative answer to the problem. They hypothesis is tentative and subject to testing. A real live situation needs to be used to testing the hypothesis. If evidence warrants, the hypothesis is rejected. New data or information then need to be gathered. This result in a new hypothesis which is again subject to testing in a life-like situation. If results indicate, the hypothesis may then be accepted.

There are numerous reasons pupils need to learn to write information essays. New information has come out on a topic and the learner believes others need to be informed of the new content. Perhaps, there is a need to inform individuals about the necessity of selected current events items that have just come of the news network. The major purpose here being to inform learners and others about the newness of the situation. Information then is being shared. There is so much new information coming out that it is difficult to stay abreast of what is new. We certainly do live in an information age and individuals feel so limited when they can only learn to know a small amount what is new content. If we think to internet and all the information that is therein, it baffles the individual who thinks of possible ways to learn as much as possible. Newspapers and news magazines attempt to keep individuals informed as to what is going on. But the amount of information coming therefrom is overwhelming. There are selected pointers that may be provided pupils when writing the information essay. These are the following:

1. Try to be as objective as possible when reporting information. The information does not represent opinions, feelings and subjective thoughts;
2. Remember that the writer is writing for human beings and not automations;
3. Write facts, not opinions, to be presented in an appealing way;
4. Delimit the topic to what can be accurately covered and in detail. Overly broad topics may be too complex to cover as compared to a more delimited approach;
5. Cover your delimited topic in a comprehensive way be discussing the five w's—who, what where, when and why. Shallow and survey methods of reporting information may not stand up under scrutiny. Depth coverage of information will influence the reader much more so as compared to survey procedures;
6. Be as accurate as possible in reporting information. Sources of information need to be checked for reliability and accuracy;
7. Make certain that the information being reported is new and not something that is a rehash of previously presented ideas;
8. Have pupils perceive the new information being reported as related to what as known previously;

9. Sequence ideas presented effectively so that readers perceive the relationship of new knowledge to what was presented previously;
10. Use drawings, diagrams, figures and illustrations to report information clearly and accurately.

In an information age, pupils need to be able to present content accurately and in depth. The information needs to be as factual as possible and yet it needs to be presented in an appealing manner. It is always important to secure learner attention in reading written work.

Writing to Describe

Descriptive writing is very important to a pupil. Why? Each pupil needs to learn to describe something as accurately as possible. In conversing with others individuals are asked to describe something such as a car, bicycle, house, and/or a place, among others. When pupils are ready they should have sample opportunities to describe something that is purposeful in their lives. When going to the doctor's office, we are asked to describe how we feel, what the pain is like and the kinds of foods we like to eat frequently. When engaged in descriptive writing, the writer needs to be as accurate as possible when describing an object a musical performance and/or a delicious meal at a banquet, among other things.

Generally, a good conversationalist can converse well and in conversing, decisions enter in. There are selected excellent pointers that may be given in order that pupils write well in descriptive writing:

1. Have something worthwhile to describe. Worthwhileness is an important concept to stress in writing since pupils do better in writing when a purpose or reasons are involved in writing work;
2. Have a peer evaluate the descriptive writing product to notice accuracy, in particular, in the written product;
3. Appraise the sequence of ideas in the descriptive writing. Good sequence or order of sentences can assist to clarify the descriptive writing product;

4. Have major ideas be supported with details, whose ideas are of lesser value but do add emphasis upon the major ideas;
5. Use adjectives wisely in your writing since these words describe nouns used as subjects and objects;
6. Develop pupil interest as much as possible when writing to describe. Due to interest factors, the reader might continue to pay attention to the entire written product;
7. Use adverbs effectively to describe. The descriptive adverbs modify verbs, adjectives and other adverbs within the framework of descriptive writing;
8. Check for meaning within the written product. Meaningful statements assist in improving any descriptive writing product;
9. Pay careful attention to the mechanics of writing such as correct punctuation, capital letters, spelling of words and indentation of paragraphs among other items;
10. Proofread and modify weaknesses in the descriptive writing paper.

Narrative Writing

Narrative writing tells a story. Pupils need to do much reading of narrative stories so that they will understand the elements that go into this type of writing. Thus, there needs to be good models of narrative writing for pupils to emulate. Much interest then might be developed in the writing of narration. Interest is powerful factor in learning. Interest in writing might well propel children to pupil forth effort in narrative writing. Pupils, too, need to perceive reasons for writing narrative content. These reasons should be stated deductively by teachers as well as inductively. There are times when prizes and awards in extrinsic motivation allow a pupil to really buckle down to write narrative forms of stories.

When readiness factors permit, the pupil with teacher guidance may begin using the elements of writing narrative accounts.

There are definite pointers for the teacher to point out to pupils when narrative writing is in the offing:

1. Have pupils understand the important ingredients of narrative writing by reading stories that clearly point out what narrative writing is;
2. Permit pupils to use a familiar story for revision and thus stress, heavily, sequence of happenings in the story;
3. Provide quality continuity when pupils are heavily involved in writing sequential happenings in narration;
4. Read aloud narrative accounts so that pupils understand sequence in narration;
5. Guide pupils to choose a character that will be fully described in the narrative account;
6. Assist learners to write a setting for the character that will interest the reader;
7. Help pupils write a theme for the story. The theme will be the underlying message in narrative writing;
8. Let pupils develop a point of view in terms of someone telling the sequential events in the writing;
9. Have pupils write a plot which tells what actually happened in the story. The plot must keep the reader reading to find out what really happened in the story;
10. Use conversation in the story whereby quotation marks indicate what a character said at a specific time.

As is true of all writing done by pupils, the teacher needs to have conferences with pupils individually and collectively so that optimal progress for each pupil is possible. A writer's workshop might assist individuals to improve in the area of writing.

Writing to Assert

Information written by the learner, at times, will need to be backed up with logic and evidence based upon research. Assertions go beyond opinions, feeling and subjective knowledge. The assertion attempts to prove selected ideas, concepts and generalizations. Quality reasons given by the writer to make these assertions include strong and consistent logic, as well as good research which is accurate and reliable.

Sometimes, a writer believes that too many people have inconsistent ideas that are based on partial truths and poor research. The record then needs to be straightened out. There are selected pointers for pupils to become more proficient in developing written content which does hold water:

1. The central idea of the essay must be the assertion, not opinions, feelings, attitudes and subjective thoughts;
2. Vocabulary terms in the essay should be clear and meaningful. Peers and the teacher who proof-read may need to point out the fallacy in logic used as well as terms that are vague and fail to communicate;
3. With critical thinking, the essay may need to be analyzed into important parts which then make it possible to take out and weaknesses in the assertion;
4. Ample evidence must be given to substantiate the assertion;
5. The evidence presented at diverse places in the essay needs to be sequential and related, not in terms of isolated fragments;
6. Evidence presented needs to be written in a manner readable to the audience or target group;
7. Research information may be presented in terms of graphs, charts, illustrations, tables and figures;
8. The summary of the essay needs to present a generalization which draws conclusions, supporting the assertion;
9. The assertion made will need to be written in a serious manner, but in a way which facilitates the reading thereof;
10. Clarity in writing and direct communication is necessary.

Oral discussions whereby pupils need to defined statements made, could be a pre-requisite in writing assertion essays. These learning opportunities provide background experiences for pupils in being able to defend statements made. Assertions should be backed up with supportive information which is logical and research based.

Evaluation Within an Essay

Individuals seemingly are always evaluating ideas, objects and statements made. Their worth and accuracy is then being evaluated. Quality criteria need to be used in the evaluation process. Otherwise, the evaluative statements may have little worth. There are definite pointers that may be given to assist the writer in writing an evaluation essay:

1. There needs to be clarity on what is being evaluated;
2. Comparisons need to be made between and among comparable items. Apples and oranges should not be compared since they are different fruits and the comparisons a writer makes depend upon the feelings and subjective ideas of the evaluator;
3. Evaluative statements should be valid in terms of topic presented in the essay;
4. Clarity in the criteria used to judge the worth of something is a must;
5. There seems to be an opposite and equal reaction to many statements made in society. The writer must allow for other points of view, presented by listeners, that may have much merit;
6. Statistical devices should be used to support evidence in the evaluation process, such as tables, charts, graphs, figures and research data;
7. Sequential statements should be made to support the evaluation process;
8. Evidence to support an evaluation should be significant, not minor ideas nor trivial content;
9. Bias and prejudice need to be avoided in the evaluative statements;

10. Defend what has been written, based on logic, reason and objective data.

Writing Business and Friendly Letters

Business and friendly letter writing are two kinds of written work which have high utilitarian values. Most people write both kinds of letters to serve personal needs.

The business letters needs to have a heading to show where it came from such as the street and its number, the city and state as to its origin and the present date. Convention indicates these items should be on upper right hand side of the business letter. The inside address should be located on the left hand side of the letter. The inside address indicates to whom the letter is written, street address, city and state with zip code number. The greeting is directly below the inside address. The body is the major part of the business letter and pertains to what is being order in terms of merchandise or other requests, followed by the closing and the signature. Thus, a model business latter might look like the following:

Heading

D-43, S.V.N. Colony
Guntur 522006
Andhra Pradesh
India

August 15, 1996

Inside Address

Bowen Book Company
1849 Skyview Hall Drive
Kansas City, Missouri 69981

Greeting

Dear Sir:

Body

I would like to request a price list of current books you have on education. Your prompt attention to this would be greatly appreciated since our class is studying the educational systems of different countries.

Thank You

Closing

Sincerely Yours

Signature

D. Bhaskara Rao

The friendly letter has the same format as the business letter above, except the inside address is not necessary. The reason for this is that in friendly letter needs to contain personal experiences of the writer which would be of interest to the receiver of the letter. I would suggest here that the writer of the friendly letter include such items as the following:

1. hobbies and interest being pursued;
2. vacations that were taken;
3. weekend trips experienced.
4. a new addition to the family;
5. gifts given and received during holidays, birthdays and other special events during the year;
6. an unusual event or happening.

Before a letter is sent, careful proof–reading needs to be in the offing. Politeness is involved when business and friendly letters are carefully and accurately written. Receivers of letters need to be clear as to the meaning of content written. Writing in long hand needs to be proofed in terms of clarity in hand-writing. It is difficult to write legibly in long hand. Pupils should have ample experiences in using the word processor when conveying information in business and friendly letters.

Writing to Persuade

There are occasions when individuals need to persuade others in writing as well as orally. Selected educators have stated that persuasion is the most important kind of essay writing. Frequently, there are no right or wrong positions on an issue. Therefore, the individual, having strong feelings about one side of the issue, may use persuasive powers to have others, who initially disagreed, change their minds. When voting for officer at any level of government, the candidates running for office take different positions on an issue. Each candidate attempts to persuade voters to accept his/her position when voting. Liberals versus conservatives, agriculture versus business, pro-choice versus pro-life, as well as pro-labour versus pro-business provide opportunities to hear and determine how each person stands on an issue. The position taken may represent how the candidate will vote in an election.

Some pointers that may assist pupils in being able to persuade others include the following:

1. Select a position on an issue which you agree with wholeheartedly, Write a persuasive essay to support your contention. Attempt to influence others to accept your point of view;
2. Write the essay for a selected audience. The audience should tend to believe the other side of the issue;
3. Do possess clarity in terms of where you stand. Your position should be very clear in the essay;
4. Argue, using logic, to substantiate your thinking on the issue;
5. Focus on the one issue so that your argument will be stronger and more influential;
6. Provide evidence which strengthens your point of view;
7. Appeal to the feelings and emotions of the reader when presenting your argument(s);
8. Establish credibility in your writing so that readers will wish to share your position on the issue;
9. Sequentially, order your statements to support your point of view on the issue. The best supportive statement comes toward the end of the essay. The attention of the reader must be kept so that the most powerful influence comes toward the end of the essay;
10. Clarity in the writing of ideas is important with a variety of vocabulary terms used to convince others.

Redundancy in writing makes for less influence over the unconverted reader. Arguments given must be direct, logical, and used to obtain converts from the uncommitted.

Being able to influence others is very important in a democracy. There are many ideas and points of view on the many issue in society. Peaceful means of resolving these issues is important. Too frequently, violence is resorted to in society to influence others toward a certain position or point of view. The pro-life versus pro-choice issue is a good example. There needs to be rational means with debate and persuasion used to convince others to join a particular group having a specific point of view. Democracy in society emphasizes the freedom to express and listen to diverse sides of an issue. The atmosphere here must be such that listeners and readers might make up their own minds, after hearing the different point of view on an issue.

Finding Time to Write

If pupils are to become proficient writers, when will there be time to do much teaching of writing? I have noticed student teachers and cooperating teachers use different time schedules to permit increased time for writing. Numerous elementary school teachers indicate that there needs to be a scheduled period of time to have pupils be actively involved in writing for different purposes. Perhaps, two to three thirty minute periods are then given to teaching writing each week. Here, pupils are provided guidance and direction in writing. A definite type of writing might then be emphasized such as narrative or expository writing.

A second approach in finding time to teach writing is to relate writing with all curriculum areas in the elementary school. For Example, there are many writing activities then that can be stressed in the social studies. Poetry writing might then be correlated with a thematic unit in the social studies (Ediger, 1997).

Third before the school day begins, there could be writing instruction as well as writing projects for pupils. Pupils may write collaboratively or individually. It is good to provide choices for pupils as frequently as possible.

Fourth, pupils need to be encouraged to write in the home setting. Through parent/teacher conferences, a away may be worked out whereby the home setting becomes conducive to pupil writing. Definite goals in writing for pupils to achieve might be discussed with parents.

Fifth, writing clubs have been successful in many schools. These clubs meet after school. The Writing Club has specific goals for learners to attain in writing. Sharing of written products might be an end goal to stress. Pupils may learn from each other and challenge learners to achieve at a more optimal level in writing.

Sixth, pupils should definitely be encouraged to write when assignments and tasks have been completed. Some of the finest writing comes from pupils when they write in their spare time during the school day!

Conclusion

There are many kinds of writing activities for pupils. Pupils need to develop proficiency for a variety of types of writing. Hopefully, pupils individually will achieve more optimally in writing. With writing experiences, pupils engage in reading also. Writing and reading cannot be separated. What is written will be read. Sometimes the re-reading is done many times since the end product needs to be proofed and become a quality written product.

We would like to end the writing and reading connection by indicating ways to motivate writers to increase proficiency in print discourse. How might pupils then be motivated to increase writing skills and products?

1. Developing a classroom that is very rich with materials which encourage writing by pupils;

2. Encouraging pupils to write content pertaining to their very own interests and purpose. The content then for writing comes from the learner;
3. Providing rich experiences from which pupils enjoy writing in their diverse manifestations;
4. Showing interest and respect for pupil's writings;
5. Buildings on the interest of pupils to encourage participation in many purposes in writing;
6. Building a classroom environment for writing that is free from ridicule, embarrassment and fear;
7. Giving adequate time before, during and after the school day for pupils to truly become proficient in writing;
8. Assisting pupils to use the mechanics of writing well without losing out on quality ideas for written expression;
9. Helping pupils to feel confident when sharing ideas from writing;
10. Evaluating pupils progress in writing which encourages, but does not destroy interest in written work (Tiedt, 1983).

A quality programme of evaluation needs to be in evidence to appraise pupil progress in the language arts and reading. This is true also in appraising pupil achievement in motivation. The teacher needs to evaluate, continuously, pupil progress in motivation. Motivation needs to be there to have pupils attain worthwhile objectives in the language arts/reading curriculum (Ediger, 1996).

REFERENCES

Ediger, Marlow (1997), *Teaching Reading and the Language Arts in the Elementary School.* Kirksville, Missouri: Simpson Publishing Company, 135-44.

Ediger, Marlow (1997), *Social Studies Curriculum in the Elementary School,* Fourth Edition, Kirksville, Missouri: Simpson Publishing Company, 168-83.

Ediger, Marlow (1996), *Elementary Education,* Kirksville, Missouri: Simpson Publishing Company, 107-17.

Eduiger, Marlow and Bhaskara Rao, Digumarti (1996). *Science Curriculum* New Delhi: Discovery Publishing House.

Ediger, Marlow (1998), *"The Principal of the School",* Reading Improvement, 35: 45-48.

Tiedt, Iris M. (1983), *The Language Arts Handbook,* Englewood Cliffs, New Jersey: Prentice-Hall, 184.

9

Speaking and the Language Arts

Pupils who are far along in their speaking vocabularies tend to do well in reading. These pupils speak clearly and have a large vocabulary for their age levels. Each pupil needs to receive guidance and assistance to achieve as optimally as possible in oral communication. Hopefully, achievement in oral use of language will also assist pupils to do well in reading.

The oral communication curriculum needs to have clearly stated, worthwhile objectives of instruction. Pupils individually need to be encouraged to take part in formal and informal experiences involving oral use of language. Learners need to attain as optimally as possible? Expectations should be high, but feasible, for achievement. Those who are deficient in oral communication are at a disadvantage in school and in society were there are expectations for each learner to be able communicate needs, wants and wishes. To be successful in society, especially at the work place, individuals need to be able to express themselves in an efficient manner. Promotions at the work place depends upon many factors, inducing the ability to communicate well orally.

The teacher must be creative and think of diverse ways and approaches in helping pupils do well in speaking effectively with others. Literacy and oracy skills are complimentary. With oral communication, there needs to be a listener. What is said orally and listened to, can be recorded in written discourse. The recording here involves reading and attaching meaning to abstract symbols making for words, sentences, paragraphs and larger units of written expression.

...research on topical reading acquisition shows that reading is built on a foundation of oral language competence—in other words, not just on phonology but also on vocabulary, grammar and so on. The idea that reading can be taught exclusively or even primarily through the visual modality, without regard to these foundational linguistic skills, is not consistent with what is known about the process of reading development (Spear-Swerling and Sternberg, 1996).

Critical Listening to the Spoken Voice

Speaking involves a listener to ideas expressed. Critical listening to a speaker is important. Ideas need to be analyzed into component parts to become meaningful. Ideas may be expressed to manipulate individuals in numerous ways.

First, the glittering generalities approach might be used by a speaker. Here, the positive aspects of a topic are covered only. The information presented by the speaker leaves many loopholes that need to be filled. If a speaker states that "we need to become more democratic", but does not define 'democratic' nor is it said how this goal of being 'more democratic' is to be fulfilled, facets of content are lacking. The speaker merely states how wonderful a life can be with increasing emphasis placed upon democracy as a way of life. Over generalizing is in evidence and the positive side is mentioned only with vague statements.

Second, a bandwagon approach is used by a speaker. The speaker indicates that everyone agrees with him/her and needs to join the crowd, be it in buying of cereal, a specific car, a type or brand name of clothing, or of a personal computer. Others are joining the crowd and the listener needs to do the same. Charisma and a persuasive tone of voice with appealing content may be in the offing with the band wagon approach.

Third, a testimonial procedure may be used. Thus, a famous personality may endorse a product wholeheartedly, meaning the listener also needs to buy the product endorsed by the testimonial.

Fourth, deck stacking approaches are used. Thus, a product is advertised as being very nutritious with multiply vitamins. The speaker does not say which vitamins and how many are involved.

Fifth, a positive association approach is to entice consumers. Thus, a soft drink is advertised with an attractive woman nearby as well a luxury house in the background. The soft drink advertisement has nothing to do with the unusually pleasant surroundings. An association is to be made by the reader between the soft drink to be consumed and the beautiful surroundings. The speaker/advertiser hopes that the soft drink will be purchased increasingly so, due to the appealing environment, even though it is unrelated.

Sixth, a plain folks setting is provided with the product being emphasized, which is to be sold. The ordinary people concept is stressed due to the thinking that most individuals are common in society and not ivy league college/university graduates. Historically, the common man (or woman) has been glorified in being able to rise through the ranks from poverty to riches and fame. Thus, if plain folks like and support a product, then the majority of individuals in a nation should also prize the product highly.

Seventh, an upper class appeal can be enticing to some people. An appeal in a commercial is then made to going higher on the socio-economic level. A new product being advertised then needs to be purchased to rise on the socio-economic ladder in order to compare with wealthier individuals who have larger, spacious homes.

Eighth, name calling is used by some when the other person or side disagrees with the personal ideas being presented (Templeton, 1997). A person then might be called a 'leftist' with communist connotations. Or an individual may be labelled a Nazi. I (Ediger) was called a Nazi, during my junior and senior high school years—1940-1946, before and during World War Two by a few persons. We had German services in church and being a General Conference Mennonite, I was a conscientious objector toward participation in war. These two traits, German services in church and being a conscientious objector, made a person a Nazi. Another name used here was to call a person a 'Hitlerite', referring to Adolph Hitler, Germany's dictator from 1933-1945.

Pupils need to be aware of the dangers of name calling, not only to the receiver of the negative name, but also what it does to have hatred within the caller of these names. Both lose here in that the self concept of the individual might be lowered due to being on the receiving end of the name calling as well as being the name caller. Respecting and being a caring person are so necessary for the welfare of all in society. Being filled with hatred, psychologically, seemingly is not good for anyone in society. In the oral communications curriculum, there are basic criteria which need to be followed so that all feel valued and prized. These criteria are the following:

1. each person needs to be treated with respect in school and in society;
2. all need to participate actively in developing rules and regulations for classroom conduct;
3. pupils individually should be involved in appraising student conduct in terms of these standards;
4. standards for pupils in the classroom to abide by may be modified and change as the needs arises;
5. safety, security, belonging and esteem needs should be met for each learner.

Teaching and learning should be based on the best theories available in education (Ediger, 1996). We will now discuss learning opportunities in oral communication for pupils to achieve the five objectives above.

Using Puppets

The use of puppets can be a good way to assist pupils to express themselves more proficiently when using oral communication. Shy, withdrawn learners tend to feel more relaxed in speaking when puppets are used. We recommend, if at all possible, that pupils make these puppets, bit sack puppets, sock puppets and/or stick puppets. The puppets may be used in different units of study in an integrated curriculum. Thus, if pupils are studying a farm unit, they may make stick puppets pertaining to different kinds of livestock. Speaking parts may be developed, based on pupil background knowledge, for a committee presentation to the rest of the class members or within a neighbouring classroom of learners. Or, in studying life on a assembly line in a factory, pupils may develop speaking parts for the different roles of involved workers. Assembly lines have fewer and fewer workers due to automation. Here, pupils may do research using needed reference sources to discuss how the role of the worker has changed due to automation. Effective oral use of language should be in the offing. Puppets may be made and used to play different roles of participants in the discussion. There is novelty and newness involved in the use of puppetry. Individual pupils tend to forget their shyness and reservations when participating in role playing with puppet use. We would like to suggest the following pointers when stressing puppetry as a part of the learning activities provided in ongoing lessons and units of study:

1. emphasize quality art work when puppets are being made. Multiple intelligences emphasizes that talents in art work should be prized highly by all in the learning community;
2. an integrated curriculum in reading and the language arts may be emphasized when art work receives its due emphasis in worth and value;
3. speaking activities need to be carefully developed in an ongoing lesson or unit of study;
4. pupils need to practice their speaking parts after the role of each has been decided upon by pupils, with teacher guidance;
5. standards and goals for oral communication need to be carefully defined. Each pupil should be challenged to achieve as optimally as possible.

Speaking parts may be recorded by cassette or videotape to be reviewed by participants in the puppetry activity as well as by those who were observers. May be, there are parts in speaking that will result in being revised and modified. The new approach, as modified by feedback from the audio-visual presentation, might be tried out in the classroom. Developing interest in puppetry use should be an end result and not to destroy interest in learning. It is so very important to develop and maintain a powerful factor in learning and that is pupil interest.

Using Role Play Activities

Pupils at a very young age love to play different roles in the pre-school years. What child does not like to put on the parents' shoes and role play the parent? These kinds of activities are very excellent to emphasize on the elementary school and higher years of schooling. Thus, high school students love to have roles in plays which are put on for the public as well as for students. Adults try out for parts in local play performances. It is motivator to perform in front of others. Those who participate in plays also have made lasting friendships from these performances.

We believe all should have opportunities to be in plays, if they so desire. Elementary and secondary school pupils seemingly feel quite relaxed while performing in front of groups. As adults, more seem to have fear in getting up in front of others. In the elementary school years, performing within a classroom can be very rewarding. The threat a criticism should not be used when role playing is used as a learning opportunity. The teacher needs to develop standards for pupils to follow in classroom role playing so that positive attitudes toward others is developed. Rôle playing may stress a story from literature or a biography in history.

With creative dramatics, no speaking parts are written down. Pupils decide cooperatively upon who will play which role. It is good to give everyone a chance for a role playing. Each person in the creative dramatics activity needs to have the content well in mind when playing a specific role representing an individual in literature or in history. This is especially important since no play parts are written, but rather individuals play their respective role and orally provide the speaking parts when sequence demands it.

In formal dramatics, pupils collaboratively in a committee write play parts for each person in the literary or historical context. The parts may be memorized or read to the class or audience. Listening, speaking, reading and writing are stressed in this learning experience.

In addition to creative and formal dramatics, pupils may engage in socio-drama. With socio-drama, pupils play the role of another person to see how it feels to be in someone else's shoes. For example, if a pupil has been ridiculed, that individual and the one who did the ridiculing change roles. Thus, each person may attempt to feel how it feels to be ridiculed as well as the one who did the ridiculing. Feelings experienced need to be discussed. Hopefully, pupils will learn the consequences of belittling others.

Pointers for pupils to remember in role play activities are the following:

1. try to feel the role that is being played;
2. use voice inflection with stress, pitch and juncture when communicating orally;
3. use gestures and facial expressions as non-verbal factors in communication;
4. speak clearly and accurately when oral communication is in progress;
5. use feedback from the observers and from video-tape to improve the next dramatization.

Committees in the Classroom

There are many occasions in school and outside the school setting whereby pupils need to be capable in a discussion setting. Relevant decisions are made when working together with others to discuss important ideas. Discussions may break down if involved people do not stay on the topic, but digress to the irrelevant. Ideas need to circulate within the committee doing the discussing and not between the chairperson and one other person and back to the chairperson in that repeated sequence. All need to participate and no one dominate the discussion. If content is not presented clearly and accurately, there will be wasted time in obtaining meaning from what is being said. Respect for the ideas of others needs to be in the offing.

Pupils may change off in terms of being leaders within the committee endeavours. The teacher may appoint different leaders or the committee itself may select leaders. The leader needs to try to secure comments fro all members, Hardly might one consider it a committee decision of one or two members do all the deliberating. Leadership qualities also stress a desire for all to participate, but no one dominating also stress a desire for all to participate, but no one dominating the discussion within the committee settling. A pleasant tone of voice needs to be used by discussants with clarity of ideas presented for the discussion. Questions need to arise by participants when comments and problem areas are not clear and distinct.

Children's literature provides excellent opportunities for interesting topics to discuss. The following, among others, are fascinating areas from children's literature for pupils to discuss:

1. ***Character:*** What are the clues to characters suggested in the writing? From what is said or the action taking place, what inferences can be made about the individual? Why does the character act the way he does? What are his values? Did anyone change in the story? Why?
2. ***Setting:*** Can you see where the story is happening? How do those in the story is happening? How do those in the story act because of the setting? Is there a basic struggle between the people in the story and the nature of the place where they live?
3. ***Mood—feeling—tone:*** What words are used to tell you how the writer feels? What is the tone of voice of the story-teller? Is it serious? Humorous? Is this is true experience?

4. ***Story Pattern:*** What would you tell it you had only the first paragraph to guide you? Can you tell what happened by reading only the first paragraph? Is there a theme or lesson that the writer is illustrating? Who is telling the story? What differences does it make? (Anderson and Lapp, 1979).

The voice plays a major role in holding listeners' attention. Good speakers change the speed of their voices. Vary loudness, pitch their voices attractively, and avoid mannerisms that affect listeners negatively.

Young persons need to experiment with variations in speed, pitch, loudness and tone, Probably, the best way to do experiment is to record an oral report on tape. This technique is especially good if the presentation is a team endeavour, for group members can listen to themselves is playback, assessing their vocal expression, the overall organization and clarity of their presentation and their general knowledge of the topic...

Effective communication is as dependent on the body as it is on the dynamic use of the voice. The use of visuals is one way to encourage gesturing and movement of the body in oral reporting. The student who uses a time line to show relationships will point to each entry on the line as he/she talks; the student who works from the map will point to locations on it. Pointing, moving forward and holding up are all non-verbal devices necessary when using a visual, These gestures add action and force to a presentation.

If the school or community owns a cam corder, it can be used to videotape presentations for eventual self study. Each student views his/her contributions to a programme and evaluates it in terms of questions as: Did I make eye contact with my audience? Did I gesture automatically? Did I change my facial expressions as required? In viewing a videotape, young people often can spot their problems and without prompting improve on them during future reporting sessions (Hennings, 1994).

Pointers to stress for committee endeavours to function well include the following:

1. Listening carefully to ideas expressed carefully and provides the background information so necessary for a discussion group to function well;
2. Developing a sense of community is vital so that group cohesion is possible;
3. Quality sequencing in ideas expressed makes it easier for all to follow the discussion;
4. Evaluating periodically of what has been covered assists the group to notice achievement;
5. Respecting each other's ideas helps release the creative thoughts of committee members.

Giving Oral Reports

Pupils should have ample opportunities to present oral reports in front of the classroom. To give quality reports, pupils need to have the subject matter well in mind pertaining to what will be reported. An outline continuing the salient points of the oral report provides assistance to the speaker. Video-taping the oral report provides ample opportunities pertaining to securing feedback on the presentation. The reporter needs to observe the speed with which ideas can be presented so that all listeners may obtain the contents as readily as possibly. Quality stress helps the speaker to get ideas across to peers. Stress emphasizes saying words louder or softer in oral communication. To say a word louder tends to place emphasis upon that word. It draws attention to that word with louder stress. Pitch emphasizes pitching words higher or lower so less of a monotone voice is in evidence when speaking. In music, there are notes that are higher or lower on a scale and the reader of music needs to pay attention to the pitch of each note in order to read music accurately. The speaker also needs to raise and lower and lower the voice to use it effectively in oral communication. A third factor that is relevant in speaking is to emphasize juncture. With quality juncture, pauses are indicated at the proper place in ongoing subject matter. If a reader or reporter does not pay careful attention to commas, periods and question marks, among other punctuation marks, there will be misinterpretation and run on sentences and words may result. Pupils with teacher guidance need to practice giving reports using the concepts of stress, pitch and juncture.

Some pointers to emphasize when giving oral reports are the following:

1. Go over oral report with pupils to determine what makes for an effective presentation;
2. Assist pupils in working on quality presentations in reporting orally to the class;
3. Have pupils work in dyads, two working together, to refine methodology in giving oral reports;
4. Have pupils present oral reports in small groups of three to four pupils to develop confidence and poise in the given of these reports;
5. Let pupils appraise their own videotape results of oral reporting in terms of desired criteria.

Oral Reading to Classmates

Pupils need to have ample opportunities to read orally to others in the school setting. Too frequently, oral reading has stressed the round robin approach whereby pupils in a class have been placed into three different ability levels in reading. The teacher works with one of the three groups at a time. One facet of instruction here is pupils taking turns reading orally to the teacher. The teacher then may evaluate reading skills possessed by each learner and those needing more assistance for improvement. This approach is used somewhat routinely each sequential day of instruction. Boredom and the routine set in. Pupils here do not have a chance to practice oral reading skills in terms of desired criteria.

Oral reading to an audience has a different goal. Here, each pupil may practice reading a selection until it is suitable to read to a larger audience including pupils in the classroom, other classrooms and to parents. Peers in practice sessions may listen to the oral reading and provide suggestions, in terms of desirable criteria, for improvement. There may be five or six pupils who have modified/refined a selection for oral reading.

Reader's theatre is very similar to the oral reading experience just discussed. In reader's theatre, five or six pupils may practice reading play parts written out, as is true of formal dramatics. Each person accepts his/her role in the play and reads with voice inflection, stress, pitch and juncture. The play parts are good enough to present in front of an audience, such as classmates, parents and others interested in the presentation. Pupils individually may hold their very own book as they take their respective turn in reading orally. Generally, pupils in reader's theatre sit in a semicircle on tall stools so they are clearly visible to listeners. A reader then role plays the part being read. The oral reading experience then has elements of the traditional round robin approach as well as dramatic qualities. Thus, the involved pupil needs to play the character in the story as if he/she is an alive person making decisions.

There are definite pointers that may be used by teachers in having pupils read well orally:

1. Learners need ample time to practice reading a selection orally unit it has been refined and mastered;
2. Guidance needs to be given pupils in using proper enunciation and pronunciation;
3. Content must be conveyed clearly and accurately to observes;
4. Each pupil's presentation needs to be evaluated in terms of making progress over that of previous performances;
5. Self evaluation is important and, especially if videotaping of a performance is being emphasized;
6. Pupils should be encouraged to enjoy oral reading and read more literature as a result;
7. Teachers need to model good oral reading of stories and other print discourse to pupils (Ediger, 1997).

Giving and Following Directions

In society, people are asked to give directions when going to a specific place. We think it is frustrating to a person when asking where a place is located and there is a vagueness or a lack of knowledge in the response. We believe individuals can become better observers of landmarks so that helpful answers may be given to those asking for directions. Pupils should be given much time to practice giving directions in order to reach a specific destination. Pupil/teacher planning may be used to indicate which landmarks are important to know in a community or area. The following landmarks are important and were brain stormed by a class of fifth grades:

1. parks and school buildings;
2. selected stores and offices;
3. major highways and streets;
4. museums and libraries;
5. the train depot and airport;
6. important bus stops;
7. selected churches and governmental buildings.

To assist pupils in becoming mcre conscious of following directions, the following projects were completed by pupils with teacher guidance in an ongoing unit of study:

1. making a relief map;
2. developing a diorama;
3. working a written exercise;
4. completing a test;
5. developing a selected dish of food;
6. learning to play a game;
7. making a simple musical instrument;
8. providing a set of directions for others to locate or find a specific object;
9. performing a folk dance.

Quality listening needs to be practised by pupils in all curriculum areas. The integrated curriculum is then in evidence. In the reading curriculum, pupils need to distinguish between letters and sounds when analyzing words for proficient reading. Thus, reading emphasizes good listening by pupils, not only to hear diverse phonemes clearly, but also to develop much background information for reading different selections. Comprehension of content in reading comes from diverse sources such as listening to a related discussion covering content read or new subject matter to be read.

Extemporaneous Speaking

When readiness permits, pupils tend to enjoy extemporaneous speaking. Here, pupils may be given at random a topic to speak on. A topic from the current unit being studied in reading may suffice. The involved learners are given three minutes, or more, to prepare a talk on the topic. If pupils have been reading on the topic 'Animals of the Artctic', a learner may be given the topic of 'Polar Bears', at random. The involved pupils then prepares a talk in the allotted time given. Recall of information is necessary. The pupil needs to think quickly on foods eaten, habitat, raising of offspring and dealing with enemies. The pupil then must arrange the items sequentially to report orally to the class. The talk may be videotaped and critiqued by a group of classmates. The pupil realizes that knowledge needs to be recalled rather quickly and thinking on one's toes is important. The talk needs to be given clearly and sequentially.

Pointers that may be given to aid pupils to achieve more optimally in speaking include the following:

1. The teacher needs to be a model in quality speaking activities;
2. Pupils should have numerous opportunities to choose their very own topics for oral communication endeavours in the classroom;
3. Learenrs need chances to appraise their progress in oral communication;
4. Diagnosis of pupil deficiencies is necessary so that remediation may occur;
5. Peers working together may assist each other to achieve in oral communication endeavours.

Using the Telephone

Much use is made of telephones in society. Messages may be given clearly and effectively. With answering machines, the receiver of calls may return each when convenient. The answering machine is handy for school personnel since messages may be left on the voice recorder to be returned at a more opportune time. Cellular phones has expanded opportunities for the making of phone calls. With cellular phones, calls can be made and responded to, outside the home setting. I believe it is the school's responsibility to develop within pupil's knowledge, skills and attitudes to use telephones successfully. One of my student teachers together with the cooperating teacher wrote and implemented the use of the following criteria pertaining to telephone use:

1. be polite in all telephone conversation;
2. speak at a rate where optimal communication may take place;
3. communicate loudly enough so that the receiver many hear the message clearly;
4. clarify contents where this is needed;
5. be a good listener!

Conclusion

How does quality oral communication assist pupils to become good readers? With oral communication, pupils practice using words, phrases, sentences, and paragraphs. There should be good sequence in what is said (Ediger, 1997). Meaning needs to be inherent in messages conveyed. What is said might be written down and read by the listener. These features are inherent in all reading that is done. Oral communication requires a listener. The listener provides feedback to the speaker in terms of quality communication. There is oral communication that is directly related to reading such as oral reading and reader's theatre. There are numerous speaking activities that pupils should become proficient in. These include use of puppets, role playing, committee endeavours, oral reports, oral reading extemporaneous speaking and giving directions. Additional experiences for pupils to engage in within the speaking and oral communication arena include engaging in discussions, interviewing and making introductions. Speaking and listening are integrated and, in reality, not separate areas of communication. For convenience of instruction, speaking and listening may be separated to emphasize what can be done in each area to assist teachers in guiding major optimal pupil progress.

The section on oral communication may be ended by listening salient objectives for pupils to achieve. These are:

1. to converse with others courteously and easily;
2. to take part in discussions, sticking to the topic and accepting the thinking of others;
3. to sequence information properly and use it effectively;
4. to plan, develop and carry out an interview effectively and courteously;
5. to be competent in the use the telephone;
6. to use parliamentary procedure appropriately when participating in meetings;
7. to provide clear directions, announcements and explanations;
8. to tell stories with quality sequence and in an enthusiastic manner;
9. to introduce individuals properly to each other;
10. to participate actively in choric reading;
11. to take part in dramatic experiences in ongoing lessons an units of study (Greene and Petty, 1975).

REFERENCES

Anderson, Paul S. and Diane Lapp (1979), *Language Skills in Elementary Education,* 296.

Ediger, Marlow (1996), *Essays in School Administration.* Kirksville, Missouri: Simpson Publishing Company, 136-41.

Ediger, Marlow (1997), *The Modern Elementary School.* Kirksville, Missouri: Simpson Publishing Company, 192-93.

Ediger, Marlow (1997), *Teaching Reading and the Language Arts in the Elementary School.* Kirksville, Missouri: Simpson Publishing Company, 158-59.

Greene, Harry A. and Walter T. Petty (1975), *Developing Language Skills in the Elementary Schools.* Boston: Allyn and Bacon, Inc., 172.

Hennings, Dorothy Grant (1994), *Communication in Action.* Boston: Houghton Mifflin Company, 224.

Spear-Swerling, Louise and Robert J. Sternberg (1996), Off Track—When Poor Readers Become *"Learning Disabled"* Westview Press, 46.

Templeton, Shane (1997), *Teaching the Integrated Language Arts.* Second Edition. Boston: Haughton-Mifflin, 349-50.

10

Listening and the Language Arts

Listening carefully to ideas expressed orally by others is important. This is important for a number of reasons. Respect for other individuals and their thinking is then revealed. It is a way or means of developing new learnings. Feelings of belonging may be achieved when interacting with other human beings; listening is important in the process.

There are many situations in life in which carefully listening is important. The following, among others, represent some of these situations:

1. Conversing with others;
2. Participating in a discussion;
3. Interviewing visitors and guests.
4. Making introductions;
5. Participating in a dramatization;
6. Answering questions raised by others;
7. Listening to a lecture or explanation;
8. Listening to musical recordings;
9. Responding to sounds in the environment pertaining to one's safety;

   Reacting proficiently to sounds in the environment requiring selected responses.

Diverse levels of listening are the lot of pupils on an individual basis:

1. Hearing sounds of words but not reacting to the ideas expressed: a mother knows that Daryl is speaking;
2. Intermittent listening—turning the speaker on and off: hearing one idea in a sermon but none of the rest of it;
3. Half listening—following the discussion only well enough to find an opportunity to express your own idea: listening to a conversation to find a place to tell how you handled a child;
4. Listening passively with little observable response: the child knows the teacher is telling him once again how to walk in the hall;
5. Narrow listening in which the main significance or emphasis is lost as the listener selects details that are familiar or agreeable to him: a good Democrat listening to a candidate from another party;
6. Listening and forming associations with related items from one's own experiences: a first-grade child hears the beginning sound of *Sally*, *says*, and *said*, and relates it to the letter *s*;
7. Listening to a report to get main ideas and supporting details or follow directions: listening to the rules and descriptions of a new spelling game;
8. Listening critically: a listener notices the emotional appeal of words in a radio advertisement;
9. Appreciative and creative listening with genuine mental and emotional response: a child listens to the teacher read *Miracle on Maple Hill* and shares the excitement of sugar making.

Principles of Learning Applied to Listening

The psychology of learning has much to offer in providing guidelines for an appropriate environment facilitating the development of listening skills. The teacher must follow recommended guidelines pertaining to teaching and learning which aid pupils in developing needed skills in listening.

1. Learning activities should be interesting to encourage improved listening on the part of pupils. Too frequently, experiencing in the classroom have been boring and result in poor listening.

   Dawson, Zollinger, and Elwell list the following appreciative listening activities, among others, which might well capture learner interests:

   "Oral reading will often be the background for responsive listening as the listeners (1) sketch an original cartoon of a character or situation portrayed in a story; (2) pantomime, activate puppets, or dramatize spontaneously in response to a story just listened to; (3) individually tell or write an original ending to a high-quality story; and (4) make sound effects with rhythm band instruments as the teacher reads a poem or story portraying different kinds of weather or rates of motion; for instance, as a character strolls, walks briskly, stumbles, lopes, pauses and walks softly, races and leaps to safety.

   Storytelling, too, gives opportunity for the children to learn to listen appreciatively and creatively, for instance, they (1) tell chain stories in which each participant carries on from where the preceding speaker stopped; (2) witness the first act of a play planned and presented by a committee, then spontaneously make up the next act; (3) listen for leads in prepared stories told by members of a special committee, these leads to suggest spontaneous stories on the part of the listeners; and (4) for advanced pupils, keep notes of the ideas suggested by the poems and stories presented by the teacher or their classmates."

   The teacher must know as much as possible about the interests of individual pupils. Learning activities related to unit titles may be based on pupils' interests. Thus, learners having hobbies such as collecting coins, stamps, rocks, pennants, and other items, can bring these to school pertaining to a unit on hobbies. As learners tell about their hobbies, skills pertaining to listening are involved. Pupils need to listen carefully to the presentation of others. They also must listen to questions of listeners pertaining to specific hobbies being presented.

The teacher then should attempt to select learning activities which stimulate learners in wanting to listen carefully to ideas being presented. Content discussed in films, filmstrips, slides, and other audio-visual materials on the understanding level of pupils can aid learners to become better listeners. Problem solving activities may guide pupils to improve their listening vocabularies. Ideas are shared when pupils in committees identify problems, obtain needed information, and revise necessary hypotheses. Problem solving activities may generate much interest in learning on the part of pupils.

2. Teacher-pupil planning can aid learners in listening. Teaching very often has amounted to lecturing and explaining. Thus, a one-way street of communication is in evidence. Eventually, pupils may lack purpose in learning since there are few opportunities to ask questions in terms of what is valuable to pupils. Pupils, of course, must perceive reasons for learning. Teacher-pupil planning means that learners participate in actively presenting ideas as well as listening to content. Pupils might then have a voice in determining what is to be learned as well as how the learning is to take place. They may also be involved in assessing their own achievement. Thus, pupils become participants in determining the elementary curriculum. Thus, pupils become participants in determining the elementary curriculum. The concerns of pupils should be in evidence in teaching-learning situations in the class setting. If the concerns of pupils become an important part of the elementary curriculum, purpose is then involved in learning.

3. Variety in learning experiences can help to develop needed skills in listening. Sameness in learning experiences generally forces listening in turning off to ongoing learning activities. If improved listening is to take place within pupils, learning activities must be varied. There are more kinds of experiences that can be provided for pupils than ever before. It behooves the teacher to select those which help pupils to listen more attentively.

4. Pupils must receive direct practice to achieve at an optimum rate is listening. Learnings that pupils have developed pertaining to listening should be applicable and transferable to new situations. The teacher needs to provide experiences for pupils where skills in listening can be developed. Developed skills must be relevant and useful. Thus, the teacher might have pupils listen to various sounds in the environment when taking an excursion on or near the school grounds. Learners may identify the sounds as to their source or origin. The teacher as well as pupils might record diverse sounds and have learners in the class setting identify their cause or causes. The teacher also, could have learners put their heads on their desk and not see the source of sounds, while the teacher crumbles paper, pours water into a tumbler, and taps, a pencil. Pupils can guess what made each of these sounds to occur. Hopefully, as a result of direct experiences pertaining to the identification of sounds, pupils will transfer learnings to new situations. Improved listening might then occur in the classroom setting.

5. The teacher must provide for individual differences in listening. Each child differs from others in many ways such as in height, weight, energy level, health, capacity, and achievement. The teacher must make definite provisions for individual differences in the class setting. To be sure, selected pupils will be better listeners as compared to others. Two pupils may even be quite similar in capacity and achievement;

however, one of these learners will comprehended content better in learning activities involving listening. When differences exist in capacity of two pupils, generally the pupil with the higher capacity should achieve better in listening activities, all things being equal. The ability to comprehend well in learning activities involving listening may well depend upon factors such as the following:

(a) background information of pupils;

(b) interest in the topic being presented;

(c) motivation of pupils in desiring to learn;

(d) content being presented on the understanding levels of pupils;

(e) sequence of ideas being presented;

(f) methods used in presenting ideas;

(g) enthusiasm of the presenter of content;

(h) impression made by speaker on listeners;

(i) use of appropriate gestures, facial expressions, and body movements of the speaker.

6. The teacher must accept each pupil regardless of race, creed, or socio-economic level. Pupils come to school representing diverse socio-economic levels. The home situation may or may not have the following benefits educationally for pupils:

(a) reading materials for pupils;

(b) discussing content with children in a meaningfully way;

(c) having an atmosphere of empathy and respect;

(d) children being involved in the making of decisions;

(e) parents reading to themselves and thus setting a model for pupils;

(f) parents taking pupils to visit places of importance such as museums, circuses, and other points of interest;

(g) appropriate clothing for children;

(h) nutritious meals for members of the family;

(i) concern for health and safety of children.

The home situation must provide what is of benefit to children. However, as is will known and documented, selected pupils lack having needed experiences in the home which make for a sound educational background. Pupils may come to school lacking proper fitting and clean clothing. It may then be difficult for some teachers to accept these individuals as having worth. Each pupil must feel he/she is wanted and valued in the school setting for optimum achievement to take place. A child that feels he/she is not a part of the class will hardly achieve optimal development. All pupils must be accepted by the teacher; each child can then be guided to realize optimal development. This is true of the language arts area of listening as well as other curriculum areas.

7. Pupils should be actively involved in learning for the highest achievement in listening to occur. A passive receiver of information cannot achieve to his/her optimum in listening. Pupils need to have a stimulating environment in order that improved listening habits may result.

The teacher must emphasize proper balance among diverse learning activities to stress pupils growing in listening, speaking, reading, and writing. This definitely means that the listening vocabulary should not be deemphasized. Too frequently, skills objectives in listening have not been stressed adequately in teaching-learning situations. The classroom teacher must stress the importance of having pupils achieve relevant objectives pertaining to listening. If learning centers are used in the classroom setting, the following might serve as a model:

(a) ***A discussion center:*** Here, pupils could discuss a selected picture, from among others. The pictures should stimulate curiosity and involve learners in a lively discussion at the learning center. Active participation on the part of pupils is to be desired in learning experiences involving listening. At the discussion center, pupils could also discuss relevant issues in the current affairs programme. Issues being discussed should provide for situations in which pupils have an inward desire to listen attentively;

(b) ***An audio-visual station:*** Pupils in a committee could view selected filmstrips, films, and slides pertaining to ongoing units of study. Following the presentation, learners could discuss and present their findings to the total class. In the discussion, learners need to present ideas as well as listen to the thinking of others;

(c) ***A listening center:*** Pupils may listen to cassette recordings of their choosing related to specific units being studied presently. A task card could be an inherent part of the center. From the card, pupils individually may select sequential activities to complete. Each pupil might then be assessed in terms of having understood and gained ideas through listening when responding to selected questions on the task card;

(d) ***Oral reading and storytelling center:*** Here, pupils in a small group may listen to stories being read orally or to stories being told by learners or by the teacher. Careful listening is important in this teaching-learning situation. Hopefully, the stories read and told make for active involvement in listening.

Chambers and Lowry wrote:

> "***Active listening*** *is specialized listening. It is listening to receive special, important information. This is listening with a definite purpose. The conductor listens actively as he rehearses his orchestra. The physician listens actively through his stethoscope. The athlete listens actively to directions from his coach. Active listening implies readiness, listening for a special purpose. Children listen actively to a spelling list being read by a teacher, since after they hear a word on the list, they are required to write in on paper.*

Active listening does not comprise most of the child's listening efforts. Often he does not know how or when to listen actively. He will usually need clues so that he can listen in an active way. A good teacher will provide these clues. She many times will have a device that will bring children's attention to her, so that they will be able to participate in active listening. Such a device as calling for attention and waiting until all eyes are toward her and quite prevails is a common one. Preschool and kindergarten teachers many times will strike a chord on the piano or ring a special bell to bring children to attention so they will listen in an active manner.

It is probably wise also to tell children that they will receive directions or other information that is important to them. It is good to simply tell them that they need to listen carefully! What the teacher is actually doing is structuring their listening. They are told to listen carefully, and why they are to listen carefully. Sometimes it is necessary to present the information and/or directions more than once. After they have been given, many teachers will ask a student to repeat what they have heard, so that additional reinforcement is provided. Active listening is specialized listening. Teachers must realize that some children will not know how to listen in this way and will need help in learning this skill.

***Passive listening** describes that level of listening that does not require the attention, the concern for detail, or any specific requirements of active listening. This kind of listening is largely an unconscious process and contrasts with active listening, which is largely a conscious process. Passive listening is the kind of listening that one does as he listens to the radio, aware of the sound, but not paying great attention to it. One responds to classroom 'hum' in a passive way, aware that it is present, but not consciously concerned with it. The everyday sounds of the world are heard in a passive way. They occur and pass with little attention from the listener. Only when the listener is given a clue that what he is hearing is of importance to him will this unconscious, passive listening become active and conscious.*

Most of the younger's listening (and the adult's for that matter) is of a passive nature. He is aware of sound activity and accepts it passively. His environment teaches him to be activily aware of certain sounds for his protection or to satisfy needs. Other sounds will go relatively unattended.

Objectives in Listening

Dallmann lists the following do's and don'ts for teachers in the area of listening:

1. Speak in a pleasant voice, one to which the pupils can enjoy listening;
2. Build upon the listening experiences that the child has had at home and/or in earlier years at school;
3. Remember that listening is more than hearing, and help the boys and girls to recognize the fact that attention to a speaker's words often requires thinking;
4. Encourage the listener not to be so absorbed in his own ideas about a point the speaker has mentioned during the course of his talk that he will not note subsequent points the speaker makes in the rest of his talk;
5. Be a good listener yourself. When a pupil or other person is speaking, show be your behaviour that you are listening to the speaker. Some teachers spend much of the time that they should spend in listening by watching members of the audience. This is bad practice because boys and girls may develop the habit of not listening as they note the teacher's inattentive manner;
6. Guard against giving instructions such as "Let's all pay attention." Rather, indicate for what the pupils should be listening;
7. Avoid the practice, in which some teachers engage, of repeating directions or explanations unnecessarily. Otherwise the pupils may develop poor habits of listening, as they realize the teacher will most likely make his explanation more than once. Or the pupil may be bored by that which the teacher repeats. However, the teacher should be careful that he makes his points clear. At times, for example, after the teacher has given a direction of more than one step, a pupil may be asked to make application of it for demonstration purposes, to insure that the point is made clear to those who are listening;
8. Discourage interruption of the speaker, even if he makes an error in speech or in facts presented or in deductions from facts he presents;

9. Don't encourage fake attention. The teacher might lead a discussion on the fact that merely looking intently at the speaker does not guarantee good listening. He can help the pupils to understand that a person looking intently at the speaker may sometimes feel justified in letting his mind wander rather than concentrating on what the speaker is saying.

Objectives for pupils to achieve is listening must be selected carefully. Only relevant objectives should be stressed in teaching-learning situations. Following the selection of objectives, learning experiences must be selected for pupils. Ultimately, assessment must take place to determine if the objectives have been realized. If objectives have not been achieved, the teacher needs to determine causes. New or modified learning experiences may need to be selected so that pupils can achieve the stated objectives. Or, the original objective(s) may need to be omitted or stated at a less complex achievement level.

The following, among others, may be relevant objectives for pupils to achieve in listening:

1. to recall factual information, main ideas, generalizations, and summary statements;
2. to attach meaning to content presented by others;
3. to utilize learnings obtained within new situations such as in problem-solving activities;
4. to analyze content critically in terms of separating opinion from facts, inaccurate statements from accurate statements, and imaginary situations for situations involving reality;
5. to listen creatively with the intent of achieving new, unique, novel ideas;
6. to listen attentively to ongoing presentations;
7. to listen to ideas of others in an atmosphere of respect;
8. to desire to improve in the area of listening;
9. to diagnose one's own difficulties in listening and working toward remedying these deficiencies;

10. to listen proficiently to diverse types and kinds or oral presentations such as in conversations, discussions, interviews, and in the making of introductions;
11. to develop adequate background information so that goals in listening can be realized to their optimum;
12. to evaluate ideas expressed by others in terms of desirable criteria.

The teacher also needs to have objectives which are relevant to use in teaching-learning situations. Thus, the teacher may emphasize the following objectives involving listening:

1. Presenting content on the understanding level of pupils;
2. Varying the kinds of learning activities to promote optimum pupil achievement in listening;
3. Working in the direction of pupils enjoying ongoing learning activities to increase listening potential;
4. Providing for individual differences among learners in listening;
5. Valuing the worth of each learner so that an adequate self-concept may result;
6. Helping pupils develop respect toward others.
7. Developing a relaxed environment free from threats and tension.

Learning Experiences and Listening

> *Imagine you are in a vast conventional hall filled with an immense display of the latest, brightest, and best educational materials; film strips, tapes, movies, magazines, workbooks, photographs, craft kits, cutouts, stencils, and textbooks. Except for these items spread in colourful array, the room is empty. Until one human being enters the scene, walks, stops, looks, and touches, all the materials are nothing but inert matter, just as the magician's props are nothing but objects until used by the individual who can change them into something wonderful.*

> *Creative teachers can transform ordinary learning into a magical moment. They can translate routine lesson plans into memorable experiences. They can present facts in such original ways that the facts fuse with other, deeper understandings and result in exciting discoveries for the student.*

A variety of learning experiences must be provided for pupils so that stated objectives in listening can be achieved.

The teacher may select and read interesting stories and library books to pupils. Periodically, stimulating questions might be asked of pupils pertaining to content read to evaluate achievement in listening. Questions asked should not hinder in developing improved skills in listening.

Pupils in committees may take turns reading-selected stories to each other. The content of these stories can be discussed within the committee. The teacher then has opportunities to assess each pupil's achievement in listening.

The teacher, as well as pupils, might engage in the telling of stories. Pictures, objects, and charts may be used in the learning activity. Following the telling of stories, pupils with teacher guidance may discuss major generalizations achieved in the listening activity.

Selected intervals of time may be used to provide direct experiences for pupils in listening. Thus, pupils may tell of sounds heard presently in the class setting. Pupils could bring to class an object that would make a certain sound; listeners not seeing the object may guess the source of the sound. Learners individually might also make selected sounds without the use of objects. Other pupils, having their eyes closed and heads on their desks, may determine the cause of these sounds.

Pupils with teacher guidance may develop appropriate standards pertaining to listening. Periodically, pupils could evaluate their own personal achievement in listening in terms of the agreed upon guidelines.

There are many kinds of learning activities to assist pupils in becoming better listeners. The activities must be interesting, purposeful, meaningful, and provide for individual differences. The following, among others, may provide experiences for pupils requiring skill in the area of listening:

1. discussing content read from reference sources;
2. evaluating the results of a science excitement;
3. planning a mural, frieze, or diorama within a committee;
4. making and evaluating relief maps, models, and toys relating to an ongoing social studies unit;
5. working cooperatively in solving a mathematics problem involving a new process;
6. assessing cooperatively in an atmosphere of respect, written or oral reports presented in reading;
7. planning well balanced meals in a unit on nutrition in the health curriculum;
8. assessing achievement in small groups toward achieving objectives in physical education, art, and music, as well as in other curriculum areas in the elementary school.

In Summary

It is important for teachers to follow important principles of learning when guiding pupils toward improved skills in listening. Objectives which pupils are to achieve in listening should be carefully selected and relevant from the learner's own unique perception. Experiences pertaining to listening should assist pupils to achieve desired objectives. How well pupils listen in any given situation may depend upon the following; (Smith):

1. the child's maturity level;
2. the child's general ability;
3. the child's interest in the topic at hand;
4. the child's previous experience with the material being presented;
5. the type of material being presented;

6. the listening 'climate' created by the teacher;
7. the children's rapport with the teacher or the speaker;
8. the quality of the teaching;
9. the attitude and ability of the teacher (or speaker) to relate to the child;
10. the demands made on the child during the listening period;
11. the child's listening readiness;
12. the child's established listening habits;
13. the child's ability to adjust to any abnormal or unpredicted situation;
14. the physical-emotional tone of the room;
15. the child's acquired listening skills;
16. the adjustment of speed of reception with the speed of delivery;
17. the creative set to listen;
18. the child's general health and the social-emotional climate of his home.

REFERENCES

Anderson, Paul S., and Diane Lapp. *Language Skills in Elementary Education*. Third Edition. New York: The Macmillan Company, 1979.

Applegate, Mauree. *Easy in English*. Elmsford. New York: Harper and Row, Publishers, 1960. Chapter Four.

Chambers, Dewey Woods, and Health Ward Lowry. *The Language Arts*. Dubuque, Iowa: Wm. C. Brown Publishers, 1975.

Chenfeld, Mimi Brodsky. *Teaching Language Arts Creatively*. New York: Harcourt Brace Jovanovich, Inc., 1979.

Dallman, Martha. *Teaching the Language Arts in the Elementary School*. Second Edition. Dubuque, Iowa: Wm. C. Brown Company Publishers, 1976. Chapter Four.

Dawson, Mildred, Marian Zollinger, and Ardel Elwell. *Guiding Language Learning*. Second Edition. New York: Harcourt, Brace and World, Inc., 1963.

Dawson, Mildred A., and Frieda Hayes Dingee. *Children Learn the Language Arts*, Second Edition. Minneapolis: Burgess Publishing Company, 1966. Chapter Five.

Ediger, Marlow. "Good Listening Habits a Must," *The Oklahoma Teacher*. (February, 1968), 18-19.

Fox, Sharon E., and Virginia Allen. *The Language Arts*. New York: Holt, Rinehart and Winston, 1983.

Newman. Harold. *Effective Language Arts Practices in the Elementary School: Selected Readings*. New York: John Wiley and Sons, 1972. Chapter Four.

Shane, Harold G., et al. *Improving Language Arts Instruction in the Elementary School*. Columbus: Charles E. Merrill Books, Inc., 1962. Chapter Five.

Smith, James. *Adventures in Communication*. Boston, Massachusetts: Allyn and Bacon, Inc., 1972.

Strickland, Ruth G. *The Language Arts in the Elementary School*. Second Edition. Boston: D.C. Health and Company, 1957. Chapter Six.

11

Phonics and the Language Arts

Word recognition skills help readers identify words while reading. One skill is sight word recognition, the development of a store of words a person can recognize immediately on sight. Use of context clues to help in word identification involves using the surrounding words to decode an unfamiliar word. Both semantic and syntactic clues can be helpful. Phonics, the association of speech sounds (phonemes) with printed symbols (graphemes), is very helpful in identifying unfamiliar words, even though the sound-symbol associations in English are not completely consistent. Structural analysis skills enable readers to decode unfamiliar words using units larger than single graphemes. The process of structural analysis involves recognition of prefixes, suffixes inflectional endings, contradictions and compound words, as well as syllabication and accent. Dictionaries can also be used for word identification. The dictionary re-spelling that appears in parentheses after the word supplies the word's pronunciation, but the reader has to know how to use the dictionary's pronunciation key in interpret the re-spellings appropriately.

Children need to learn to use all of the word recognition skills. Because they will need different skills for different situations, they must also learn to use the skills appropriately.

An overall strategy for decoding unfamiliar words is useful. The following five step strategy is a good one to teach:

1. use context clues;
2. try the sound of the initial consonant, vowel, or blend in addition to context clues;
3. check for structural clues;
4. use phonics generalizations to sound out as much of the word as necessary; and
5. consult the dictionary (Burns, Roe and Ross, 1996, 152-53).

There is considerable debate pertaining to how much phonics should be taught in the reading curriculum. Whole language approaches tend to minimize the teaching of phonics. Advocates of whole language believe that pupils will learn to read well when holism in content read is emphasized. For example, pupils together with the teacher here look at a Big Book that all can see clearly to discuss the illustrations. This activity assists pupils to obtain background information so that the resulting print will be understood better. Pupils also speculate on what the print material in the Big Book will be about. The pulls and the teacher then read aloud the contents in the Big Book. Pupils may see the printed words as the oral reading activity progresses. If they do know them or they don't, pulls can determine what each word is through reading aloud together and follow along in the print material. Re-reading is recommended since all pupils have their favourite stories and like to hear them again. Before I was able to read to myself, I liked to hear the Katzenjammer Kids comic strip read over and over again. The countries therein were quite predictable since the Katzenjammer Kids always did something mischievous; the father and the captain never liked to work while mama did all the work.

Big Books read with children should contain predictable content in the pupils have security in knowing something about what will happen in the story. With re-reading and predicable content, pupils learn to identify many words. These identified words become sight words. With a core of sight words in the repertoire, pupils may then read content at a more sophisticated level. With the Big Book approach, pupils are not hindered in sequential thinking when attempting to recognize an unknown word. Enjoyment of the story being read should then be in the offing. If pupils are stumbling along with word recognition, they may learn to dislike the act of reading. Rather, pupils need to focus upon interesting content contained in the Big Book. There are teachers who teach some phonics along with Big Book use. Thus, there may be games that pupils play in phonics related directly to the content read. Pupils then study words which have the same beginning letter and sound. They may compare short and long vowel sounds in words following a pattern such as: cap—cape, hat—hate, fat—, nap—nape and can, cane, among others. Teachers in whole language also stress words that end alike and words that rhyme. By having pupils find which word, for example, starts like 'bat', pupils may enjoy the phonics learning activity. It is not drill in a complete scope and sequence programme of phonics, but rather learners locate words with a pattern and these words came from print materials read.

Phonics Integrated with Content from Reading

The view that reading consists of its simultaneous application of many different skills has important implications for our understanding for the successes and failures that readers experience as well as the kinds of educational programmes that we should implement. The reason for this is that in reading, as in all cognitive activities, there are many roads that lead to Rome. There are many paths to successful reading and hence many paths to successful reading instruction. On the other hand, failure to read may result from deficiencies in any of the sub-skills of literacy. On the other hand, readers with strong skills in one facet of reading are bound to be able to compensate for possible weaknesses in other skills. We already have seen, for example, how second language readers use their comprehension, and inferential skills to compensate for a lack of vocabulary and word identification skills. Thus, it is true that readers not only can fail to accomplish literacy for many different reasons, but also can succeed for different reasons (Van Den Broek, 1996).

We do not agree with a phonics programme that has a scope and sequence of its own whereby lesson after lesson emphasizes phonics. Why? 1. The lessons become much too abstract for young pulls on the primary grade levels. 2. Phonics is separated from the act of reading whereby reading for ideas should be the key component of a quality reading programme. 3. Pupils experience much drill when phonics becomes a separate subject area. 4. Teachers find it difficult to obtain pupil interests in sequential lessons in phonic. 5. Learners have a difficult time to determine reasons for all the emphasis upon 'How' to read.

An approach in the teaching of phonics needs to stress reading for content and ideas as well as mastering key concepts pertaining to word recognition. There needs to be rational balance between whole language and phonics. Now we are left with the problem of what makes for balance between whole language and phonics. Now, we are left with the problem of what makes for balance between the two—phonics and whole language. We would give much more importance to reading for ideas as compared to phonics. Why? We read to secure ideas, not to associate sounds with symbols. Relating sounds to symbols emphasizes keys to unlocking unknown words. It is not an end in and of itself. Phonics should never be taught as an end, but it is a means to an end. If phonics knowledge and use is more important than being a tool to unlock unknown words, then we are stuck with a strong scope and sequence programme in phonics. Phonics then may be taught for its own sake. Here, we believe a mistake is made when phonics is conceive to be good for its own sake whether it assists pupils in reading well or not. Compare that line of thought with phonics being a tool to use when needed to determine the word that is not being identified.

Sometimes, even with strong context clues, a pupil cannot identify an unknown word. Perhaps, in these cases, a pupil may unlock an unknown word through identifying the initial consonant and then using context clues. A strong case can be made for emphasizing phonics as needed. If a pupil then cannot identify a word after being given adequate opportunity to do so, the teacher may need to stress selective facets of phonics which are useful here, such as the initial consonant 'm' when the word 'modify' is encountered and not identified. There is that teachable moment when the teacher needs to emphasize what is salient and in this case, a phonetic element. Phonics also may be taught in the context of basal reader use. Thus, when pupils are to read a story or selection from the basal, the teacher may print on the chalkboard in neat manuscript style the new words pupils will encounter when they are to read silently or orally. Generally, these new words will come from the manual section of the basal. The teacher points to each new word as he/she and the pupils pronounce them. This procedure may be used more than once per lesson if the need exists. The point is that pupils should be able to recognize these same words when reading. It still will be necessary as the act of reading is in evidence for the teacher or a good reader to pronounce words not known to the teacher. The pupil needs to be helped after allowing not known to the reader. The pupil needs to be helped after allowing five seconds, in general, before the unknown word is pronounced. Pupils not knowing a word should attempt to the best possible to determine it during these approximate five seconds. When pupils have ample opportunities to see the new words in near manuscript print, prior to oral or silent reading, the chances are they will identify many of these in the ongoing reading experience.

What about a phonics programme that has a scope and sequence of its very own? Pupils should realize that a consonant sound is made with an obstruction by the speaker between the throat and the lips. This is true of all consonant sounds. When thinking about the teaching of single consonants, the teacher or committee of teachers need to decide when these should be taught. There are individual consonant letters that are very consistent with their individual sounds. The following consonants are very consistent between grapheme/phoneme—b, d, f, h, j, i, m, n, p, r, s, t, v, w and y With high frequency of use, I would stress the importance of pupils learning the following consonants: b, d, m, n, p, r, s, t, and w. These consonants have very few exceptions to being consistent between symbol and sound. The following are some exceptions:

1. the letter 'b' is silent in the word 'debt';
2. the letter 'p' is silent in the word 'pneumonia';
3. the letter 's' sounds like a 'z' in the word 'resides';
4. the letter 'w' has a 'wh' sound in words such as 'why'.

'what', and 'when'. When I was an undergraduate student in a teaching of reading class, the instructor mentioned strongly that the 'wh' sound is made with pronouncing the 'w' and then at the same time blowing the light out as a candle. We think in most cases we cannot distinguish between the two initial consonant of 'w' with the words 'where' and 'when'.

In context, then, single consistent consonants, between symbol and sound, need to be taught. These are very helpful for learners to use in addition to context clues to unlock unknown words. Functional use should be made of these consonants. They are not to be learned for their own sake, but rather for application and use.

Short vowel sounds are next in importance for pupils to study. The consonant/vowel/consonant pattern are relatively easy for many pupils. These sounds are common in such words as the following: run, sun and bun. These words pattern with a short 'u' sound. Ran, ban and man pattern with the short 'a' sound. Hen, men and pen pattern with the short 'e' sound. Sit, pit and hit pattern for the short 'i' sound. Cot, lot and tot pattern with the short 'o' sound.

Long vowel sounds can have a pattern when taught to pupils. For example, there are numerous words that follow the consonant/vowel/consonant/silent 'e' (CVC silent e) pattern, such as bake, make, fake, sake and lake. Vowel digraphs include sail, pail, mail and rail, there are two vowel letters that come together with the first being long and the second silent in sound.

Initial consonant digraphs taught by the teacher may assist many pupils to become proficient in word recognition. Generally, two consonant letters make for one sound. These individual letters cannot be taken apart and make sense, such as the following: 'th' as in *thought*; 'sh' as in *shine*; 'ch'as in *chair*; and 'ph' as in *phone*. The words listed here for the consonant digraphs are commonly used words. The consonant digraphs listed are used very frequently. Within context, there are pupils who need assistance here since the separate letters do not make for consistency between symbol and sound.

Ending consonant digraphs are more difficult for pupils to master as compared to those coming in the beginning. Many pupils have been guided to improve reading through identification of ending consonant digraphs such as: ch as in *bench*, sh as in *push* and th as in *width*. Games may always be played with pupils to see if they can provide additional words that have a beginning or ending consonant digraphs. One of us observed a student teacher and her cooperating teacher have pupils brainstorm consonant blends and pupils wanted the lesson to continue beyond closing time. There was excitement and interest in continually naming more consonant blends.

Consonant blends or clusters are made up of two or three letters, each making its separate sound. The sounds come rather close together. There are pupils who have difficulty making these blends of two consecutive letters with their individual sounds. Here are some common blends: bl as in *blow* and *blue*; cr as in *cry, crystal* and *crow*; fr such as in *fruit, frail* and *fry*; sn such as in *snow*, snail and snake and str such as in *street, stray* and *strike*.

Phonograms are interesting for many pupils to experiment with. Phonograms are short words found within a larger word. Examples of pupils discovering phonograms are the following: *at* as in hat, *eat* as in seat and *ate* as in skate. Sometimes a new 'unknown' word is not impossible to identify. Thus, the word may appear unknown, but the learner knows enough about phonograms that he/she can identify of the word correctly.

There are pupils who face an 'unknown' word until they notice familiarities therein, such as a prefix. There are very common prefixes that hold true quite consistently. These include *un* meaning *not* such as unpopular and *im* meaning not such as in impolite. The unfamiliar becomes familiar when pupils notice suffixes such as *less* as in child*less* and *ful* such as in cap*ful*. By noticing the familiar such as the root word and adding either the prefix and/or suffix, many pupils can determine what the new word is.

Diphthongs may cause selected pupils problems in word recognition. Why? Here are two vowel letters that are together and yet their sound is different then any short or long vowel sound as well as being different in pronunciation. The following are examples: *oil* (the oi letters make a unique sound) and *oy* as in oyster (the oy make a unique sound also). These sounds are not like the individual letters or like a short or long vowel sound would make.

Another problem in sound/symbol relationships are words governed by a final 'r'. Notice the following words: *fir, fur, fer,* a syllable as in trans*fer*. The first word 'fir' refers to a fir tree. The second 'fur' refers to the hair on an animal, such as 'The dog had shaggy fur'. The third 'fer' is common as a suffix to many words. Sometimes, there are no governing principles in analyzing an unknown word. With the sight method in oral cooperative reading by pupils and the teacher, an unknown word becomes a known word. The following words, for example, follow a spelling pattern, but their individual pronunciations certainly do not: though, through, tough, bough, cough and dough. These words are spelled in an irregular manner and must be learned as sight words, even though a spelling pattern is there.

We generally oppose in teaching phonics prior to the time it is needed. To be functional. Phonics should be taught when the need arises. Thus, when a pupil is reading silently or orally, he/she may need assistance on word identification. There is that teachable moment in time when a pupil might well benefit from selected phonics learnings. Thus, if a pupil is reading. "The Henry family liked to take—during holidays', the pupil may not know the word in the blank space. When using context clues, there are many words that would fit in according to meaning theory. The words that do not begin with the correct initial consonant can then be eliminated. If the pupil does not know the sound that goes along with the initial consonant letter, he/she may now be taught the grapheme/phoneme correspondence.

There is another suitable time to teach phonics and that is when learners may see pattern pertaining to the word not identified in oral or silent reading. Not always, of course, are there patterns in evidence. But, when a pupil does not identify the word 'soil' in reading, he/she may be assisted to notice words which pattern such as boil, toil and spoil. The patterns approach has helped many pupils to identify unknown words when reading. Then too, a pupil who does not identify the word 'soil' when reading may be asked to give other words that begin like 's' or end like 'l'. Why is this important? The teacher may then appraise if the pupil can see and hear these phonemes/graphemes.

The question always arises as to the teaching of phonics to pupils who truly cannot hear sounds. A colleague of one of us as a sophomore in college in teacher education could not hear sounds. He was an avid reader and comprehended well. At the same time he was doing student teaching during his sophomore year for a sixty hour certificate, he was called down during a lesson taught. The calling down occurred in front of pupils being taught. The student teacher had stated in the elementary school class that a vowel sound in reading was long when actually it was a short vowel sound. A colleague felt very badly for this happening and was ready to quit student teaching. At the last moment he decided to continue and be certified with a sixty hour certificate for teaching. This colleague had taught for forty-two years at the time he was dying of cancer. His teaching was done on the fifth and sixth grade levels where phonics instruction in reading was minimal. He seemed to have done well as a classroom teacher. This teacher should no doubt rely very heavily upon whole language approaches when teaching pupils. This might not always be possible when the pendulum swings to a heavy dose of phonics for all pupils. One thing my colleague did during his teaching years was to mark vowel sounds carefuliy before each day of teaching. He checked with a dictionary as to the accuracy of the making.

Basic Principles in Teaching Phonics

There are basic principles that teachers should adhere to when teaching phonics to primary and intermediate grade pupils:

1. Pupils should be ready for the new lessons to be taught. This would include learners having an attention span adequate in duration. They should be able to hear likenesses and differences in sound;
2. Pupils should experience lessons in phonics that are taught in an interesting manner. This would mean that drill would be greatly minimized and stimulating games would receive primary emphasis in the teaching of phonics;
3. Pupils need to experience sequence in ongoing lessons and units of study. One of the most important factors in teaching is that pupils perceive learning activities as being sequentially more difficult and yet readiness is there for attaining goals in phonics instruction;
4. Pupils need to be attentive during the time phonics is taught. If pupils are not attentive, they will not benefit from ongoing instruction. A teaching strategy needs to be in evidence whereby pupils develop and maintain their attentiveness;
5. Pupils should experience success in learning. If pupils experience failure, the chances are they will not benefit much from phonics instruction;
6. Pupils should receive feedback on how well they are achieving in phonics instruction. In this way, pupils know what they need to concentrate on in phonics lessons;
7. The teacher needs to monitor pupil progress in phonics. Thus, there are indications that pupils are achieving and learning if careful monitoring is done;

8. Pupils need to use what has been learned in phonics; otherwise phonics may be learned for its own sake. The only reason for teaching phonics is for pupils to become capable readers and spellers. Knowledge needs to be used and application made to new situations encountered;
9. Pupils need to assist each other in learning about and using phonics in reading instruction;
10. Pupils should appraise themselves personally to notice progress in phonics knowledge acquired and application made;
11. Teachers need to evaluate themselves to notice what pupils have achieved and work for improved instruction;
12. Objectives chosen for phonics instruction need to be relevant and achievable by learners;
13. Learning opportunities in phonics should provide for individual differences regardless of ability levels and socio-economic status;
14. Evaluation techniques should be aligned with the stated objectives so that the objectives provide direction for instruction;
15. The phonics programme needs to be assessed frequently and modified to provide the best instruction possible for each pupil.

We need to emphasize again that phonics should be taught as a means to an end, not an end in and of itself. The end being to produce readers who enjoy reading and like to solve the problems through the act of reading.

Philosophies of Phonics Instruction

There are diverse philosophies of education stating how phonics should be taught. One philosophy stresses the basic idea whereby there is essential information that needs to be taught to all pupils. Phonics is conceived to be the basics by selected authors in education as well as teachers. These individuals believe that phonics is rather consistent between symbol and sound. Thus, the grapheme/phoneme correspondence makes it so that teachers can be certain that consistencies to exist between symbol and sound as pupils learn to read.

Advocates of the basics believe that there is a core of phonics principles and generalizations that pupils should learn and use. More people then would learn to read than ever before, according to advocates. A strong scope in phonics needs to be identified. The scope or breadth of phonics content to be taught needs to be identified. Specialists in phonics instruction should be on committees to choose *what* is silent to teach pertaining to phonics. These phonics learnings might be graded so that pupils and parents would know what the minimal level of achievement should be for pupils to achieve on a grade level or at the end of a semester. The determining of *when* phonics objectives should be emphasized in teaching stresses the concept of sequence. Thus, there are phonics objectives that would be taught on the kindergarten, first and/or second grade level. There are teachers who emphasize a very strong programme of phonics instruction with a well developed scope and sequence.

Reasons given for a strong programme in scope and sequence in phonics are the following:

1. the English alphabet is rather consistent in stressing each grapheme (symbol) equals a phoneme (sound);
2. the key to success in reading is becoming an independent reader and that is through the study and use of phonics;
3. once the graphemes/phonemes have been mastered, pupils can do more and more independent reading;
4. pupils can enjoy ideas in reading when studying and using phonics. It is not an either/or situation such as either studying and using phonics versus obtaining ideas and enjoying reading;
5. phonics instruction can be made enjoyable with games and stimulating exercises. The teacher may use a phonics text or workbook in teaching and still promote pupils interest in learning to read.

There seems to be general agreement that good auditory and visual discrimination are pre-requisites for learning sound-symbol relationships. We know that children must be able to distinguish one letter from another and one sound from another before they can associate a given letter with a specific sound. Visual discrimination refers to the ability to distinguish likenesses from differences among letters and auditory discrimination refers to the ability to distinguish likenesses and differences among sounds. To achieve these skills, children must first understand the concepts of like and different among forms. Also to achieve auditory discrimination, children must first have phonemic awareness or the awareness that speech is composed of separate sounds (phonemes). They must be able to hear sounds within words or they will be unable to form mental connections between sounds and letters (as quoted in Burns, Ross and Roe, 1996).

Somewhat toward the opposite end of the continuum, there are teachers who believe in holism, only in the teaching of reading. They stress pupils reading the entire story or reading selection without having lessons on phonics. These teachers believe that phonics instruction destroys interest in reading. Thus, pupils with teacher assistance should read the selection together. In this way, all pupils can orally read the content and identify all words. Re-reading is also stressed so that pupils and the teacher read over again the same selection. Generally stories chosen are quite predictable in that pupils have some idea of what will occur in sequence. Predictability of content assists pupils to ascertain what the unknown words are in pronunciation and in meaning.

Individualized reading is a holistic approach in reading instruction. The teacher here needs to have a rather large supply of library books from which each pupil will select sequential content to read. Learners generally select sequential books to read that are interesting and on their own unique reading level. Positive attitudes should be an important and on their individual reading level. After the completion of reading a library book, a conference is held with the teacher to determine comprehension and reading skills of the pupil. Attention is paid to phonics individually or in a committee when pupils reveal a need for help. It is important to notice that pupils reveal help needed as they read orally to the teacher a chosen selection. Assistance is provided pupils then as the need arises in reading and not before any selection is to be read.

Reasons given for using whole language approaches in teaching phonics within a quality reading programme are the following:

1. Pupils learn phonetic elements within context as library books are read and holistic procedures in reading are emphasized;
2. Ideas acquired are the major ingredients of a good reading programme for pupils. With interest and purpose in reading, the pupil hurdles many difficulties in reading, including associating sounds with symbols;
3. Pupils need to read to become better readers, not study phonics for its own sake;
4. The whole is greater (content in reading) than the sum of the parts (phonics);
5. Phonics is a tool to be used to obtain ideas from reading, not an end in and of itself.

In a psychological reading curriculum which is child centered, the pupil is strongly involved in a selecting objectives, learning opportunities, and evaluation procedures. This is the heart of a pupils centered curriculum in reading. Humanism as a psychology of learning is then being emphasized. A humane reading curriculum, according to its advocates, stresses the individual learner being involved in decision making in the reading curriculum. The pupil is at the center of developing the reading curriculum (Ediger, 1997).

Behaviourism and the Reading Curriculum

Behaviourism a psychology has had much influence in education. With behaviourism, objectives for pupil achievement are stated prior to instruction and in measurable terms. Teachers can even announce prior to teaching what pupils are to learn from the lesson. It is very precisely written in the objectives as to what each pupil is to learn. The learning activities are aligned with the objectives. The teacher then ultimately measures, after instruction, what pupils have achieved that was stated in the objectives. A pupil either achieves or does not achieve an objective since each is stated very precisely. Reasons given for using behaviourally stated objectives in teaching are the following:

1. Learning standards are written with precision so there is certainly in knowing what pupils are to learn or have learn;
2. Careful selection is given to objectives when each is very important and carefully defined in measurable terms;
3. Clarity is involved when communicating pupil results to parents. The results can be given in numerical terms;
4. Much attention can be paid to sequencing of objectives so that pupils experience as much success in learning as possible;
5. Pupils receive continuous feedback on how well they are achieving.

Phonics objectives for pupil attainment may be stated precisely or behaviourally. Careful selection of phonetic elements to be taught needs to be inherent in the stated objectives. A good teaching strategy needs to be in the offing so that pupils may achieve the sequential objectives. The teacher ultimately appraises pupil achievement to notice if objectives have been achieved.

Conclusion

There are numerous decisions to make in the teaching of reading. First, which objectives should pupils achieve? There are implications here for stressing holistic approaches in teaching of reading versus analytical procedures. The objectives chosen will reflect 'one's beliefs pertaining to the teaching of reading. Under which conditions do pupils learn to read best? Second, which learning opportunities should be selected so that pupils will achieve the stated objectives. This includes the role of the basal textbook in the teaching of reading. In addition to basals, there are many other materials in reading instruction as learning opportunities such as the use of CD ROMS, computer packages (drill and practice, tutorial, games, simulations and diagnostic approaches), Big Books, picture books, library books, encyclopaedias, filmstrips and slides with accompanying print materials, among others.

Third, how should the reading curriculum be organised? There are numerous procedures available such as a separate subjects approach involving reading and literature only; correlation such as reading/language arts and social studies taught as being related; fused curriculum such as reading/ language arts, social studies, science and mathematics, taught as being related. The inter-disciplinary reading curriculum integrates subject matter from all disciplines of knowledge. Problem solving procedures are best to use in inter-disciplinary approaches in instruction. Regardless of the academic discipline, that subject matter is used which assists in solving a problem.

The role of the reading teacher is to stimulate pupils to identify problems within the framework of a stimulating environment. After a problem has been clearly identified, related information is gathered to solve the identified problem... Based on the data, a hypothesis is developed in answer to the problem. The hypothesis needs to be specific so that it can be tested. The hypothesis is tentative, not an absolute. With further reading experiences, as well as use of audio-visual activities, the pupil with teacher guidance tests the hypothesis. The hypothesis, as a result of testing, may be accepted as is, refuted or modified... Problem solving skills are usable in all curriculum areas, as well as in the societal arena...

Curiosity of the learner is salient when he/she selects a library book to read. With curiosity, interest accrues. Interest in a particular topic may well spur pupils on to a greater desire to read (Ediger, 1997).

Fourth, how should pupil achievement be evaluated? There are many techniques to use in evaluating pupil progress in reading. These include standardized and norm referenced tests, teacher written tests, teacher observation, anecdotal records, checklists and rating scales, pupil self-evaluation, as well as peer appraisal! The purpose of evaluation is to determine how well the pupil achieving in reading. A philosophy of constructivism in evaluation may also be emphasized in that pupils reveal in context what has been achieved in word recognition techniques and in comprehension. This can provide feedback to the teacher and the pupil in deciding upon what he/she needs to emphasize as objectives.

A quality reading programme then stress the following:

1. Each pupil begins at a point where he/she is ready to achieve as optimally as possible;
2. The learner experiences continual progress successfully in reading;
3. The four vocabularies—listening, speaking, reading and writing—are integrated in a quality reading programme;
4. Word recognition skills, such as phonics, syllabication, context clues and structural analysis, are taught within a framework of interesting content to be read;
5. Major emphasis is placed upon reading literature, not analyzing words into component parts;
6. Multimedia approaches are used to motivate pupils so that an inward desire in learning to read is inherent;
7. Problem solving, critical and creative thinking, as well as application are salient concepts stressed in teaching reading;
8. The best sequence is used to guide each pupil toward optimum achievement in reading;
9. Learning to read as a life time endeavour is stressed;
10. The use of relevant research results is important in the teaching of reading (Ediger, 1997).

REFERENCES

Burns, Paul C., Betty D. Roe and Elinor Ross (1996), *Teaching Reading in Today's Elementary Schools*. Boston: Houghton Mifflin Company, 114.

Ediger, Marlow (1997), *Teaching Reading and the Language Arts in the Elementary School*. Kirksville, Missouri: Simpson Publishing Company, 32.

Ediger, Marlow (1997), *Teaching Reading and the Language Arts*. Kirksville, Missouri: Simpson Publishing Company, 37.

Ediger, Marlow (1997), "Perspectives in Teaching Reading", *Reading Improvement*, 34(2), 52-53.

Ediger, Marlow and Digumarti Bhaskara Rao (2002). *Elementary Curriculum*, New Delhi, India: Discovery Publishing House.

Van Den Broek, Paul (1996), "On Becoming Literate: The Many Sources of Success and Failure in Reading", the *first R. Every Child's Right to Read*, Graves, Van Den Broek and Taylor, (Editors), 193.

12

Vocabulary Development and the Language Arts

Developing a rich listening, speaking, reading and writing vocabulary is important in all curriculum areas. In the reading curriculum, in particular, a quality vocabulary needs to be achieved by each pupil. One reason that pupils do not read well is that they do not posses a functional vocabulary for reading. Enriching and developing pupil vocabularies should be a major goal in each academic discipline. The following are reasons for teachers guiding learners to possess a rich vocabulary:

1. Subject matter and ideas are expressed with more clarity and accuracy;
2. Proficiency in the work place might well depend upon individuals having a quality vocabulary;
3. Individuals seemingly have more prestige if their listening, speaking, reading and writing vocabularies are adequately developed;
4. Greater enjoyment of reading is in the offing if a person has a rich functional vocabularies;
5. Vocabulary development is salient in problem solving. A person with a rich vocabulary should have a better opportunity to develop his/her vocabularies;

6. Conversations carried on with other persons require a rich vocabulary. There needs to be an appropriate number of words used that carry intended meanings;
7. Variety in selecting words to convey accurate meanings is necessary in speaking and writing, the outgoes of the language arts;
8. Use of diverse terms and concepts in speaking and writing adds variety to quality communication. Vocabulary development becomes a tool to take in, such as listening and reading, as well as provide communication to others within the framework of speaking and writing.

Very closely related to the background knowledge required for reading a text is vocabulary knowledge... By about the third grade and certainly by the fourth grade, most of the selections of the newer reading programmes are drawn from independently published materials, as compared to selections created by a publisher for inclusion in their series. The newer basals are virtually anthologies. Authors of the selections are professional writers using the best words available from the general vocabulary to communicate their ideas. Thus, the kind of vocabulary control found in the older basals is not in evidence in current programmes. The sophisticated vocabulary in the selections from the newer basals has both positive and negative potential for students. The negative potential is obvious—too many unfamiliar words will cause comprehension problems. The positive potential is also obvious—children can add words to their store of vocabulary.

Vocabulary development strategies created for each story lesson begin with the identification of a subset of words that developers believe may cause meaning or decoding difficulty. These words are listed in the teacher's manuals. By the third or fourth grade the programmes assume, competent decoding: most of the words noted in the teacher's manuals are of the meaning variety difficulty. These words become 'target words' for vocabulary development activities. Traditionally, the development of word meaning is attended to by instructional events that occur prior to reading, during reading and after reading... (Beck, 1984).

Developing the Vocabulary of Learners

The reading teacher needs to select quality objectives for pupils to achieve in the areas of vocabulary development. These objectives need to emphasize that is relevant and functional in vocabulary development. Certainly, pupils should be able to use what has been learned. Learning should not be for its own sake but rather be for personal use and application in society. Important vocabulary terms should be acquired by pupils. Adequate time must be given in choosing what pupils need to learn in vocabulary development. This cannot be hurried, because vocabulary development emphasizes that which must be learned in depth, not survey approaches.

Objectives pertaining to vocabulary development need to stress securing the interests of pupils in ongoing lessons and units of study. Ways of developing and maintaining pupil interest in learning must be emphasized in vocabulary studies. If pupils do not reveal interest in learning, they will not achieve as optimally as possible.

There needs to be objectives reflecting pupils working collaboratively. Within the cooperative endeavour, pupils listen to others and use oral communication with opportunities to achieve in vocabulary development. There are definite social goals here in that pupils need to learn to work harmoniously with others. And yet pupils also should be able to work by the self and achieve on an individual basis.

Vocabulary development emphasizes that pupils seek purpose in learning. Purposeful learning in vocabulary development means that pupils perceive reasons for learning. I think that one cannot stress too strongly that vocabulary development for pupils should have as a goal that purpose is involved in learning. Purposeful learnings have as a goal that pupils perceive the values inherent in vocabulary activities. If these values are lacking, the teacher should stress other vocabulary development lessons for learners.

Objective in vocabulary development need to emphasize the importance of meaningful learnings. If meaning is lacking, the chances are pupils will memorize terms and concepts for testing purposes only or largely. Meaning stresses the importance of pupils understanding that which has been learned. Use cannot be made of a new vocabulary terms unless understanding of prerequisites in vocabulary terms is prevalent. With prerequisites, background information is needed to attach meaning to vocabulary terms being studied.

Objective in vocabulary development for pupils should emphasize pupils experiencing the concept of providing for individual differences. There are pupils who learn more rapidly that others while some pupils take more time to learn the same content/skills as written in the statement of objectives. Each pupil regardless of socio-economic level must be accepted as a human being and taught in a manner which provides for all pupils.

Learning Opportunities to Achieve Objectives

To achieve vital objectives in vocabulary development, the teacher needs to select worthwhile activities for pupils. These activities need to be selected carefully so that each pupil's achievement is as optimal as possible. Pupils should not be labelled as being fast, average, or slow learners. Rather all should be accepted and develop feelings of belonging to the group.

To achieve objectives in vocabulary development. We recommend selected learning opportunities that student teachers and cooperating teachers whom we supervise have used successfully.

Each day the teacher should read aloud to pupils during story time. The book chosen should interest pupils and keep their attention. Voice inflection using proper stress, pitch and juncture should be in the offing when the teacher reads during story time. Words should be pronounced clearly and accurately. The teacher should have good audience contact with listeners. For young children, it is especially good to show the book's illustrations to pupils as the library book is being read. Throughout the story time activity, pupils should understand an increased number of facts, concepts and generalizations. Knowledge received provides background information for more complex ideas that should be forthcoming. Knowledge is sequential and cumulative for learners. A love for learning by pupils might be a further end result when the teacher reads orally to pupils during story time.

A second activity stressed pupils discussing ideas obtained from listening to the library book read or from personal reading pursued. Through discussion participation, pupils should learn effective ways of working within a small or large group setting. Pupils should learn to be polite, accepting and cooperative in the discussion learning activity. Being a good listener, valuing the thinking of others and actively participating in a polite manner should help a discussion to move forward in quality. Thus, the processes of being a member of a discussion group need to be emphasized continuously.

Then too, during the discussion, pupils should achieve quality ideas, facts, concepts and generalizations. Learners need to stay on the topic to achieve subject matter learnings during a discussion. Straying from the topic at hand merely wastes time. Ideas need to circulate within the group so that all have opportunities to participate. Active participation by each pupils should be an objective. Use of language during a discussion helps pupils to achieve more optimally in speaking. This translates content acquired to be used to comprehend subject matter in reading. The content and vocabulary gained by the learner might then provide background information for reading. Generally, what pupils are able to discuss represents meaningful subject matter. The subject matter might then provide the necessary knowledge, prior to reading, which helps pupils to understand increasingly complex vocabulary read.

Third, it is good to have once or more listening centers in the classroom. There are excellent cassette tapes related to an ongoing lesson on unit of study. Information gleaned from listening to a tape may guide pupils to answer related questions contained at the center. The information might well assist pupils to use this as background content to understand better what will be read from a basal or library book.

At the listening center, pupils may choose sequential tapes to listen to, for a variety of purposes. These purposes might well be the following in listening for:

1. facts, concepts and generalizations;
2. information to use in problem solving;
3. critical thinking purposes such as separating facts from opinions, accurate from inaccurate information and fantasy from reality;
4. opportunities to do creative thinking in the reading curriculum such as coming up with novel, unique ideas and originality in thought;
5. obtaining directions in reaching a certain place;
6. securing a main idea when relating facts, concepts and generalizations;
7. obtaining the setting of a story;
8. securing ideas pertaining to characterization within a writing;
9. determining the plot of a selection in reading;
10. understanding the theme of the speaker.

Fifth, the reading teacher needs to have one or more speaking centers in the classroom. Listening (discussed above and speaking are interrelated. We will mention some activities here that emphasize speaking more than listening.

1. Giving oral reports on library books read, related directly to the ongoing lesson and unit of study being taught. The oral report should follow good sequence in content presented. The ideas need to be presented clearly and at an appropriate rate of speed so that listening comprehension is optimal. The pupil presenting the oral book report needs to have the content well in mind. An outline, in proper form, should be used to convey the contents therein. The presenter of the book report should have good eye contact with the audience. Reading for enjoyment and for solving problems are two purposes in having pupils become proficient in reading.

2. Having pupils video-tape their individual oral book reports given to the class. Here, pupils individually or with a peer may appraise the quality of the oral report given. Standards used to appraise may be the same as under number two above. The contents of the videotape may also evaluate distracting mannerisms of the speaker such as rubbing the nose excessively. It is good to have the presenter appraise the quality of his/her own oral report in terms of quality standards. Vocabulary terms are developed from the reading of library books as well as from the oral presentations given of library book content.

3. Interacting with audio-visual materials to locate information for problem solving. The AV materials may include video-tapes, CD-ROMS, films, filmstrips, large illustrations, snapshots enlarged for class viewing with an opaque projector, internet and worldwide web, as well as computer packages. Among others, with pupil interaction with AV materials of instruction, there are many opportunities to gather information for a committee project such as developing a mural. The mural must be planned cooperatively with all participating and no one dominating collaborative endeavours. After the planning, the implementation of the plan comes in sequence. With implementation, each pupil on the committee does his/her fair share of the work. The project represents the best work each pupil can do. Thus, neatness, accuracy and attractiveness become key ingredients when appraising the mural. Art work correlates well with reading. Through art, pupils may reveal what has been learned. Vocabulary development is definitely inherent in planning, implementing and appraising the project.

Sixth, ample emphasis should be placed upon pupils doing much writing. With writing, pupils read their own written products as well as read those of other learners whose works are posted on the bulletin board. Reading and writing cannot be separated from each other but are complimentary. There are numerous forms of written work that pupils may engage in Journal entries should be written freely to indicate what had been learned in a given lesson. Diary entries may be written each day and should be dated. These diary entries portray what pupils learned for a day. As pupils write these diary entries, they read written content. In this way, pupils also review that which was learned previously from reading and re-reading diary entries covering subject matter learned. Additional written work may included the following:

1. ***Logs:*** Logs summarize what was contained in diary entries for one week. Clarity of ideas and proper sequence is important in writing logs;
2. ***Book Reports:*** These relate to an ongoing lesson or unit of study. Meaningful content in an appropriate order must be inherent in the written work;
3. ***Outlines:*** Here proper style needs to be used such as Roman numerals to indicate main ideas, capital letters in sequence to indicate subordinate ideas and Hindu-Arabic numerals to reveal details. The subordinate ideas relate directly to the main ideas whereas the details tell more about the subordinate content. Outlines are very helpful to use in giving a report on a certain topic to classmates. Thus, the oral report will have improved sequence to ideas presented as well as if the pupil forgets certain ideas, the outline is there to aid memory in oral communication;

3\. ***Poems:*** Poetry written in any lesson should relate to an ongoing lesson or unit of study. There are opportunities for pupils to write poetry in each curriculum area. There can be unrhymed verse written such as free verse. Or poetry written may contain rhyme such as couplets, triplets, quatrains and limericks. Poetry written may also include a selected number of syllables per line such as Haiku (5-7-5 syllables for each of three sequential lines). Tanka contains 5-7-5-7-7 syllables per line for each of five lines.

It is quite obvious that there are many writing opportunities for pupil pertaining to each curriculum area and within each lesson taught. Pupils engage in much reading, re-reading and proof-reading when engaging in writing experiences. Vocabulary development opportunities are numerous.

Seventh, pupils may engage in developing a dictionary. Even though there are pictured dictionaries, grade level dictionaries, unabridged dictionaries, as well as glossaries in basal textbooks, it can be highly profitable for pupils individually or in committees to develop their very own dictionaries. Why? Perhaps, there are many new words brought into the lesson or unit of study by the teacher. It is good to alphabetize these new words and write meaningful definitions for each. Dictionary entries need to be functional so that they may be used as needed to obtain contextual information. It is good for pupils to be able to alphabetize and re-read the necessary entries.

Eighth, pupils and the teacher should engage in story telling activities. Content for the story needs to follow a certain order to be meaningful to the listener. Thus, sequence of ideas in story telling is important! A clear speaking voice with proper enunciation helps the oral presentation to be more effective. Having a pleasant speaking voice with quality eye contact with listeners assists in the communication of the story. When pupils hear stories told, especially pertaining to a specific library book at an interest center, interest in reading that book tends to be generated. Background experiences are also developed within pupils for reading additional books in ongoing lessons and units of study.

When engaging in story telling, pupils should be developing poise and gracefulness in the process. Pupils need ample opportunities to appear before others in informal and formal experiences. No doubt, skills and attitudes are being developed here that will have life-long values and worth. Shy pupils, in particular, need to appear before others in a variety of roles so that feelings of poise and worth are inherent. The confidence that can come from these experiences might well have carry over values to other endeavours.

Tenth, reading co-operatively in small groups can provide much enjoyment and interest in literature. Being with others is a favourite learning style of selected individuals. They prefer to work together rather than working on an individual basis. Pupils too receive practice in reading. Cumulative practice should make for increased knowledge, skills and attitudes toward reading. With co-operative reading, three or four pupils may take turns reading a library book. If one copy only of a library book is available, sequential pupils may read aloud as the others in the group listen carefully to the contents. The contents may also be tape recorded so that individual pupils may re-read the library book. Then, if a word is not known in identification, the recorded voice provides the needed information.

If multiple copies of a library book are available, the small group of three or four pupils may follow along in their own library book as the sequential oral reading takes place. Thus, one person reads aloud as the others in the committee follow along in their own library book. Shared reading experiences has many intrinsic rewards for pupils. There should also be ample opportunities for those who like individual endeavours to read a book by themselves.

Eleventh, there should be many objects and items at an interest center whereby pupils may discuss each. I have observed many aquariums and terrariums in classrooms which provide stimulating situations for pupils to provide content for an experience chart. Sometimes a teacher has numerous potten plants in the classroom which may provide pupils an opportunity for informal conversation and also ideas for an experience chart. A rich learning environment helps pupils to think about the contents. The resulting ideas assist pupils to use oral language, engage in written work, read about similar situations or subject matter and/or listen to the thinking of others. A stimulating environment needs to be in the offing so that pupils have purposes for engaging in reading and language arts activities. For example, on the early primary grade level, pupils may observe and experience objects on an interest center. They may then provide content to the teacher who in return prints in neat manuscript letters what pupils have said and discussed. After the write-up of the contents, the pupils with the teacher pointing to words and phrases being read may comprehend the ideas presented into his experience chart. This approach is sound in that:

1. pupils have the background information to begin with by looking at and discussing objects at the center;
2. pupils present ideas for the experience chart. Learners then have chances to speak and to listen to others. What is said should be meaningful since it is based upon personal experiences pupils. When the teacher points to words and phrases, he/she together with pupils read orally content from the experience chart. Here, young learners should be developing an enriched vocabulary with a larger basic sight vocabulary. These sight words become the building blocks for future reading activities. The contents of the experience chart may be re-read as pupils desire. Many pupils like to read over again what has been read previously. Practice here assists pupils to retain basic sight words better than would otherwise be the case.

Twelfth, a quality spelling programme should help pupils to become better readers. There are numerous places where spelling words in vocabulary development may come from for pupils to master. Individualized spelling stresses learners mastering a reasonable number of words that come from what was missed in spelling words correctly from every day writing occurrences. The teacher needs to decide here how many of these misspelled words can be spelled correctly within a week or whatever the designated time would be. Words may also come from a quality basal spelling text, new words in a lesson for pupils to master as listed in the basal reader, words that research states are important for pupils to master in spelling such as the Dolch list (1955). A pupils practice the correct spelling of words, they are becoming involved in vocabulary development and reading, learners need to see print as often as feasible in order to become good readers. Spelling need not be dull and dry with memorization of words. Rather pupils should experience interesting activities by:

1. using these words in writing letters to parents and friends, developing a related cross word puzzle and playing games with peers;
2. working with peers in learning to spell words correctly. Co-operative learning may be a preferred style of learning for selected pupils;
3. pantomiming the meaning of selected words. This could involve the playing of charades whereby a pupil chooses a word for spelling at random from a box, pantomimes it and then asks others in the classroom to identify which word is involved;
4. dramatizing the spelling word. A pupils may select a spelling word at random and use puppets or marionettes to dramatize its meaning. Classmates may guess what the spelling word is. Creative dramatics may also be used. Here, the pupil chooses a word at random from a box and uses words and actions to indicate which word is being focused upon. The word wanted is not mentioned orally in the creative dramatics presentation. Several pupils could also be involved in this activity.

How much of the spelling curriculum should stress inductive and how much deductive thinking? We would suggest a balance between the two approaches. Thus, when using a spelling textbook in teaching, the teacher assigns words for pupils to master. This is a deductive approach. Furthermore, the teacher has pupils learn a strategy for learning to spell these words such as:

1. looking at the spelling word carefully;
2. saying the word accurately;
3. saying clearly the parts of the word, such as pronouncing each syllable carefully and accurately;
4. writing the new word without looking at it;
5. comparing the written word with that contained in the basal spelling textbook.

The teacher here is emphasizing a deductive method of spelling words correctly. Why is this a deductive approach? The teacher has determined what and how pupils are to learn.

An inductive approach stresses pupils being involved in curriculum development such as, pupils seeing how many homonyms or synonyms to find in a homonym/synonym hunt. Pupils might have suggested this activity when studying a unit containing a few of these words. Also, the teacher may have suggested the activity and pupils individually or on teams volunteered to see how many could be found. The sky is the limit in the number to be located. Perhaps, the teacher needs to have a balance between deductive versus inductive approaches in having pupils learn in the area of spelling. If a basal spelling text is used and there are a few rhyming words in a weekly list, pupils could locate additional ones to go along with those given in an inductive approach in learning. With a deductive procedure, the teacher may challenge gifted learners with additional words to master in spelling in addition to those listed in the next. By studying the correct spelling of words, pupils should increase their skills in vocabulary development and reading.

Thirteenth, we recommend pupils learn to spell relevant words contained in computer packages. There are drill and practice activities, tutorial, gaming and games, simulation and diagnostic/remedial packages. Reading teachers need to evaluate each package carefully to determine which relevant words in spelling pupils should master. Use should be made of spelling words for retention to take place. Spelling words may be used to write:

1. friendly and business letters;
2. notices, announcements, plays, reports, poems and stories;
3. names and addresses;
4. birthday greetings and holiday messages;
5. notes of sympathy and condolence.

As pupils participate in these writing activities, they need to proof-read content. The skills of reading are very much in evidence then. The spelling curriculum should be based upon words that pupils need to learn to spell. The needs of pupils are very important when developing any curriculum area. Beyond the goals of learning to spell words correctly are skills in reading for a variety of purposes that should be upper most in the minds of learners. Narrative, expository and creative writing should all be emphasized in ongoing lessons and units of study. Vocabulary development is an essential part in any listening, speaking, achieve as optimally as possible in vocabulary development and its related component—reading.

What then should be guidelines to use in assisting pupils in vocabulary development?

1. Word study should be integrated with prior knowledge and with learning in the content areas;
2. Word study should involve intensive 'deep' study of some words, involving many exposures to the words in meaningful contexts, both in and out of texts;
3. Teachers should engage in direct teaching or modelling talking explicitly about word meaning and structure;
4. Students should be actively involved in instruction; an important side effect of this involvement is the development of favourable attitudes toward words and word learning;
5. Students should be taught strategies for learning new words independently;
6. Teachers should introduce words in meaning 'families' so that semantic and structural relationships among the words are made explicit.

These principles are more applicable at the intermediate grade levels and beyond, when student's cognitive development has advanced to the point where they can explicitly deal with increasing conceptual abstraction. Nonetheless, you will see aspects of these principles at work; in work study at the primary grade level as well... (Templeton, 1997).

Conclusion

There are numerous opportunities for pupils to engage in vocabulary development. Each curriculum area provides these learning activities to increase proficiency in the use of vocabulary terms. The teacher needs to establish objectives, learning opportunities and evaluation procedures within individual academic areas to guide pupils in acquiring a rich listening, speaking, reading and writing vocabulary. The objectives of instruction need to stress relevant, functional words for pupils to master. Learning opportunities in vocabulary development should assist pupils to achieve the stated objectives. These activities need to be interesting, purposeful and meaningful. Evaluation procedures to appraise learner performance in achieving objectives need to be valid, reliable, varied and encourage further learning.

In evaluation Ph.D theses for Sri Ramakrishna Mission Vidayala College of Education in India, the author of the study listed the following sequence in vocabulary development (Ayyappan, 1997).

The confrontation phase emphasizes the teacher presenting relevant data pertaining to the concepts as well as important related definitions. Students then generate questions pertaining to the concept or vocabulary term. Phase two is the concept information phase. Here, students compare the attributes given and relate them to form the concept of vocabulary terms taught. Learners discuss with other pupils the distinguishing features to identify the concept.

In phase three, the teacher obtains responses from pupils in a stimulating discussion. Pupils then identify similarities and differences from the information presented. Pupil hypotheses are then appraised involving the tentative concept. In phase for stressing the concept development phase, the teacher presents related tasks for pupils to complete pertaining to the concept stressed. Probing of pupil knowledge pertaining to a concept is important. References are also made to the textbook while discussing the concept. The major classroom interactions are:

1. Teacher interaction/introduction/information;
2. Activities for pupils include media interaction, consulting text, and peer interaction whereas feedback includes evaluation and teacher interaction (Ayyappan 1997).

One of the finest procedures in vocabulary development, one of us have observed in supervising student teachers and cooperating teachers, was the Hilda Taba inductive method used with a class of sixth graders. Here, the two teachers had pupils view a filmstrip on *Life on a Manor*. The teachers, after having pupils view the contents in the filmstrip, asked:

1. Tell us in a single word or phrase what you learned from watching the filmstrip. The following responses were given by pupils; castles, moats, draw bridge, the mill for grinding grain, oxen pilling a plow, peasants cutting wheat by hand, peasant cottages, the three field approach in farming, fallow, boblemen, tournaments, page, knight, guilds, apprentice, master and wars;
2. How would you combine or join together the concepts you mentioned for number one above? Here, a variety of answers were given in and for open-ended question. One grouping of vocabulary terms given by pupils was the following:

Oxen pulling a plow, peasants cutting wheat by hand, the three field approach in farming and fallow were joined together.

3. What name would you give to the joined together vocabulary terms? The answer provided was 'cultivating the soil'.

REFERENCES

Ayyappan, R. (1997). *Concept Development in Electronics at Higher Secondary Level*. Coimbatore, India: Bharathiar University, Ph.D. Thesis

Ediger, Marlow and Digumarti Bhaskara Rao (2001). *Teaching Reading Successfully*. New Delhi, India: Discovery Publishing House.

Templeton, Shane (1997), *Teaching the Integrated Language Arts*, Second Edition, Boston: Houghton Mifflin Company, 287-88.

13

Spelling and the Language Arts

Pupils need to become good spellers to communicate effectively with others. Spelling is a tool to use to make known personal needs as well as to communicate feelings and appreciations. Correct spelling of words will always be necessary, even with the mass amount of technology available to many in society. Why? A person does not always have a computer at a specific place to process words. If the word processor is available, individuals still need to spell words reasonable close in accuracy for the spell checkers programme to work and be effective. Thus, if a word is misspelled greatly, spell checkers will not list the needed correct spelling of the word on the monitor. Then too, sometimes, it is more convenient to use long hand in writing rather than starting a computer up and using the attached printer. A personal message written in long hand may convey information to the reader better as compared to a printed document. How then might pupils be assisted to become proficient spellers?

Guidelines for Teaching Spelling

We would like to state selected guidelines which good teachers have used successfully in the teaching of spelling. First, pupils should understand the meaning of words to be mastered before studying their spelling. Meaning theory suggest that if pupils understand context, they will learn more effectively and depth learning may then be in evidence. Teachers need to take time for pupils to give definitions and/or be able to use a word contextually within a sentence. Some words are difficult to define and should then be used by the learner in the meaningful sentence. If a word can be defined and a pupil is ready to explain the meaning, he/she should do so. We believe that being able to use a word in a sentence and with a clear meaning, the learner is then ready to study the correct spelling of that word. We hope that words mastered in spelling will also be retained in memory for reading content as well as for writing in different academic areas. It is good if a pupil makes use of spelling words in many ways such as in reading those same words in literature, social studies, science and mathematics content. If pupils do not identify words correctly or a halting procedure is used in reading, the chances are comprehension will suffer in the process.

Second, the teacher needs to provide a variety of learning opportunities to assist pupils in learning to spell words correctly. Do I approve of the use of spelling textbooks that is good or bad, but it depends upon how they are used by pupils and the teacher. There can be selected fascinating activities for learners within the confines of a spelling textbook that has been carefully chosen. Thus, here are activities that truly benefit and make spelling enjoyable. For example, in one lesson in a spelling textbook, there are the usual list of words for pupils to master. How are they to achieve this task? One approach in the text is to have pupils fill in blank spaces in sentences given, whereby the words for the fill in, come from that list. Pupils can be very attentive in doing this when application is made of the new words to be mastered in spelling. Seemingly, many pupils are interested in this activity even though it does occur generally in each weekly lesson. We think that the activity has variation each week due to changing words that are used to fill in the blank spaces within sentences. The teacher should always observe pupils to notice if boredom sets in and, if it does, to switch to a different experience. The teacher cannot do a perfect job of varying activities when boredom sets in, but he/she can do the best possible to keep pupils on task. With twenty to thirty pupils in a classroom, it is difficult to provide for individual needs of all pupils. Additional tasks in a textbook to be used to help pupils learn to spell words correctly are cross word puzzles that used words from the weekly list in the spelling text. Friendly and business letters are to be written using selected words from the spelling list. The teacher needs to be creative in text use in teaching spelling by thinking of and implementing other learning opportunities than those indicated in the weekly lesson.

Third, we believe that pupils should develop a definite methodology in learning to spell words. A good speller, no doubt, has a workable method of learning to spell words correctly. Those who do not spell words correctly, in many cases, may need a new methodology in mastering the correct spelling of words. We like the method that many pupils have used correctly in learning to spell. Thus, the pupil needs to look at the new word carefully. It is doubtful that a teaching strategy will work if the pupil here does not look at the word carefully if pupils are truly focusing upon a word to acquire in correct spelling. Next, the pupil should pronounce the word correctly. Spelling errors are made due to inaccurate pronunciation of words. Hopefully, the pupil will listen to all the sounds with that word being studied for mastery in spelling. Involved sounds need to be associated with the correct graphemes or symbols. The learner then should practice writing the word once. The written word may then be checked with the correct spelling. Too frequently, pupils are asked to write a word five or ten times immediately; the word written might be misspelled then ten times. Better it is, to write the word once and check accuracy of spelling. Once the word is spelled correctly, the pupil may wish to write it several times in a contextual situation.

Fourth, pupils need to perceive reasons for learning to spell a given set of words, be if from the textbook or from other sources. Purpose is vital for success in learning to spell words correctly. The teacher may say why it is important to learn to spell words correctly in a specific lesson. A deductive approach is then in evidence. Inductive procedures may also be used such as a teacher asking questions of learners so that the latter understands the merit of learning to spell a given number of words correctly. Extrinsic rewards are used by some teachers to motivate pupils to study and master the new set of words in spelling. Thus, a teacher may say how many words need to be spelled correctly by Friday to receive a prize. These prizes are generally visible to pupils. Learners then know what to do to receive the award. We recommend that if extrinsic awards are given for learning, pupils should, as soon as possible, feel a desire from within to learn to spell words correctly as an intrinsic motivational device. The extrinsic rewards should be removed as soon as possible and not become a crutch or lever used to spell words correctly.

Fifth, pupils should learn to spell words correctly in a contextual situation. The new words are then used in functional situations. Words and their correct spelling and meaningful within a practical endeavour. We recommend that pupils determine useful ways to spell words correctly within contextual situations. The learner may then use the new words when writing an invitation for his/her birthday party. Further uses include writing business an friendly letters, content in greeting cards, prose and poetry, poetry, narrative and expository accounts, short stories, announcements and thank you notices, among other functional writing activities.

How many words should a pupil learn to spell correctly per week? This depends upon the present achievement level of the involved learner. To be sure, too many words may be required for a pupil to master in spelling. The opposite extreme would be too few words are learned to spell words correctly in a given time interval. The teacher needs to observe each pupil and notice what a reasonable number of words might be. There is nothing sacred about mastering twenty spelling words per week in the third grade, for example. It is important always to challenge pupils to do their very best in all curriculum areas.

Sixth, the spelling curriculum should be as individualized as possible. To some educators this means that each pupil should have a unique set of words to master in spelling. These words may come from those the learner misspelled from diverse writing activities the preceding week. The number of words in this list must be adjusted to fit the abilities of the individual learner so that too many or too few words are not required for mastery within a designated time. This seems to work fairly well in the spelling curriculum provided that learners do not refuse to use words in writing unless they are spelled correctly. The reason for doing this pertains to keeping the number reasonable of those words misspelled and needing to be studied for mastery. Another approach that might be used pertains to adjusting the number of words from the spelling textbook that need to be spelled correctly per week. Pupil A then may find it easy to learn to spell all words correctly plus a bonus list of words per week. Pupil B might be able to spell ten of the twenty words correctly per week. Once Pupil B has experienced success, he/she might become motivated to increase the number of words spelled correctly per week. We have noticed that pupils who are successful do volunteer to do more work then formerly and go beyond minimal levels. It takes time and effort for the teacher to make these adjustments for individual pupils. But with good teaching, teachers attempt to provide for individual differences among learners in the classroom. Even though the spelling curriculum is individualized, there may be pupils who wish to work collaboratively. Learning styles differ from one pupil to another such as wanting to work intrapersonally or by the self as contrasted with interpersonal or committee work. Here, pupils should have a voice in how they wish to study and learn, individually or in a group, to achieve more optimally in spelling.

Seventh, we recommend that creatively be stressed in pupils learning to spell words. So often, spelling is taught as role learning and memorization. Rather, the pupil should have ample opportunities to spell words correctly within creative poetry and prose written or within plays and stories written Here, we recommend that pupils evaluate correct spelling of words after the creative product has been completed, not during the writing endeavour. Pupils may wish to assist each other when correct spelling of words is emphasized at the end of the creative writing experience.

Eighth, we recommend strongly to provide incentives for pupils to volunteer to learn to spell more words correctly, then those assigned or even going beyond the bonus words. It is surprising what pupils will do to put forth effort when the sky becomes the limit. Intrinsic motivation certainly can come into being when pupils feel rewarded and successful in learning. The teaching of spelling is not known to be the most stimulating curriculum area, but the teacher can work in the direction of it becoming motivating and challenging.

Which Words Should Pupils Master in Spelling?

This question has been debated for a long time. There are teachers who assume that the spelling text alone contains salient words for pupils to master in spelling. The text has had a long history of use in teaching and learning situations. We have looked at spelling texts that came out in the early 1930s. These books had lists of words only for pupils to memorize in spelling per week. There were no suggested learning activities. The teacher each week needed to work out all learning activities that would assist pupils in learning to spell each word correctly. Presently, there are teachers who believe that no spelling texts be used and believe better teaching is an end result. A well chosen textbook should definitely not hinder good teaching. Ingenious teachers can stimulate pupils to learn with interesting activities that capture pupil attention. No textbook needs to be followed religiously in terms of the recommendations in the manual. The good teacher chooses from among the different activities stressed in the manual section. Additional learning opportunities are brought into the teaching and learning situation that provide for individual differences among pupils. No writer of quality materials would suggest following the manual 100 per cent. Writer realize that the teacher is the one to implement the teaching suggestions and must vary the kinds of learning opportunities provided for pupils so that securing the attention of pupils is there and pupils are actively engaged in learning. No using a basal textbook, in and of itself, does not make for good teaching. The teacher is there to study and implement teaching strategies that assist pupils to attain relevant objectives in the spelling curriculum.

If the teacher uses words for each pupil that the latter missed in everyday functional writing, the teacher still needs to have quality approaches in teaching so that individual pupils learn and achieve. Pupils need to be motivated when attempting to master the spelling words missed in daily writing. The number per week to be mastered needs to be adjusted to what a child can achieve in a reasonable manner. Certainly, a pupil may experience failure if too many words need mastering or become bored if too little is expected in a given time interval.

There have been successful teachers whom we have observed that emphasize spelling words that have been chosen for pupils to master which are based on research study of pupils' writings were selected by the teacher within a list for mastery learning by local pupils. The Dolch List (1954) has been used in teaching spelling by many teachers, even though it is not a recently developed list. This list has 220 words that Dolch's research found should be learned by pupils as sight words. This might then cut down on the number of errors that pupils make in spelling as well as in word identification in reading. These are the most frequently occurring words in spelling errors in pupils' writing, according to Dolch. We feel the Dolch List still has much merit because these words are commonly used by pupils in everyday writing and reading today. The word list is not divided by grade levels but is contained in one listing. We recommend that teachers study pupils' writings to notice which words are used most frequently. Teachers should be involved in doing research and may come up with a revision of the Dolch List. With personal computers in the school and in the home, the statistical procedures, we believe, have been greatly simplified and become user friendly. With personal computers and assistance from educational researchers, teachers now have more opportunities to engage in research and attempt to solve classroom problems than even before.

There are numerous statements of objectives in spelling that educators have developed over the years. We believe the following are worthy for teachers to emphasize in the curriculum:

1. Assist pupils to master those words which are needed in order to express oneself clearly and accurately in writing;
2. Guide pupils to achieve good study habits which assist the learner to pursue diverse kinds and type of writing experiences. Preservance is a key concept here. Pupils need to establish plans in writing, work toward their achievement and personally monitor progress. We have noticed pupils who attempt to give up too soon on assigned or voluntary written work. Encouragement by peers and the teacher will go a long way in motivating learner achievement. Pupil pride in achievement aids in setting higher goals in spelling within the writing activity;
3. Develop within pupils a set of standards in learning that will help pupils to spell words correctly. These standards involve using phonics to make associations between symbol and sound where this consistency is in evidence. Pupils also need to learn to spell selected words by sight when the consistency between symbol and sound and sound just is not there. Correct pronunciation of words is important so that spelling errors are not made due to that factor;
4. Help pupils to realize that correct spelling is a social courtesy and incorrect spelling may reflect negatively upon the pupil;
5. Direct quality teaching to have pupils, when ready, learn keyboard skills to use the personal computer to engage in writing. This is necessary for all pupils. Spell checkers can do much to minimize spelling errors when word processing is used. Computers are increasingly becoming user friendly;
6. Provide friendly assistance to pupils who need help in spelling so that success can be stressed as much as possible in the writing curriculum. A good speller in the classroom may also provide this help. If the latter approach is used change or rotate who gives the assistance. Each pupil also needs to pursue his/her own interests in purposeful learning;

7. Emphasize the interest factor by letting pupils choose the topic to write on, regardless of the purpose involved. Thus, if pupils are to write limericks, the learner may select within that framework the contents of the limerick. Interest goes a long way in providing effort for learning;
8. Let pupils work together in the writing activity involving spelling. Observe that each is participating actively in the spelling/writing experience;
9. Involve pupils in self-evaluation as well as the teacher participating actively in appraising learner progress. Collaboratively, a learning community may be developed that stresses quality writing in the curriculum;
10. Establish quality sequence in pupil learning to spell words correctly. If pupils are involved in determining which words need to be learned in spelling, a psychological spelling curriculum is in evidence. Sequence then resides within the learner, not in other sources. Should the teacher determine sequence in pupil learning to spell words, a logical approach is in evidence since the teacher determines the order of learning activities for pupils (Ediger, 1988).

Pupils should definitely realize that spelling and reading are related, not isolated entities. Being able to spell more words correctly as time goes on should reflect learners' increasing abilities to become better readers. The goals of spelling and reading instruction should develop confidence in the learner to achieve at a higher level commensurate with inherent abilities of the involved pupil (Ediger, 1998).

Cautions in Learning to Spell Words

There are selected cautions that teachers need to be aware of when teaching spelling. Pupils and the teacher should not go overboard on phonics when correct spelling of words is being emphasized. Thus, there are numerous words that lack consistency between symbol and sound such as my, pie, buy, sigh, kite, white and bye. Each of these words contains the long *i* sound and yet that sound is spelled differently from word to word.

Second, pupils need to learn to spell vital words that are truly useful. Too frequently, words listed in a spelling textbook may not be important enough for pupils to learn to spell. We believe the teacher needs to study word lists in spelling texts, if used and ascertain the worth of learning to spell each word. There is so much to learn that it behooves the teacher to choose carefully what pupils are to learn.

Third, if pupils are to learn to spell a given set of words, they should make application of what has been learned. Much forgetting occurs of mastered words in spelling if there are no related practical endeavours, meaning that applying what has been learned is important. We believe much time is wasted in learning if pupils are tested only, on the number of words spelled correctly on Friday and yet the involved pupil perceives no practical application of these kinds of learning activities.

Fourth, too frequently, memorization of correct spelling of words is emphasized and yet meaningful experiences are lacking. Generally memorization is done for the sake of passing a test and in this case to receive a good grade from the teacher. We would like to see the evaluation process change to where more emphasis is placed upon pupils' making application of words being studied for correct spelling in ongoing lessons and units of study.

Fifth, pupils in many cases lack readiness factors for learning to spell words correctly. What are these readiness factors? Certainly, a pupil should also be able to use the new words being studied contextually in a sentence that makes sense. Pupils individually need to use the proper tools at hand to analyze parts within a word such as grapheme/phoneme relationships. For those irregularly spelled words, a basic sight vocabulary needs to be developed by learners.

Sixth, too often, pupils in a class are taught as if all possess reading for the same number of words to be mastered in spelling. Pupils are individuals, not a mass of objects. Learners come with feelings, dreams and hopes. They need to be treated as human beings with much worth. Thus, the teacher needs to help each pupil to learn as much as possible. The opportunity for pupil learning is now and we need to take advantage of these opportunities.

Seventh, there is a lack of emphasis upon diagnosis and remediation when teaching spelling. We need to determine why pupils individually are making errors in the incorrect spelling of words. Do pupils go by phonics too much when learning to spell words and yet one or more of these words are not that phonetic in sound/symbol relationships? Is legible handwriting a cause for improper; spelling of words? Pupils need to experience as much success as possible so that motivation is there to learn, grow and achieve.

Technology and Spelling

There definitely is room for technology use in the spelling curriculum. Its use is one way to strengthen teaching and learning in ongoing lessons and units of study. Computer use should be made available to teachers and learners. The software content of the computer should not duplicate with other materials of instruction, but should provide learning activities which also assist pupils to improve in the area of spelling. There are drill and practice exercises which truly help pupils to achieve more optimally. Words here need to be highly useful with strategies of learning that provide for each pupil's ability level. The drill and practice experiences give learners an opportunity to rehearse the correct spelling of words. There are needs for drill and practice so that pupils may practice and retain the correct spelling of words at a more optimal level of achievement. Much of what we remember has been presented to us in different ways using a variety of learning activities. Here software and computer use can provide this variety with innovating ways and procedures displayed on the monitor. Also, there are numerous games that pupils may engage in individually or collaboratively that stress the correct spelling of words, as shown on the monitor. These games may provide wholesome competitive activities between two or three sides. Thus, in rotation, one side may score points for the correct spelling of one or more words whereas the two other sides or single side, in sequence, may come back with spelling other words correctly to score points. The winner has the most words spelled correctly. Games in spelling are good for pupils to play competitively, if appropriate attitudes are in evidence.

Tutorial software programmes provide new words for pupil mastery, as shown sequentially on the monitor. Diverse learning opportunities are provided so that pupils may master these new words in spelling. Also, there are simulations that attempt to represent life-like situations whereby pupils are to engage in problem solving in virtual reality. The encounters here are quite realistic and provide for situations involving higher levels of cognition such as critical and creative thinking as well as problem solving. At the same time, pupils are engaged in attempting to spell words correctly. Since a more utilisation situation is involved in simulations, pupils tend to find these activities to be challenging and real.

We find that pupils engaging in using the word processor to write creatively or functionally is one of the better ways to stress correct spelling of words. Here, pupils need to be proficient in spelling during the actual composing situation when using the words processor. It is true that spell checkers does provide much assistance in helping pupils make corrections in spelling. However, the commands provided by the learner in writing content into the computer need to be very close in correct spelling or spell checkers cannot provide the correct spelling on the monitor of the word processor. All pupils, when ready, should master use of the word processor to write prose, poetry, or utilitarian content. Mehlinger (1997) asks the following provocative questions when using computers in the curriculum:

1. How would teachers teach if textbooks were replaced by small multi-media devices that serve as both computer and communications tool?
2. What would school libraries be like when students have access to the libraries of the word?
3. How would teaching change when students can contact experts who know more about a single topic than the teacher?

These are three excellent questions that need pondering for all educators. We recommend both technology and textbooks, carefully chosen, be used to provide for individual differences among learners. Diverse kinds of materials need to be used in teaching and learning. Individuals possess diverse learning styles and the professional teacher attempts to harmonize instruction with pupil learning styles. Bermman and Tinker (1997) discuss a seminar method of instruction with the use of technology:

Many teachers who experiment with on-line courses report being overwhelmed with enrolments of 10 or 12 students because they set up e-mail conversations with each student. The better model is more than a seminar, in which the teacher determines the topic and activities, encourages substantive interactions among students, monitors and shapes the conversation and promotes an atmosphere in which students respond to one another's work. This model results in more conversation, is far more likely to be constructivist and builds on the rich learning that takes place in groups.

Collaborative endeavours that stress the learning of correct spelling of words within purposeful writing activities certainly do emphasize positive ways in the use of technology. Interactions among learners do tend to make for higher levels of cognitive endeavours within the framework of critical and creative thought as well as problem solving.

Handwriting, Spelling and Print Discourse

Illegible handwriting may be major cause for incorrect spelling of words. Handwriting as a separate subject is receiving much less emphasis than formerly. When attending the elementary school years from 1934 to 1942, handwriting received considerable time for instruction; approximately, fifteen minutes per day was spent in handwriting instruction. We learned to write in the air to form individual letters correctly. The making of ovals so that no line was crossed with another received much emphasis as did push and pull exercises, again with no strokes crossing each other. May be these activities had something to do with the transfer value in becoming better handwriters. We truly doubt if this was the case, however. Probably, more time should have been given to the actual writing of prose and poetry, as well as other forms of print discourse. Thus, use needs to be made of what has been learned in handwriting experiences.

What might the teacher do to assist pupils to improve in handwriting? Here, the teacher needs to give much attention to child growth and development characteristics. A lengthy period of time given to handwriting instruction may not harmonize with psychomotor skills and readiness of the learner. Much tension may be built up by the learner if he/she is required to write extensively. Activities may be changed so this does not occur, such as changing to a reading experience. It is always good procedure in teaching to observe the attention span of pupils to notice when sequential activities need to be changed. We strongly recommend handwriting be taught within an ongoing activity involving purposeful writing. Application might then be made of what is being emphasized in terms of objectives of instruction. Handwriting and content written become one, not separate entities.

The objectives of handwriting need to be chosen carefully so that relevance is in evidence. The making of ovals and push/pull exercises were eliminated from the elementary school curriculum some time ago due to lack of significance involved. To spend hours and hours on drill pertaining to a set of letters certainly is misusing teaching time. We believe legibility is a key concept to emphasize in the handwriting arena. A pupil does not need to conform specifically to models of upper and lower case letters of the alphabet presented in a handwriting text. The model letters, however, may be used as a guide for pupils to develop legibility in handwriting. If we can read a pupil's written products readily, then we are satisfied with the quality of his/her handwriting. If illegible handwriting is in evidence, then objectives of instruction need to be developed and implemented so that the child becomes a writer of legible content.

Pupils should feel successful in ongoing experiences. Thus, a pupil is making progress over his previous work in handwriting. Learners should not be compared with each other in legible handwriting. Why? Pupils individually are at different achievement levels in using neuromuscular skills. Teachers need to develop interest within pupils in achieving at a higher level in handwriting. Three kinds of objectives need to be stressed in handwriting. These are knowledge objectives whereby pupils have the needed content about legible letters, words, phrases, sentences and paragraphs to write in a illegible way; skills objectives whereby learners use what has been learned; and attitudinal objectives in which learners develop positive feelings in wanting to improve over previous levels in handwriting.

More specifically, objectives of instruction in handwriting should achieve the following:

1. how to form letters legibly;
2. how to align letters appropriately;
3. how to space letters and write properly;
4. how to stress proper proportion of letters within words;
5. how to achieve overall legibility in written discourse;
6. how to appraise the self in the quality of handwriting exhibited;
7. how to emphasize neatness in all written products as final copies.

Skills objectives should emphasize the following:

1. form letters and words illegibly;
2. align letters and words properly;
3. appropriate proportion of letters and words;
4. proper spacing of letters and words;
5. self-evaluation in achievement in general as well as specific skills in handwriting;
6. neatness in the handwriting arenas.

Attitudinal objectives for pupils to achieve should place importance on the following:

1. desiring to improve in the area of handwriting;
2. wanting to improve in the area of letter formation;

3. developing positive attitudes toward having proper proportion;
4. feeling a need to space words and letters properly;
5. voluntarily assessing personal achievement in handwriting;
6. emphasizing neatness in activities involving handwriting;
7. respecting the progress of others in handwriting.

There needs to be proper balance among understandings, skills and attitudinal objective in handwriting. Pupils do need knowledge pertaining to what makes for quality handwriting, but the knowledge needs to be implemented as skills. Hopefully, positive feelings as attitudes within learners will develop as a result.

Quality Handwriting Across the Curriculum

Good handwriting that is legible needs to be stressed throughout the different curriculum areas in the school setting. Thus in mathematics, written work of pupils becomes difficult to evaluate unless good handwriting is there. Good handwriting needs to infiltrate numerals written as well as story or words problems composed by learners. Reports written such as biographies of famous mathematicians provide more opportunities to have pupils practice proper handwriting skills.

In science, pupils individually or in committees may write up the results of a science experiment, a method of procedure in doing an experiment, a report written on a self selected topic in science, bar or line graphs developed on temperature readings on a daily basis, notes written on content read in science from a well known encyclopaedia, an outline written from a variety of reference sources in science, criteria written on being an effective member of a discussion group in science, as well as summaries on main ideas obtained from a video tape.

In social studies, pupils may write business letters to order free and inexpensive materials pertaining to an ongoing unit of study, friendly letters to pen pals, generalizations involving content read from diverse reference sources, relevant facts in reaction to a question raised by pupils in the classroom, as well as announcements to other classes to come to visit the pupil's classroom to observe completed projects related to an ongoing unit of study in social studies. Additional learning opportunities involving handwriting in the social studies include the following:

1. Speaking parts for pupils involving early days of Puritans in the New World;
2. Directions written for making a relief of the continent being studied in the social studies;
3. Standards may be written for evaluating an oral report;
4. An outline might be written to cover content pertaining to conclusions reached on an important selection read from social studies materials;
5. Hypothesis written involving one or more hypotheses written in a problem solving activity;
6. Notes taken on a selection in reading in the social studies.

In the literature curriculum, there are many opportunities for pupils to practice handwriting, including the following:

1. Labeling objects in the classroom in a reading readiness programme;
2. Using handwriting texts as the need arises, such as for a model in the writing curriculum;
3. Developing experience charts written by pupils with teacher guidance in a reading readiness class;
4. Writing ideas involving reading for a variety of purposes, such as from critical reading, reading to follow directions, factual reading, reading for a sequence of ideas, creative reading, reading for main ideas and reading to develop generalizations;

5. Pupils need ample time to practice forming letters correctly, writing letters and words with proper alignment, slanting letters correctly, spacing words and letters properly and using proper proportion of letters;
6. Pupils with teacher guidance need adequate time to write news articles. The resulting newsletter could be sent home weekly, bi-weekly, or monthly on important happenings in class.

In the health curriculum, the following writing experiences involve handwriting:

1. Learners may take notes on a talk given by a physician pertaining to improved health practices in everyday living;
2. Main ideas might be written on a set of slides or illustrations presented by a registered nurse on improving healthful living in the community;
3. Each pupil might write a personal experience chart pertaining to content from a filmstrip related to a facet of healthful living;
4. Letters may be written to the city council making recommendations on improving a polluted area;
5. Menus may be written for a week on implementing balanced diets in the school lunch programme;
6. Business letters may be written to order free and inexpensive materials relating to an ongoing health unit of instruction.

Conclusion

Handwriting errors certainly may cause spelling errors. The teacher needs to do much diagnosing to ascertain why pupils misspell words in writing. Writing needs to be emphasized in all curriculum areas. Improved communication results when quality spelling and handwriting are involved. Courtesy is also inherent when the learner exhibits the best spelling and handwriting in ongoing contextual writing activities. Purposeful writing experiences propel pupils to put forth effort to attain worthwhile objectives. Quality knowledge, skills and attitudes as three categories of objectives should be achieved by pupils. Pupils need to practice much writing so that increased proficiency is in evidence. The writer has treated spelling and handwriting within the broader perspective of writing. Spelling and handwriting skills can best be developed in context within the writing activity. Successful learners in writing will increase their abilities in spelling and handwriting. Careful selection of objectives, learning opportunities and evaluation procedures need to be in the offing.

REFERENCES

Ediger, Marlow (1998), "Goals of Reading Instruction", *Experiments in Education*, published by the SITU Council of Educational Research (in India), 11-19.

Ediger, Marlow (1988), *Language Arts Curriculum in the Elementary School, Kirksville,* Missouri: Simpson Publishing Company, 73-81.

Dolch, Edward W. (1955), *Methods in Reading*. Champaign, Illinois: Garrard Publishing Company.

Mehlinger, Howard D., "The Next Step", *Electronic School*, A22-A24.

14

Punctuation and the Language Arts

Proper punctuation is vital in reading/writing. It clarifies what has been written and makes written content more meaningful. There are a plethora of ways to interpret written subject matter unless the content is properly punctuated. If commas, for example, are omitted, it would be difficult or impossible to determine how many people attended an event such as, "John Mark Ruth Elaine and Bob attended the play". There could be as many as five in attendance or as few as three. Once the commas are put in proper place, the sentence is clarified as intended such as, "John Mark, Ruth Elaine, and Bob attended the play". In oral communication, there are brief pauses between words to indicate commas for the above named sentence. In written communication, there are diverse punctuation marks to indicate, among other things, pauses within a sentence. When should punctuation signs first be taught in the public schools? The answer is it depends upon the child's readiness for learning these abstract symbols. Certainly, by grade one, many students may benefit from meaningful instruction.

Personalized Reading and Punctuation

Young primary grade students seemingly enjoy personalized reading. First, these students need to experience items and objects so that they have something to talk and write about.

Background information is needed. The teacher may place selected objects on a learning center. After viewing and discussing these interesting objects, students may present ideas pertaining thereto for the teacher to record on the chalkboard or in a word processor. Students may then see their ideas recorded or talk written down. As each idea is given within a small group setting, the teacher may assist students to notice where a punctuation mark is placed, such as in the following situations:

1. When there are words in a series as in, "At the picnic, they ate ham, sandwiches, lettuce salad, and bread." If the teacher does not say why commas need to be added, the sentence would lack meaning. Without commas, there could be as many as five items at the picnic or as few as three, depending upon where the commas are placed;
2. When there are complete thoughts which need to be separated with the use of a period as in— "The picnic was enjoyed by all. Each person was very hungry." If a period was not placed at the end of each sentence, the words would read— "The picnic was enjoyed by all each person was very hungry". "The picnic was enjoyed by all each person—" initially, sounds different in meaning as compared to the two sentences being separated properly by a period;
3. When there are different types of sentences such as an interrogative sentence whereby a question mark needs to be placed at the end of the sentence as compared to a different end punctuation mark. As talk is recorded, the teacher may state why the question mark is necessary (See Ediger, 2001, 120-123).

In the above examples of recorded sentences, the teacher calls student attention to where and why the punctuation marks are needed. Learning about punctuation marks is done in context, not is isolated tasks such as in drill and memorization of punctuation mark usage. Students are learning punctuation within the framework of ideas they presented and with meaning theory being in evidence. Learning of proper punctuation is then useful and has utilitarian values. Proper punctuation is applied in a functional situation, not in isolation from practice.

Writing for a Variety of Purposes

Written work for early primary grade students may well emphasize the personalized approach such as in using reading and writing connections. Ideas written then come from the learner, not from external sources. The following sequential purposes in writing may then be stressed within a functional situation:

1. *Business and friendly letters:* Here, for example, the learner needs to perceive reasons for separating the day of the month from the calendar year with a comma—September 6, 2002, otherwise it would read September 6, 2000;
2. *Poetry, rhymed and unrhymed:* In adding imagery, the student needs to use commas at appropriate places, e.g. The clouds, looking like pillows in the floating sky, appear to be made for sleeping. There is clarification here of a creative comparison being made when using a comma such as clouds—looking like floating pillows in the sky;
3. *Prose with its elements of characterization, setting, plot, irony, theme and underlying messages:* In describing a character, there may be words in a series which need separation with comma use such as, "Anthony, was reckless, a careless spender of money, haughty, lacked imagination, and impulsive." If the commas were omitted, the student may perceive a lack of idea organisation and clarity;
4. *Invitations answering the questions of why, what, and where:* Each of these questions need answers, separated by periods in order that run on sentences are not in the offing;
5. Announcements containing essential information;

6. Formal dramatization parts whereby the inherent content comes form the basal text or form a library book. Each character's speaking part needs to be set of with quotation marks, otherwise it is difficult to separate what a character says from the rest of the background content needed in writing play parts;
7. A written report on a library book read or on a selected topic in science or social studies;
8. Outlines, summaries, and/or conclusions drawn;
9. Diary and log entries;
10. Editorials and commentaries;
11. Evaluations developed to appraise the self in personal achievement. Each evaluation statement needs to be clearly written with proper punctuation used inside individual statements and at the end of the assessment item (See Ediger, 1996, 17-18).

Students may perceive a need for using proper punctuation by looking at non-examples, as in the following:

Roger a carpenter liked to work in the outdoors his hard work brought him success in many cases he became very hungry by lunchtime and liked french fries hamburgers cheese pizza and a soft drink.

The above writing may be punctuated by students and reasons given for each punctuation mark used. The corrected writing then includes the following revision:

Roger, a carpenter, liked to work in the outdoors. His hard work brought him success in many cases. He became very hungry at lunch time and liked frènch fries, hamburgers, cheese, pizza, and a soft drink (Ediger, 1997, 29-30).

The reading/writing connection is important for meaningful learning to occur. What is and has been written can be read. What has been read may be summarized in writing. The student needs to perceive that knowledge is related and the language arts areas can be integrated into all curriculum areas.

Diagnosis and Remediation in Reading/Writing Connections

In context and sequentially, the student should become increasingly knowledgeable and skillful in the proper use of punctuation. The following are selected basics which students need to learn and use in order that clarity in reading and writing is in evidence:

1. Separating words in a series with commas, as in "For dinner, they had chicken, turkey dressing, jello salad, and peas." If the commas were omitted, it would be difficult to say how many different food items were in evidence at the dinner;
2. Using proper and punctuation marks in sentences as in
   (a) using a period to end a sentence which states a fact or opinion;
   (b) using a question mark to indicate that an interrogative sentence is in evidence;
   (c) using an exclamation mark to show strong feelings;
   (d) using a period to end an imperative sentence indicating a command or request.
3. Using commas to separate an appositive/appositive phrase from the rest of the sentence, *e.g.* Bob, a brick layer, is sick today;
4. Using a comma to set apart an introductory dependent clause from an ensuing independent clause: After the game was over, Bill felt tired. There is a pause then after the dependent clause; otherwise the two clauses would run together in a somewhat meaningless fashion;
5. Using a comma after a direct address, "Alicia, my cousin is here." Compare that sentence with "Alicia, my cousin, is here." The two sentences are quite different in meaning depending upon where the comma is placed;

6. Using quotation marks to set apart a direct quote from the rest of the sentence, "Oscar ran a good race, but lost," said Emmett. Notice the comma after the direct quote;
7. Separating individual words which show strong feeling as in the following: Don't Stop! Contrast the previous two words with the following in meaning: Don't stop! Or, 'Run!' she cried.

with 'Run?' she cried (See Ediger, 1996, 34-35).

Ideas in writing come first, in importance, from the student. What has been written may then be proof read and punctuation marks added as needed. The mechanics of writing should not be emphasized first, followed by ideas developed by the student. The written content needs to be there in order that students might correctly punctuate the product. Nor, should punctuation be stressed during the time ideas are written because the student may not concentrate on the major purpose of writing and that is to convey information to others.

Criteria to Use in Teaching and Learning

There are definite criteria from the psychology of learning which should be used in teaching punctuation to students. First, there needs to be a purpose for having students learn proper punctuation. That overall goal is to write clearly and distinctly. Otherwise the reader will be uncertain as to intended meanings in the written script. If a student's purpose is to write about a birthday party and states that, "John Mark Edward Lee and Kent Dean were at the party" how many were there in total? There could be as many as five and as few as three, depending upon where the commas are placed to separate names of persons attending. Purpose for learning is vital. The teacher may state clearly, prior to writing, what the purpose is for the ongoing lesson and that may be to separate words in a series. Examples and non-examples may be written on the chalkboard or in the computer to indicate what happens to meanings when incorrect punctuation is used as well as when correct punctuation is used.

Second, interest in learning is important. Attentive students will learn more as compared to those lacking interest. Thus, the teacher needs to implement teaching strategies, whereby students become engaged in learning about punctuation in the reading/writing connection. A variety of learning opportunities is important here. Variety needs to be in the offing to encourage active learner participation as well as meet personal needs. Active participants achieve at a higher rate as compared to passive recipients. Identifying and solving problems pertaining to punctuating sentences correctly needs to be stressed. All students need to become interested in teaching and learning situations. The teacher then needs to attend to the diverse styles of learning in the classroom (See Searson and Dunn, 2001).

Third, students should have chances to reveal learnings in diverse ways. Students individually may then may reveal if, for example, they desire to indicate knowledge about punctuation learnings individually or collaboratively. Each person has strengths and weaknesses in learning; some will like to work by the self whereas others will wish to work in a committee or group setting to indicate what has been learned in punctuation (See Gardner, 1993).

Fourth, motivated students learn more than do the unmotivated. There are different methods which may be used to motivate students. One way is to give honest praise to individual students for quality achievement is punctuation. A second way is to provide extrinsic rewards for doing well. The teacher should observe that students do not become hooked on these extrinsic rewards, but they are used as a means to an end and that end being to achieve more optimally. Intrinsic motivation is the best approach to use for motivation in that a student learns because he/she wishes to do so. Success in learning is another motivator in that the leaning opportunities provided students are sequenced appropriately so that continual progress on the part of each learner is emphasized. Each previous learning acquired is then related directly to the next step in achievement and progress.

Fifth, meaning theory is salient to emphasize in teaching punctuation. Punctuation must make sense to students. It is not taught for the sake of doing so, but rather to assist learners individually to communicate effectively in writing. What is taught must be understood by the student so that meaningful learning accrue. Hardly can students learn about interrogative sentences unless the background information is there so that the end punctuation mar can be placed correctly. The question mark then indicates that a question has been raised when communicating with others.

Sixth, individual differences need to be provided for. Students individually are are different places in punctuation achievement. Selected students will need more time, for example, in learning about dependent clauses as compared to others. Some will need more concentrate experiences in learning about punctuation as compared to others. Then too, there will be students who are quite advanced in punctuation knowledge and skills and may achieve more from the abstract, even initially, in the instructional sequence.

Seventh, selected students are more aggressive in a positive manner in pursuing tasks as compared to those who are more passive in their responses. Each student needs assistance in pursuing learning opportunities which aid in attaining optimal achievement in punctuation. Learners need to develop quality habits of learning which affect how well they will be achieving. Time on task is important!

Eighth, each student needs to persevere on an assignment or voluntary activity until its completion. Giving up does not help in learning. When needed, students need assistance from the teacher or peers to persevere and complete punctuation tasks at hand. Staying with it is a good trait for students to achieve.

Ninth, a caring learning environment needs to be in the offing. Students who feel and believe that others care for them should become increasingly proficient in achievement. With the caring attitude of students for each other, no learner should fall through the cracks. In this kind of a learning environment, students refrain from disrupting the classroom and rather help the teacher to provide assistance, and guidance to each learner, as needed. Peers also are involved in helping, assisting, and working harmoniously with others.

Tenth, quality sequence for each student in learning needs to be in the offing. Seamless learning for each student is then an ideal to accomplish. This could involve either the teacher providing ordered learnings for students when assignment are made, or learners may sequence their very own experiences, such as in voluntarily completing a task (Ediger and Rao, 2000, Chapter Ten).

Correct punctuation needs to be in evidence in order that quality communication is in the offing. Misunderstandings occur in written work when punctuation marks are not placed property in context. What is written can be read and thus emphasizes the reading/writing connection.

REFERENCES

Ediger, Marlow (2001), "Reading Science Content," *The Hoosier Science Teacher,* 26 (4), 120-123.

Ediger, Marlow (1996), "Reporting to Parents—A Classroom Newspaper," *Update*, 38 (4), 19-20.

Ediger, Marlow (1997), "Middle School Formal Dramatics," *The California Reader*, 30 (2), 29-30.

Ediger, Marlow (1996), "Middle School Multicultural Literature" *The Reading Instruction Journal*, 39 (2), 36-37.

Ediger, Marlow and D. Bhaskara Rao (2001), *Teaching Reading Successfully*. New Delhi: Discovery Publishing House, Chapter Ten.

Gardner, Howard (1993), *Multiple Intelligence: Theory into Practice*. New York; Basic Books.

Searson, Robert, and Rita Dunn (2001), "The Learning Styles Teaching Model," *Science and Children*, 38 (5), 22-26.

15

Poetry and the Language Arts

An important type of reading for elementary age pupils is to read poetry. There are pupils who love to read poetry and unfortunately others either are neutral or react negatively to its reading. My hope in this writing is that all pupils will read and react more positively to diverse forms of verse and their contents. Pupils in classrooms where I have supervised student teachers and cooperating teachers are somewhat eager to express their opinions about the study and writing of poetry. Some of the recorded comments we have written down of these opinions include:

1. I do not understand what is written;
2. I would rather read stories from library books;
3. The language used is confusing;
4. I like to read poems that rhyme;
5. I would rather do something else than read;
6. I like poetry that has animal content;
7. I like to read poetry and other literature;
8. I do not like to memorize poetry;
9. I feel that the words used in poems are difficult to understand;
10. I wish more time would be given to the study and reading of poetry.

From the above comments, it is quite obvious that there are mixed feelings toward the reading of poetry. Certainly, the teacher will need to establish objectives in which each pupil learns to love the studying and reading of poetry. This can be a difficult task and yet the teacher needs to try to get pupils actively engaged in units of study pertaining to poetry in the elementary school. We would suggest that a major goal of instruction should be to assist pupils to love and appreciate poetry. Additional objectives include obtaining meaning and understanding of poems read, desiring to write different forms and types of poems, working harmoniously with others in reading and writing of poems, increasing vocabulary development through poetry writing, improving reading skills in word recognition and comprehension (Ediger, 1997), relating poems read to different curriculum areas in the elementary school, building and developing background information to use in diverse subject matter areas in the curriculum, as well as increasing in the desire to learn grow and achieve. To write quality poetry, the pupil needs background information. The teacher needs to have a rich learning environment in the classroom. We believe in having many learning centers in the classroom so that learners may look at what is at each center. Objects, items, audio-visual aids, realia and library books with other print materials need to be located at each of these centers. The teacher needs to introduce each center briefly as well as motivate and assist pupils to move forward with achievement in poetry writing. Pupils need to browse through books containing poetry. First, lets take a look at how the poetry curriculum may be organised.

Organising the Poetry Curriculum

Teachers need to think of how to organise the poetry curriculum so that more optimal pupil achievement is in evidence. We have observed teachers teach entire units on poetry as a separate subject. The unit involved here may be entitled "Reading and Writing Poetry". Why do selected teachers teach separate units on poetry? Depth teaching might then be involved in that the focus is upon poetry only in its many forms. Here, the teacher many have pupils concentrate on rhymed, unrhymed but with a certain number of syllables per line and no rhyme and no specific number of syllables per line. When readiness is in evidence, pupils may compare and contrast diverse forms of poetry studied and written. Ingredients in poetry writing may also be emphasized here with imagery, alliteration and onomatopoeia. In the separate subjects approach of units on poetry in the elementary school, pupils may focus in depth upon what goes into the different forms of verse to emphasize poetry in its diverse manifestations.

For example, in studying imagery, pupils may learn in depth what is involved here with metaphors and similes. Thus, pupils need to understand that metaphors do not require words including *like* and *as*. Creative comparisons may then be made: The moon, a yellow flame of gold, moves rapidly in space. Here, the moon is compared creatively with, "a yellow flame of gold". This is a metaphorical comparison.

A second form of imagery is to use similes whereby the words 'like' and 'as' are used to make creative comparisons: The clouds in the sky look like sheep walking on blue grass. The smile here is "like sheep waling on the blue grass". Thus, a creative comparison is made between "The clouds in the sky", and "sheep walking on blue grass".

In addition to the separate subjects poetry curriculum, the teacher may also wish to correlate reading and writing poems with different curriculum areas. Here, the teacher attempts the best possible to have pupils directly relate each poem studied to social studies, science, mathematics and the language art areas. Thus, if the social studies unit on the Civil War is being taught, the teacher may assist pupils to read and study literature written during this war. Social Studies and literature are being correlated. Perceiving relationship of knowledge by pupils is a major goal of the correlated curriculum. There are fewer separate subjects to be taught in a given day. The elementary school curriculum tends to be crowded as it is and teachers do welcome certain curriculum areas to be correlated.

In correlating social studies and poetry, one pupil in the fifth grade wrote the following quatrain containing patterns of rhyme:

The Holy Land

Moslems, Christians and Jews
Each have their own unique views
Mosque, Church or Temple
Religion is taught as an example.

When pupils perceive that knowledge is related, it becomes easier to remember what had been learned. Why? One idea obtained triggers, off others that are related. In a separate subjects poetry curriculum, the pupil may perceive content in isolation and thereby not sense that facts, concepts and generalizations can be learned as a unity or as ideas related to each other. There are fewer separate subjects to teach if correlation of content is in evidence.

A third way of organising the poetry curriculum is to stress an integrated curriculum. Here, the teacher leans upon social studies, science, mathematics, and literature, among other academic disciplines, to provide content for poems written by pupils. Each academic discipline tends to become blurred with the integrated curriculum. Pupils then have even greater chances of understanding how knowledge can be related. Many educators would argue that pupils here should retain subject matter in memory longer due to using it and in this case not being a separate subject.

How the teacher wishes to organise the poetry curriculum depends upon many factors. These include the number of curriculum areas taught which can be emphasized satisfactorily as related by the teacher. Sometimes the integrated curriculum is also called the interdisciplinary approach for organizing instruction.

One pupil wrote the following triplet with all ending words rhyming and indicating an inter-disciplinary curriculum:

The Dome of the Rock in the Holy Land

The Dome of the rock has an octagonal design
(mathematics)

It is used for worship by the Moslems as a sign
(social studies)

With all of its beauty viewed by yours and mine
(art).

The poetry curriculum needs to be carefully developed with quality, objective, learning opportunities and evaluation procedures. In making these three decisions, the teacher also needs to think of organisations such as the separate subjects, the correlated and the integrated approach in teaching and learning.

Alliteration and Onomatopoeia in Poetry Writing

Pupils with teacher guidance should learn to use alliteration in poetry writing. Poets use this device frequently in writing. Alliteration tends to stress two or more sequential words that begin with the same sound. Learners find it fascinating to create verse whereby the two or more initial sounds are the same in an ordered way. A committee of three children collaborated on writing the following containing alliteration:

The Dead Sea in the Holy Land

With *s*alty *s*ea water at sight
And *l*ow *l*evel elevation of land
I find the *d*ear *D*ead Sea to lack life.

We feel that writing poetry with alliteration assists pupils in recognizing the role of phonics in reading. Creatively determining words that start with the same sound stresses sounds, not spelling. For example, the words *cent* and *sent* have identical sounds but these words are spelled differently with the initial consonant sound.

Another device that poets use in writing poetry is onomatopoeia. Here, words used must make the sounds that one hears in the natural environment. If one throws a rock into the water, the sound made is similar to splash! Thus, the word splash makes that sound, in degrees, when a rock is thrown into the water. A pupil I observed while supervising student teachers in the public schools wrote the following containing onomatopoeia in a science unit of study:

The Sound of Wind

Why does the wind sound like *swish, swoosh, slosh, slash* and *spash*? The unequal heating of the earth's atmosphere makes for movement of air.

The movement of molecules through the air say travel, move and go!

The underlined words in the above poem seem to indicate in degrees the sound of wind. The pupil has included onomatopoeia in the first line only of this poem.

Poems that Rhyme

One important kind poetry does rhyme. Others do not. The following are examples of rhymed verse which pupils may write when readiness is in evidence (Ediger, 1988). Couplets contain two lines with ending words rhyming, such as in the following poem:

The Forty Niners

The Forty niners went to the West
To look for gold with great zest.

One teacher mentioned to one of us while supervising student teachers that the whole word method only or largely was used when she attended public schools. Major learnings came from studying rhymed verse. In her school, the teacher would have pupils brain storm ideas on how many words would rhyme with a particular word printed on the chalkboard. These listed words were then to be used in poetry writing.

Triplets have three lines with all ending words rhyming. From a brain storming session on ideas about the zoo, a committee of three wrote the following triplet:

The Zoo

I like to visit the zoo to see large lions
We have studied these animals in science
They live in a few nations with different biomes.

The quatrain was discussed above and needs a little review. Quatrains have four lines with lines one and two rhyming as well as lines three and four rhyming. Sometimes, all ending words rhyme of the four line poem. A dyad of two pupils wrote the following within a unit of study:

An Inventor

Thomas Edison invented the light bulb with much work
His efforts helped all to see better at night with little quirk
The light bulb was here to stay
And make life better with more pay.

Selected pupils like to work together with others in the classroom in writing a poem. The number here needs to be kept small so all may participate such as a dyad of two members of a maximum of four pupils writing collaboratively.

Limericks are a very popular kind of poem for pupils to write. Generally, this poem starts with the words. "There once was a—The limerick has five lines comprised of a couplet and a triplet. Lines 1, 2, and 5 form a triplet whereas lines 3 and 4 form a couplet.

Kindness

There once was a man in a large city
Who felt sorry for poor people in a pity
His raised much money for the poor
And felt he needed much more
That wonderful man worked on a committee.

It is excellent if pupils volunteer to write poetry; however, there are learners who do not participate with intrinsic motivation and may need to be assigned to a committee which is highly accepting and provides for all pupils to succeed.

Unrhymed Verse

Many pupils are surprised that there can be unrhymed poetry which provides for interest and purpose on the part of the learner. They find free verse to be challenging and relatively easy to write. After all, pupils should enjoy reading and writing poems. Intrinsic motivation is important in all learning as an ideal. Many pupils are motivated from within and do not need inexpensive prizes as rewards for learning.

For those lacking intrinsic motivation, the teacher may need to use an award system and, hopefully, pupils will wean themselves from extrinsic motivation as time goes on. We do not count verbal praise as extrinsic motivation. Honest praise is good for pupils and should be used judiciously. We believe that quality learning takes place best with intrinsic motivation, but a few pupils will need rewards and prizes as motivators. Two pupils wrote the following haiku containing five-seven-five syllables for each of three lines:

The Goat

The goal is a joy (five syllables)
In the grass among the trees (seven syllables)
A lovely sight seen!

A tanka has two more lines, each having seven syllables:

The Tall Camel

I like to see far (five syllables)
Where camels roam in deserts (seven syllables)
And chew scarce rare feed (five syllables)
Up, away go the camels (seven syllables)
Where grass and water abound. (seven syllables)

Writing Free Verse

Free verse is a very open-ended kind of poetry. There does not have to be any rhyme nor syllabication. Many pupils enjoy brain storming lines for free verse. The following free verse was composed by four pupils collaboratively:

The Shepherd

Alone with the sheep in the field
plays on the flute to maintain entertainment
watches and cares for each and every sheep
is careful with the little lambs
herds the animals to good grass
throws stones at cement fences
does not mind being alone
relishes time with the sheep
ever faithful and kind

Conclusion

Pupils need to experience reading and writing different kinds and forms of poetry. There are rich meanings and messages in poetry. The novel use of words adds to the learning repertoire of pupils. There should be poems for pupils to read that deal with diverse topics and genres. The poems should be on appropriate reading levels of individual pupils for maximum achievement to take place. The teacher needs to read poetry frequently to pupils in an enthusiastic way. Each pupil may wish to collect his/her favourite poems for enjoyment and future reference. Pupils need to become motivated through the use of different stimuli in order to read and write more poetry. For selected pupils, reading much poetry has been a way of increasing skills in learning to read more proficiently.

REFERENCES

Ediger, Marlow (1997), *The Modern Elementary School*, Kirksville, Missouri: Simpson Publishing Company, 206.

Ediger, Marlow (1998), *Language Arts Curriculum in the Elementary School*, Kirksville, Missouri: Simpson Publishing Company, 29-36.

Ediger, Marlow and Digumarti Bhaskara Rao (2002). *Language Arts Curriculum*. New Delhi, India: Discovery Publishing House.

Rao, Digumarti Bahsakra and Pushpa Latha, Digumarti (1993). *Achievement in English*. New Delhi: Discovery Publishing House.

16

Children's Literature and the Language Arts

There are many reasons for emphasizing a quality literature curriculum for children. Reading instruction too frequently has centered upon word recognition skills such as using phonics, syllabication, structural analysis, context clues, picture clues and configurational clues. It is important for pupils to possess these word recognition skills to identify unknown words. But quality literature has more to offer than word recognition skills. Also, thinking skills are stressed such as critical and creative thinking, problems solving, as well as reading to obtain facts, concepts and generalizations. However, important these thinking skills are and they are indeed important, literature for children incorporations, but goes beyond these skills (Ediger, 1997).

Why Children's Literature?

There are many excellent reasons as to why there should be a good children's literature curriculum in the school setting. First, pupils may experience life vicariously. No one would wish to experience whatever life had to offer directly in all of its manifestations. There are too many negative occurrences which one definitely would prefer not to experience. These items include being robbed, fired from a job, death of a loved one, harsh climates for a long period of time, poverty and other negative happenings. However, pupils may experience these occurrences in a vicarious way. We learn from the experience of others. One's life consists of experiences which makes possible for new ways to respond and live. There are many choices to be made and the arena of decision making increases in options as more possibilities are in the offing. Reading then provides opportunities for vicarious experiences. These vicarious experiences might limit the negative that can occur to an individual. They do provide more indirect experiences which might be used in the decision-making arenas. Thus, there are things that one does not want to experience directly, but in a wholesome manner the experiences can be read about.

Second, choices are made in life involving standards to be used in relating to others. Values are involved in decision making. These values can be dictated to children. Many times dictated values do not work. If pupils live without a set of guiding principles they may falter and fail in possessing that which gives a person criteria or standard to live by (Leming, 1996). Children's literature can deal with the values dimension in its many manifestations. Values are secured by learners from diverse sources of children's literature may make its numerous contributions here. Children's literature may make its numerous contributions here. Children's literature needs to meet needs of pupils from different backgrounds and cultures in the values dimension. Obtaining the interests of learners is important; otherwise pupils will not be engaged in reading about and considering various values. Pupils should reveal that core values are being achieved as they interact with pupils of different beliefs and religions. Pupils need to receive insight into the structure of values and how these may provide needed guidance in relating to others in school and in society. Learners may experience unique endeavours in learning about values such as in creative and formal dramatics, pantomime and socio-drama. Positive values studied and acquired through children's literature need to be used. Application needs to be made of knowledge, skills and attitudes achieved. The practical situation provides ample opportunities for pupils to use and make application of a values system.

Third, children's literature provides avenues for relaxation and recreation. We prize very highly the ability to read well. With reading, we are able to entertain ourselves and grow in appreciation for quality literature that has enduring values. These values will provide direction for us and they will be acquired through reading for recreation and relaxation. There certainly is a refreshing component when thinking of reading during one's leisure time. To spend even a few minutes of time in reading does help one to feel renewed with energy and purpose.

Each person needs to find ways of dealing with stress. Life can indeed be very stressful. Blessed is that person who finds ways that are effective in dealing with stress. Certainly, reading can be an approach in minimizing the stressful components of life. Children's literature may well provide that avenue. Teachers, supervisors and parents should make an all out effort to assist each pupil to read well so that recreational reading may become a relevant purpose.

Fourth, reading of children's literature can be a guidance resource. Difficulties are involved when facing problems. These problems need to be identified and relevant solutions sought. Literature for children might well be a vital resource to provide assistance in counselling and guidance. Pupils face diverse kinds of problems, such as extreme shyness, aggressive behaviour, hostility, negativeness, ill-health, obesity and loneliness among others. There are books written for children which can provide assistance in dealing with these kinds of problems. Bibliotherapy as a concept stresses using library books to deal with problems faced by pupils which seem overwhelming. Teachers and guidance counsellors need to be very familiar with the wealth of library books that might well assist pupils to cope with endearing problems. We have observed in classrooms whereby teachers have suggested library books to pupils which were very helpful in dealing with an even overcoming what seemed as a major problem. For example, a girl felt she was much too tall compared to others in the classroom. She did fit into the category of being tall. After reading several library books on how individuals coped with their feelings, this girl was better able to accept herself by using personal strengths possessed to achieve, grow and develop.

Fifth, pupils can become knowledgeable about different careers that are in the offing. Career selection can indeed be a problem for many young people. Career exploration is vital for any elementary school child. The learner needs to acquire information about different careers and what is involved here when moving on to the work place as an adult.

There are numerous quality library books on careers. One of us well remember supervising a student teacher and cooperating teachers in a classroom in which two pupils did extensive reading from library books to develop a career manual. The career manual written and illustrated for fourth grade pupils contained explanations of what training is involved for the careers being studied. Drawings were made of individuals involved in each career write-up. These two pupils interviewed individuals in diverse careers. Here, pupils revealed much purpose and interest in their study. Reading of library books was central to this project. These two learners were greatly interested in careers. Later on in the high school years and beyond, these same two boys found the world of work to be enjoyable and interesting. We recommend having plenty of library books out to assist pupils with reading in the vocational and work arenas.

To learn to read well, the pupil needs to read, study and think. We have noticed effective teachers do a good job of introducing carefully selected library books to children by telling some interesting aspects of these books. Also, numerous teachers have developed excellent bulletin board displays on library books in the classroom and centralized library which capture and fascinate learner interests and provide readiness of reading. The teacher also needs to be a good story teller so that pupils perceive sequence, plot, characterization, theme, point of view and setting. Both student teachers and cooperating teachers whom one of us have supervised have told about numerous good story tellers who have come to class and engaged in the telling of stories. Story telling seemingly motivates pupils to do more reading. Sometimes, the stories told have come from a library book in school. Many pupils then wish to read this library book.

Sixth, children's literature provides a springboard for creative thinking activities on the part of pupils. After pupils have completed reading a library book, learners volunteer to do a creative dramatics activity pertaining to the subject matter. Roles are selected and learners use speaking parts spontaneously without looking at print discourse. At other times pupils individually wrote parts from a library book read. Each people then might have a role to play in presenting content written as play parts. Creative dramatics has no written script but may be based on contents contained in a library book whereas formal dramatics had parts written down for each role. The parts may be memorized and presented to the class and other classrooms of children. Quality presentations have been developed whereby pupils orally read or speak their part in sequence with others in formal dramatization. Creativity knows few bounds when children's literature provides the basis for this learning opportunity.

Seventh, children's literature may be related directly to social studies, science, mathematics, the language, arts, art, music and physical education (Templeton, 1995). There is literature written for pupils which pertains to each of these subject matter areas. In the social studies then, there are library books written on many nations on the face of the earth as well as on minority groups and diverse cultures. In science, library books on astronomy, geology, chemistry, physics and other areas other numerous in their offerings. In mathematics, library books are valuable on history of mathematics, uses of mathematics and biographies of famous mathematicians. In the language arts, there are fairy tales, myths, legends, tall tales, poetry and different novels write to meet needs of pupils. In art, music and physical education there are also interesting library books written. We always enjoy reading biographies of well known artists, musicians and basketball/football/baseball stars. There are library books written to meet interest and purpose needs of pupils as well as being on the diverse reading levels of individual pupils.

Each school needs to have ample library books in the offing which encourage reading and reflection on content read. Reading across the curriculum is an excellent concept to stress in the curriculum. One of the finest science units we observed as supervisors of student teachers and cooperating teachers stressed the title, "Our Changing Environment". Here, pupils read library books on that unit title instead of the basal science textbook. It was amazing how pupils contributed in the discussion pertaining to content read on volcanoes, hurricanes, tornadoes, wind and water erosion, as well as other natural disasters in the world of science. Pupils individually in their reading of library book content were able to relate ideas to the ongoing interaction and discussions. We wholeheartedly recommend teachers giving this procedure a try in unit teaching. Using a variety of approaches in teaching is challenging and brings in the new to pupils.

Pupils with teacher assistance need to understand and attach meaning to concepts such as setting of the story, characterization, plot, point of view, theme, irony of the situation, as well as satire. These literary concepts are used by novelists and writers in the world of literature (Ediger, 1988).

Teacher Self Evaluation in the Literature Curriculum

The teacher needs to be a good evaluator of the self in determining pupil achievement. We would suggest the following as guidelines for the teacher to assess his/her achievement in guiding optimal pupil achievement in children's literature:

1. Teacher should be an avid reader of literature, be it for children or for adults. Pupils need to realize that the teacher does much reading and does not operate on the principle that children alone are to do the reading of divers topics in literature;
2. There needs to be a literature programme that is planned with an appropriate scope and sequence. A planned literature curriculum stresses that pupils read many library books on diverse topics and on unique

individual levels of reading. The plan should include literature being emphasized across the different subject matter areas. Each unit of study taught should be integrated with library book content coming from different academic disciplines as well as from the vocational arenas. The literature curriculum should have its own objectives, carefully chosen, for pupil attainment;

3. The teacher needs to be fascinated with literature and indicate these interests to pupils. Here, the teacher may tell pupils about what he/she read as it relates to what is being taught. In sharing time, the teacher might also indicate enthusiasm for reading in general. We believe enthusiasm to be very contagious. Pupil enthusiasm for reading is motivating and stimulating to do further reading. A literate society is needed. Literacy can be stressed in any curriculum area (Ediger, 1997);

4. Pupils need to find pleasure in reading. Using leisure time wisely has been a goal of education for a long time. Wise use of leisure time is important. We would suggest that teachers work in the direction whereby reading literature becomes recreational as well as utility in emphasis. Pupils need to love reading in its diverse manifestations;

5. There needs to be rational balance between scheduled literature sessions as well as pupils reading during free time. We believe pupils need to be given ample time to read during spare time in school. Sustained Silent Reading (SSR) may also be emphasized. Here, everyone in school reads at a given time. Pupils then see models in reading to emulate. They may also notice how people of all ages become interested in reading library books and other kinds of reading materials. We have observed SSR being stressed with student teacher and cooperating teacher guidance. We believe it is one answer to problems in encouraging learner interest in reading. In SSR, individually select a library book to read. The learner, not the teacher, does the choosing of which books to read sequentially;

6. Ample time needs to be given for free reading in the classroom. Pupils do tend to enjoy reading when there is time for this activity. The free reading time may emphasize pupils choosing a library book relating to an ongoing unit of study. Thus, the free reading time relates directly to what is being studied in different curriculum areas. The learner may also choose a library book to read which is recreation in nature. With free time, pupils realize the values placed upon reading by the teacher and by the school. In most cases we have observed in supervising teachers in the schools, pupils do read and not waste time in and during free reading. The teacher may need to work with pupils who have difficulties in setting down to read sequential library books;

7. Pupils should read for both enjoyment and for information (Templeton, 1997). Both can stress assisting pupils to do well in the affective dimension. Pupils then should develop wholesome attitudes toward reading. If pupils learn to dislike reading, the chances are they will not develop the necessary literacy qualities so necessary for the twenty-first century. We believe that most individuals read well if they understand what was read from an eighth grade reader. Eighth grade readers contain content such as Charles Dicken's *A Christmas Carol,* Robert Louis Stevenson's *Treasure Island* and Edigar Allen Poe's *The Gold Bug* among others. More critics of education should pick up an eighth grade reader to notice how complex some of the reading selections are. Many would discover that an individual reading on the eight grade level can read and comprehend many kinds of recreational and vocational writings. Of course, teachers need to work in the direction of having pupils achieve as much as possible in reading and in all curriculum areas. Reading across the curriculum is important!

8. There is a considerable debate, among educators in the teaching of reading, between reading narrative versus expository materials. Previously, much stress

has been placed upon pupils reading narrative materials such as fictional and story content which has a definite sequence or order of events. Presently many reading specialists are recommending pupils reading more of expository content. Expository content emphasizes informational books that pupils should read. The information is more reality based as compared to narrative accounts. Expository reading materials cut across diverse curriculum areas. For example, pupils may read library books on volcanoes, earthquakes, as well as wind/water erosion when studying a unit on "The Changing Surface of the Earth". Information read may relate directly to the unit in science being taught presently. These same topics may provide content for reading in SSR or an individualized reading programme. Perhaps, a rational balance should be in the offing between narrative and expository reading materials;

9. The teacher should read orally to pupils each day of the school week and year. Books chosen for reading aloud to pupils should develop interest, enjoyment and motivation in that the latter develop an inward desire to read. The teacher needs to face pupils and have good audience contact while reading aloud. Voice inflection with proper stress, pitch and juncture need to be in the offing when the teacher reads orally to pupils. Pupils might then desire to do more reading on their own. Both narrative and expository books should be read to elementary age pupils. Recently, there have been educators who recommend that secondary school teachers read aloud salient facets from textbook content to pupils so that comprehension is possible. Not all secondary school pupils are able to comprehend subject matter read from their basal textbooks;

10. Library books should be ample in number to provide for individual differences in the classroom. Pupils are at different levels of achievement in reading and therefore the teacher needs to be certain that gifted/ talented, average achievers and slow readers have

access to reading materials, that are understandable and comprehendible. Accessibility is a key concept to emphasize when having pupils check out reading materials. Pupils should not feel frustrated in reading by having rigid requirements for checking out different library books.

It is a very important for library books to reflect the different interests, tastes and abilities of pupils in the classroom. Each pupils should be able to locate sequential library books to read which are of appeal, feeling and provide for the different reading achievement levels of pupils in class. Library books should be shown to and briefly discussed with pupils so that there is a desire to read. There needs to make certain that pupils realize that there is a library book to read for each and every pupil. No pupil is left out from being able to choose and read a library book. There are large illustrations with a small amount of print in numerous library books for those who face problems in reading well. For others, there is more print discourse in library books to provide for those who read at a higher level. There should also be library books to read for the talented and gifted. Provision for individual differences is a must.

It is important for the teacher to reveal to pupils his/her love for reading. The attitudes and feelings possessed by teachers toward reading are generally indicated non-verbally to pupils. The teacher needs to be certain that the message sent to children is that quality attitudes and values pertaining to reading in its diverse manifestations is in evidence. Teacher enthusiasm for children's literature is a must!

If pupils are to read library books for follow-up conferences, the teacher needs to be well informed about the contents of each book, if at all possible. I have observed student teachers and cooperating teachers whom I supervised in the public schools have an excellent knowledge of literature for children. One teacher, in particular, used individualized reading in the curriculum. She felt that if follow up conferences with pupils were to be successful after the learner has completed reading a library book, the teacher needs to be well versed on the contents of each book read by children in the classroom. This teacher had a good file of four by six inch cards in which key ideas were printed about each library book in the classroom. Her thinking was if pupils were to have quality conferences, the teacher needs to be well versed in organising content of the book, completed by the pupil and discussed in a literary setting. I agree wholeheartedly. Teachers who have good knowledge of individual library books tend to enjoy reading and they do read much children's literature. Some of these teachers should teach a class in children's literature on a university campus. So often, I hear negative comments from university students on the quality of the children's literature course. An elementary teacher may be able to do a better job of preparing future teachers from the literature curriculum. One of my cooperating teachers mentioned one time that our student teachers did not read well orally to pupils during the student teaching programme. In my Teaching of Language Arts class, immediately added a requirement for the course in that student were to read a section from a children's library books using appropriate criteria. These criteria included having eye contact with pupils when reading aloud, showing the illustrations inside the library book to pupils as the related oral reading activity proceeds, observing pupils to notice engagement with the subject matter as it is being read and pronouncing words clearly and accurately when reading orally. I like feedback from cooperating teachers in public schools who have suggestions to give to improve the curriculum. (Ediger).

Evaluating Pupil Progress in Children's Literature

One of the first things that a teacher needs to do in the classroom is to observe individual pupils reading library books. Pupils must read continuously if they are to become proficient in reading. Reading content in the basal reader and other materials of print discourse requires skill, knowledge and quality attitudes. With practice in reading diversity of materials, the pupils certainly will increase abilities to read. The pupils need to develop a positive attitude toward reading. There are numerous ways of doing this. One way is to have pupils listen to the teacher read orally with appropriate stress, pitch and juncture as well as using good audience contact. By observing learners, the teacher may notice how well pupils like what is being read. Feedback from pupils here is important. Another way is for the teacher to show pupils newly arrived library books and have pupils hypothesize as to what the contents might be. The teacher then should observe which of these books pupils chose to read on their very own. We recommend that pupils in a small group take turns reading a library book among themselves. One pupil may start to read aloud, followed by others. A creative teacher finds ways of getting pupils interested in reading alongwith developing positive attitudes toward reading. Developing an appreciation for reading children's literature is an important goal for pupil's to attain.

Reading widely on diverse subject matter areas is salient for learners. Pupils individually need to experience ideas and content diverse topics. It might be all right for pupils to read on a single topic initially to develop a desire in learning to read, but the content read needs to be broadened so that learners will find themselves more fully in a job or in life outside the work place. Thus, each pupil should find his niche in life to the best possible. A quality resource may be exploration through literature written for children. There are books written on different vocations for pupils, as well as those that assist pupils to achieve selected values and the ability to solve problems. This is continuous and ongoing throughout life. Reading on a variety of topics then is important for pupils. Hopefully, the enjoyment ingredient will be there in processes involving reading.

When supervising student—teachers and cooperating teachers, we pupils very informally why they chose a certain book to read. Pupils answer with giving purposes such as the following:

1. I like to read about themselves;
2. I enjoy reading about famous people in history, but I do like to read also about people of other lands;
3. I choose books about farming first, maybe its because my grand-parent still live on the farm;

4. My favourite library books are those that emphasize fishing and fish. My father and I go fishing very frequently in summer;

5. I read on almost any topic since I enjoy reading.

There are many purposes involved in reading. Pupils purpose is important when he/she chooses library books to read. Pupils who have narrow interests in reading as reading skills permit should be encouraged to select a wider variety of topics when choosing library books to read. A broadly educated child should be in the offing so that he/she has more options available for decision making. However, the teacher should never minimize pupils individually reading for sheer enjoyment. Pupils may need assistance to make sense out of what is being read.

From skills developed in more formal reading programmes, the child should be able to identify unknown words, especially in the use of context clues and initial consonant sounds. Then too, there are times when words need to be pronounced directly to the reader. Hopefully, there will be a short time elapse for the child to determine what the unknown word is. Independent readers is an important goal for the teacher to stress. This includes word recognition skills that are developed as well as meanings attached to content read. An ultimate goal should be for pupils to reflect upon what has been read. Analyzing content in terms of reality versus fantasy, accurate from inaccurate ideas and cognitive versus the feeling dimension needs emphasis in the literature curriculum. Hopefully, pupils will become more creative in interpretation of content read. There are numerous interpretations that can be made of content read. Then too, learners should be able to bring to bear relevant solutions to personal and social problems faced. Attaching meaning to subject matter is so very important. What is written by an author may have an agenda or personal bias and the reader needs to interpret to perceive understanding of the ideas presented in print discourse. Certainly, the pupil should be able to make use of and apply what has been learned. Use and applications can be made in ongoing social studies, science, mathematics and English units taught.

Metacognition is important for pupils to engage in. With metacognition, the pupil monitors his/her achievement in comprehension as the reading activity progresses. The child then does not read words only, but the words read mean something and it is up to the learner to bring forth meanings as abilities and progress indicate. Organisation of content read is important such as sequence, main ideas, subordinate ideas and details. Thus, the metacognition, the pupil monitors or evaluates on a personal basis if comprehension is occurring and main ideas are clarified from subordinate ideas. It is important for all pupils who read to be able to clarify with self check the progress that is being made in reading comprehension. There are pupils and undergraduate students in universities who believe that if they have 'read' the content that is all there is to reading. In other words, merely pronouncing the words and then *ipso facto* they have understood content read is a grave misinterpretation of what reading is all about. Reading is a process that involves understanding and applying what has been read There are many criteria then that teachers should be use to appraise the quality of pupils' reading children' literature.

Conclusion

We, as teachers, can assist learners to achieve in an optimal manner in reading achievement, be it in a formal or informal approaches in teaching and learning. When pupils are taught in formal reading, such as in the use of basal textbooks, they should be assisted individually and in groups to provide for continual progress and achievement. When choosing library books, pupils individually select and sequence their very own progress and achievement.

REFERENCES

Ediger, Marlow (1995), *Philosophy in Curriculum Development*. Kirksville, Missouri: Simpson Publishing Company, 13-15.

Ediger, Marlow (1997), *Teaching Reading and the Language Arts in the Elementary School*. Kirksville, Missouri: Simpson Publishing Company, 141-42.

Ediger, Marlow (1988), *Language Arts Curriculum in the Elementary School*. Kirksville, Missouri: Simpson Publishing Company, 103.

Ediger, Marlow and Digumarti Bhaskara Rao (2001), *Teaching Reading Successfully*, New Delhi, India: Discovery Publishing House.

Leming, James (1996), "Teaching Values in Social Studies Education: Past Practices and Future Possibilities', in *Critical Issues in Teaching Social Studies*, Massialas and Allen, Editors. Belmont, California: Wadsworth Publishing Company, 145-50.

Templeton, Shane (1955), *Children's Literacy*. Boston: Houghton Mifflin Company, 27.

Templeton, Shane (1997), *Teaching the Integrated Language Arts*. Boston: Houghton Mifflin Company, 209.

17

Handwriting and the Language Arts

The teacher of handwriting must select vital objectives for learners to achieve. The concept of relevance is important to emphasize in selecting ends for pupil attainment. Thus, much thought and careful consideration needs to be given by the teacher in selecting these handwriting goals. Too frequently, pupils have developed trivial and insignificant learnings. There is much to be learned during the elementary school years. In society, the 'explosion of knowledge' has been a definite reality for some time. The knowledge explosion societal trend has important implications for the classroom teacher. The teacher must select educational purposes carefully. Pertaining to writing skills, Petty wrote:

> *"Writing involves many skills and abilities. The most fundamental of these are the thinking skills or abilities, which are basic to the expression of feelings and thoughts, whether the medium is speech, movement, art, or writing. In relation to writing, these skills include collecting the most appropriate words and phrases for conveying expressions; organising these expressions into sentences that are clearly understandable; and sequencing the sentences into a meaningful whole. All of these thinking abilities are used to compose a piece of writing, with the effectiveness of any composition largely dependent on the quality of the thinking ability or skill of the composer. No written expression, not even a single sentence or a label or a short memorandum, will be effective expression unless it is well thought out.*

In addition, of course, skill in forming letters and words, in spelling correctly, in punctuating sentences properly, and in those matters of form and custom in the appearance of various types of writing are also very much a part of effective written expression. And each of these general skills or abilities consists of specific lesser ones: in handwriting the strokes needed to make the letters, spacing, rhythm of movement; in spelling, making sound and symbol associations, affixing, capitalizing, in punctuation, the strokes needed to form the punctuation marks. All of these skills require teaching and thorough practice so that they become automatic to writers and permit them to use full thinking power for composition.

The Child and Handwriting

Certainly, the teacher must give careful consideration to child growth and development characteristics when selecting objectives. If pupils cannot achieve stated objectives, modification of stated ends is in order. Handwriting objectives selected by the teacher for learners to achieve should be attainable. At the same time, the chosen objectives represent new learnings for pupils to acquire.

The length of time devoted to handwriting instruction needs careful evaluation. Early primary grade pupils need relatively short periods of time devoted to learning activities involving handwriting. Generally, their attention span is not as long as compared to older pupils. First grade pupils become tried rather soon from handwriting experiences because the finer muscles, involving the use of arm, hand, and fingers, are being developed gradually. The teacher needs to observe individual pupils to determine if learning activities need to be changed from handwriting to a different curriculum area which does not require use of the finer muscles. Intermediate grade pupils generally write for a longer period of time to finish a given reasonable assignment without excessive fatigue and tiredness setting in. However, form any age level, expectations from any individual can be too high in activities involving handwriting. If pupils perceive reasons for developing selected understanding, skills, and attitudinal objectives, energy levels of the involved person generally increase in wanting to further pursue a given learning activity. Varying approaches in teaching may also assist learners to maintain a longer attention span pertaining to teaching-learning situations involving handwriting experiences.

The teacher must remember that each child is unique in many ways and that includes rate of achievement in handwriting. Pupils feel frustrated and may learn to dislike handwriting experiences if they cannot achieve to the level expected of them. Pupils should enjoy handwriting experiences as well as have feelings of satisfaction in all curriculum areas of the elementary school.

In determining educational objectives pertaining to handwriting, the teacher needs to consider and answer the following questions:

1. Can learners satisfactorily achieve the chosen aims?
2. Will pupils feel successful in their accomplishment?
3. Can interest be developed and/or maintained within pupils in achieving desired objectives?
4. Are the stated objectives in handwriting in harmony with neuromuscular skills that learners presently possess?
5. Do the objectives guide learners to develop appropriate attitudes, as well as skills and understandings?
6. Are the objectives stated so that it can be determined if achievement in that direction is taking place?
7. Will learners feel that purpose is involved in achieving the desired objectives?

For initial instruction in handwriting Lee and Rubin wrote:

Most things we learn to do, we learn largely through imitation and experimentation, giving special attention to the more troublesome aspects. We usually arrive at our own personal adaptations and idiosyncrasies. Handwriting can be learned the same way.

Many children learn to write their names and perhaps much more before they come to school. In school, each can have a card with his or her name on it in good, clear manuscript writing, so that it is readily available for copying. When children begin dictating sentences for the teacher to write for them, they will soon want to write for themselves. Thus begins their first significant writing 'lesson'.

The teacher can write the sentences in good, clear manuscript on a strip of paper the appropriate length for the child's picture. The child takes both the strip and the picture to the writing center, places the strip just above the blank space reserved for the sentences, and copies the sentence directly below the teacher's writing.

When this procedure is repeated many times and combined with discussion during dictation, no other writing 'lessons' are needed. When a few children have difficulty with a certain letter, the teacher can group these children for a few minutes, explain the problem, and provide a good model for them to copy. They can solve the problem quickly be keeping this model in front of them as they write.

Teachers must be aware that there is a great difference in the small muscle coordination of children of this age. When a child is trying, the writing must be accepted with appreciation for progress, regardless of imperfections. If it is really illegible, perhaps larger writing—or smaller writing—would help.

Society and Handwriting

What does society expect of pupils in handwriting achievement? It is imperative that individuals exhibit legible handwriting when communicating with others. Time is wasted in reading content if is difficult to determine what others have written due to poor handwriting. Individuals like to read meaningful content which is easy to decode. This is tune of content written in friendly letters, business letters, announcements, plays, poems, stories and in letters of application in applying for jobs or positions. Legible handwriting must be in evidence. The employer generally, all things being equal, will be more influenced with content in a letter that has good handwriting as compared to illegible handwriting. It is true, of course, that letters of application in applying for positions and jobs are also typed. However there are other numerous writing occasions in which legible handwriting is a definite asset as compared to illegible handwriting. Society does place value upon individuals exhibiting quality legible handwriting.

The teacher needs to answer the following questions pertaining to what society might expect pupils to learn in handwriting:

1. Will the curricular learnings that pupils develop be useful in society?
2. Are the chosen objectives relevant pertaining to what pupils may need in terms of learnings now as well as in the future?

General Objectives in Handwriting

General objectives in handwriting state the direction of behaviour that teachers want learners to achieve over a relatively long period of time. The teacher needs to determine which understandings, skills, and attitudes are to be developed within pupils at the end of a designated interval of time. General objectives may not be achieved during the time a unit is taught or perhaps even during a school year.

Pupils should exhibit continuous progress in handwriting. They need to be taught at their present level of achievement and guided in progressing at their optimum rate of achievement as they progress through diverse years of schooling.

The following, among others, might well be important general objectives for pupils to accomplish in handwriting.

A. Understanding Objectives

1. To develop within the pupil an understanding of how to form letters legibly;
2. To develop within learners an understanding of how letters may be aligned properly;
3. To develop within the child understandings pertaining to appropriate spacing of words and letters;
4. To develop within the learner an understanding of the necessity of having proper proportion of letters;
5. To develop within the child appropriate generalizations in achieving legibility in handwriting;
6. To develop within the learner an understanding of approaches of self-evaluation in the area of handwriting;
7. To develop an understanding within pupils of the necessity of exhibiting neatness in handwriting.

B. Skills Objectives

1. To develop within the pupils skill to form legible letters in handwriting;

2. To develop within learners skill to use proper alignment in handwriting;
3. To develop within children skill to use appropriate proportion of letters in handwriting;
4. To develop in children skill to utilize proper spacing of letters and words;
5. To develop within the child skill to evaluate his/her own achievement in handwriting;
6. To develop within the pupils skill to exhibit neatness in handwriting.

C. **Attitudinal Objectives**

1. To develop within pupils a desire in wanting to improve achievement in handwriting;
2. To develop within learners a feeling of wanting to improve in the formation of legible letters;
3. To develop within the child an attitude of wanting to reveal proper proportion of letters;
4. To develop within the learner a desire to spacing words and letters properly;
5. To develop within the child a desire to assess his/her own achievement in handwriting;
6. To develop an attitude within learners of wanting to reveal neatness in handwriting;
7. To develop an attitude of respect within learners toward quality in handwriting as revealed by others in society.

It is important to emphasize balance among understandings, skills, and attitudinal objectives in teaching handwriting. Desirable attitude assist in achieving understandings and skills ends. Greene and Petty wrote the following:

"The major reason for teaching handwriting is its role in communication. Handwriting is the principal tool of written expression; for this reason it must be legible. Thus the principal objective of handwriting instruction is legibility.

Considering this objective, a teacher should not stress meaningless drill on handwriting but should strive mainly to have pupils produce legible copy. The misapplication of the principle of use and need so frequently evident is a result of the neglect of sound procedures in instruction. The principle factor overlooked is that handwriting is a developmental process that requires more than just a few years of the child's total period of growth. Simply permitting children to write as they have the need is not giving handwriting instruction nor can handwriting be taught once and then dropped from the instructional programme. Production of legible writing at a reasonable speed can be achieved and maintained only as a result of constant and meaningful practice. Thus the handwriting programme should be built around these basis goals:

Encouraging pupils to use writing as a means for effective expression.

Helping each child to discover how skill in handwriting aids expression.

Having all pupils strive for neatness and legibility with moderate speed in their writing activities.

Establishing practice periods as appropriate at all grade levels.

Analyzing the handwriting faults of individual pupils and seeking their correction.

Developing in each pupil a sense of personal pride and self-appraisal and a desire for self-improvement.

Developing correct posture and the proper use of writing tools."

Specific Objectives

Selected teachers, principals, and supervisors wish to have clearly stated objectives, as advocated by behaviourists, in teaching-learning situations. The teacher then may need to write measurable objectives in handwriting. There is relatively little leeway in determining what is to be taught when viewing specific objectives. After instruction, the teacher may determine if learners have or have not achieved the precise objectives. It is vital to have pupils achieve relevant handwriting objectives. Reasonable specific objectives need to be written for learners. Learners might then be successful achievers. Learning activities to achieve specific objectives in handwriting should be interesting, have purpose, and be on the understanding level of pupils. Provision must be made to provide for individual differences when measurably stated objectives are used in teaching handwriting.

The following are examples of specific objectives for pupils to achieve in handwriting:

1. The pupils will write three sentences using recommended alignment of words and letters;
2. The pupil will write the lower case cursive letters 'a', 'b', and 'c' correctly as presented in class by writing a sentence;
3. The pupil will write five sentences using proper spacing of letters within each word.

The teacher after instruction may assess if pupils have or have not achieved stated objectives. It is important to correlate the teaching of handwriting with other curriculum areas in the elementary school. There are many learning activities in handwriting which correlate well with writing activities in social studies, science, mathematics, reading and other language arts areas, health, music, art, and physical education. Pupils need ample opportunities to practice quality handwriting in other curriculum areas in the school/class setting.

Yelon and Weinstein wrote:

Reinforcement, in the behaviourist view, is a single most important factor in learning. The law of reinforcement, sometimes called the law of effect, defines the shaping of behaviour through reinforces. A common example is the laboratory situation in which pigeons are trained to press levers for food; the training is accomplished by providing food each time the lever is pressed. Similarly, the law of reinforcement applies to human behaviour; children may learn polite table manners, for instance, if their parents smile approvingly each time they eat correctly.

Every element of human thought and feeling, according to behaviourist learning theory, may be defined in terms of reinforcement—not just table manners but good study habits and socially approved behaviour of all kinds, even love itself. Techniques which manipulate reinforcement alter the learning process.

Learning Activities in Handwriting

There are a variety of learning activities that may be provided for learners in handwriting. Individuals differences must be provided for in any classroom. Pupils will vary much from each other in handwriting achievement. The teacher must consider the present achievement level of each child in handwriting before learning activities are selected to achieve new stated objectives. The kinds of learning activities that are selected in handwriting may well depend upon the way the school curriculum area is organised. For example, the classroom teacher may decide to teach handwriting as a separate subject with no relationship being emphasized with other curriculum areas in the elementary school. The teacher then assumes that pupils automatically will be acquired handwriting understandings, skills, and attitudes in new writing situations involving the social studies, science, mathematics, the language arts, health, music, physical education, and art. The writer definitely feels that classroom teachers must assist learners to see the uses of what has been learned previously. Thus, learners must perceive that what has been learned earlier can be utilized in ongoing learning activities.

The teacher of handwriting will definitely wish to correlate handwriting with other areas in the school curriculum. If the teacher is teaching spelling, he/she will also to emphasize quality handwriting. Handwriting errors can make for incorrect spelling of words. For example, learners who do not cross the 't' in cursive writing and leave a loop in that same letter are actually writing the letter 'l' when the letter 't' was intended to be written. The teacher then may definitely what to correlate handwriting with spelling.

Handwriting may be taught as being related to any curriculum area in the elementary school. For example, in the final product that is written in a health unit of study, a learner may exhibit improved handwriting in a report on proper dietary habits. The quality of handwriting exhibited may be assessed in terms of what the learner can reasonably well achieve. Additional examples of relating handwriting to different curriculum areas will now be discussed.

Mathematics and Handwriting

Products of learners in mathematics become difficult to evaluate if the written work is solvently done and illegible.

Thus, the teacher has an important responsibility in guiding learners to write numerals and symbols of mathematics legibly. The learner may then communicate ideas more effectively if this is done. Individuals communicate content in many different ways. Writing numerals and symbols pertaining to mathematics is a form of communication of ideas to others. It is imperative then that numerals and symbols be written legibly so that effective communication of ideas may take place. Neatness in these written products is also important.

Occasionally, learners will be writing reports in mathematics based on research. If pupils are studying the Roman system of numeration, they may wish to gather information from different reference sources and complete a written report on this topic. The best handwriting of the individual pupil needs to be expected in the final product.

Science and Handwriting

There are numerous opportunities for pupils to utilize handwriting in the science curriculum. Among these important learning activities might be the following:

1. A committee of pupils or individual learners may write up the findings of a science experiment;
2. Individually or within a committee, pupils might write a method of procedure to follow in order to conduct an experiment;
3. A report may be written on a chosen topic related to an ongoing science unit. Topics, such as 'magnetism', 'electricity', 'atoms', 'electrons', 'protons', and 'neutrons' might well make for quality content in written reports;
4. Temperature readings could be recorded on a daily basis in a unit on 'Climate in Our Community';
5. Notes may be written pertaining to a selection read from an encyclopaedia or science textbooks;
6. An outline might be written from content read using a variety of reference sources;

7. Criteria or standards ought to be written on being an effective member and/or leader of a discussion group;
8. Summaries could be written on main ideas presented in a filmstrip or film presentation relating to the science unit being studied.

Science teachers must always think of variety of learning activities for learners in order to provide for individual pupils within a class.

Social Studies and Handwriting

In a self-contained classroom or in a departmentalized plan of teaching, the teacher can stress the importance of handwriting pertaining to writing activities in the social studies. The following, among others, might provide quality learning activities for pupils:

1. Business letters could be written to order free charts, pictures, and other audio-visual aids related to the ongoing social studies unit;
2. Friendly letters might be written to pen pals. These pen pals may come from countries presently being studied in social studies, or having been studied in the past;
3. Generalizations and main ideas may be written or content read from diverse reference sources;
4. Important facts read relating to a relevant question raised by learners in an ongoing social studies unit may be recorded;
5. Announcements can be written inviting another class to observe culminating activities for a specific unit in social studies;
6. Speaking parts for a play may be written cooperatively by a committee of pupils relating to a specific part of a social studies unit. In a unit on 'Discovering New Lands' learners might write a play to interpret how explorers felt when new lands were being discovered. The play can be presented to other members of the class and to other classes of children;

7. Directions could be written in making relief maps which relate to a unit being studied. For example, if pupils are studying a unit on Australia, they might make a relief map on that country;
8. Standards can be developed by the class on giving effective oral reports. Reports may be given to the entire class by individual pupils or by a committee of children. Reports given could be assessed in light of these written standards;
9. An outline may be written relating to important conclusions reached in reading an important selection in social studies;
10. When pupils are engaged in presenting hypotheses pertaining to content in a picture, object, or problem, handwriting experiences then become a reality in functional situations in the classroom;
11. Learners may take notes relating to a discussion that has taken place.

Handwriting and the Language Arts

Handwriting is a part of the language arts curriculum in the elementary school. Handwriting thus becomes an inherent part of language arts as well as the other curriculum areas in the elementary school. Selected learning activities, among others, that pertain to handwriting in the language arts could be the following

1. Pupils with teacher assistance might label objects in the classroom in a reading readiness programme using manuscript writing;
2. Handwriting textbooks can be utilized in lessons as the need and purpose arises;
3. Experience charts might be developed with teacher guidance in a reading readiness programme. Learners may notice what is said orally can be written down in manuscript letters. Cursive writing will be introduced later on;

4. Learners can write ideas over content that has been read pertaining to different purposes in reading. These purposes involve critical reading, reading to follow directions, factual reading, reading for a sequence of ideas, creative reading, reading for main ideas, and reading to develop generalizations;
5. Pupils need ample opportunities to practice forming letters correctly, writing letters and words with recommended alignment, slanting letters properly, spacing words and letters legibly, and using proper proportion of letters;
6. Pupils with teacher leadership may write news items. The resulting newspaper could be sent home weekly, biweekly, or monthly on important happenings in class.

Health and Handwriting

Many interesting learning activities provided for pupils in the area of health could also help learners achieve important goals in handwriting. The following learning activities in health education may assist learners to improve in handwriting:

1. Learners may take notes over a talk given by a physician pertaining to improved health practices in everyday living;
2. Main ideas could be written covering a set of slides or pictures presented by a registered nurse related to improving healthful living in the community;
3. Each pupil might write a personal experience chart pertaining to contents from filmstrip relating to a facet of healthful living;
4. Letters can be written to members of the city council making recommendations on improving polluted areas;
5. Menus for a week may be written pertaining to balanced diets for individuals;
6. Business letters can be written to order free materials relating to health units of instruction.

In Summary

When writing objectives for learners to achieve, it is of utmost importance for the teacher to consider each pupil's present achievement level. The teacher also must consider trends in society and their importance in determining handwriting goals. Objectives may be stated broadly as is the case of general objectives in the curriculum area of handwriting. Specific objectives can also be written which may be achieved in a relatively short period of time. General objectives are achieved over a longer period of time. The teacher must determine rational balance among understandings, skills, and attitudinal objectives that learners are to achieve. Each category or objectives is vital to emphasize in teaching-learning situations.

The teacher must think of various methods to use in teaching handwriting. These varied approaches are necessary to provide adequately for each learner in class. Handwriting correlates well with each curriculum area in the elementary school. The pupil must exhibit improved handwriting in the final product that has been written. The child generally may not reveal improved handwriting at the time that content is being written. Ideas come first when writing content. However, the learner can always show improved handwriting in the final written product. Legibility in handwriting must permeate and be emphasized as being important in all curriculum areas in the elementary school.

REFERENCES

Dawson, Mildred A. *Guiding Language Learning*. Second Edition. New York: Harcourt, Brace and World, Inc., 1963. Chapter Seventeen.

Ediger, Marlow. "Essentials in Teaching Handwriting", *Education* (September, 1965), 37-39.

Ediger, Marlow. "Handwriting in the Elementary School", *School and Community* (April, 1972), 46.

Ediger, Marlow. "On Teaching Handwriting", *Illinois Schools Journal* (Fall, 1971), 156-157.

Greene, Harry A., and Walter T. Petty. *Developing Language Skills in the Elementary School*. Fifth Edition. Boston: Allyn and Bacon, Inc., 1975.

Lee, Doris M., and Joseph B. Rubin. *Children and Language*. Belmont, California: Wadsworth Publishing Company, 1979.

Myers, Emma Harrison. *The Whys and Hows of Teaching Handwriting*. Columbus: The Zaner-Bloser Company, 1963.

Petty, Walter T. (Editor). *Curriculum for the Modern Elementary School*. Chicago, Illinois: Rand McNally College Publishing Company, 1976.

Rose, Karel. *Teaching Language Arts to Children*. New York: Harcourt, Brace and Jovanovich, 1982.

Strickland, Ruth G. *The Language Arts in the Elementary School*. Boston, Massachusetts, 1957. Chapters Twelve and Thirteen.

Tidyman, Willard, and Marguerite Butterfield. *Teaching the Language Arts*. Second Edition. New York: McGraw-Hill Book Company, 1959, Chapter Fifteen.

Trauger, Wilmer K. *Language Arts in Elementary Schools*. New York: McGraw-Hill Book Company, 1963, Chapter Five.

Yelon, Stephen and Grace Weinstein. *A Teacher's World, Psychology in the Classroom*. New York: McGraw-Hill Book Company, 1977.

18

Evaluation of Achievement in Language Arts

The teacher must think of and use a variety of approaches in assessing pupil achievement in the language arts. Evaluation of pupil progress in the language arts should be comprehensive. Thus, many facets of a child's development are evaluated including:

(a) social development;

(b) emotional achievement;

(c) academic learnings;

(d) physical development.

The teacher must assess pupil achievement continuously. Thus, as regularly as possible, each facet of a child's development must be assessed. Evaluation must also stress the importance not only of the teacher assessing pupil achievement but also the learner and involved parents being actively involved in quality programmes of assessment. Thus, cooperative appraisal of achievement and development is important.

Evaluation of learner progress must be emphasized in terms of stated objectives. Certainly, one cannot assess learner achievement unless it is in terms of criteria, standards, or objectives.

Teacher Observation in Assessing Achievement

There are many facets of pupils learning that the instructor may evaluate through the use of teacher of observation:

1. The teacher may observe which pupils have difficulties in identifying new words in reading and work in the direction of remedying these problem areas. Specific problems in word recognition should be pin-pointed such as using context clues, phonetic analysis, syllabication, picture clues, structural analysis, and configuration clues;
2. Learner comprehension in reading may be assessed by noticing which pupils do or do not respond in identified purposes such as acquiring facts, main ideas, generalizations, and sequence of content. Critical and creative reading skills also should be assessed;
3. At a discussion center, the teacher can observe the quality of interaction among participants. Thus, pupils may be evaluated in terms of desirable agreed upon criteria in the discussion;
4. At a writing center, the teacher may observe the quality of creative ideas expressed in the written product. Pupil achievement in properly using the mechanics of writing can also be appraised;
5. When pupils present a purposeful oral report to the class, the teacher may assess the quality of the presentation using desirable standards in the evaluation procedure.

Teacher-made Tests and Pupil Evaluation

At selected intervals the teacher may wish to write appropriate test items to evaluate learner achievement. The following sample test items have been written to indicate how this procedure may be utilized in assessing pupil achievement in the language arts:

1. Which of the following words is spelled correctly?

   (a) apple; *(b)* aple; *(c)* appl; *(d)* aplle.

2. A noun is a word which may be changed from singular to plural in number.

(True-false item)

3. Matching test

(a)	nouns	—	connecting or joining words
(b)	verbs	—	may refer to a person, place, or thing
(c)	adjectives	—	words revealing strong feeling
(d)	adverbs	—	may be changed from past to present tense
(e)	conjunctions	—	modify verbs
(f)	interjections	—	modify nouns

4. Discuss important standards which need to be followed in writing a good paragraph. (Essay item)

5. ______________ contains two lines of rhymed verse. (Completion item)

There are selected standards which teachers must follow in writing test items to assess pupil achievement:

1. The terms must be written on the understanding levels of pupils;
2. Pupils must have an adequately developed writing vocabulary to respond to selected teacher-written item such as essay and completion items;
3. Items on a matching must be homogeneous; thus, the items pertain to one topic or facet of the language arts such as parts of speech only, paragraph writing only, or usage items;
4. Adequate information must be written for completion items so that learners may determine needed content relating to blank spaces. The following completion item lacks adequate content: ______________, ______________, and ______________ are ______________;

5. Test items written to assess pupil achievement should attempt to measure relevant learnings only. Too frequently, pupils respond to the irrelevant and the unimportant;
6. All responses to the stem of a multiple choice item should be plausible. There should be no clues in the stem of the multiple choice item as to which response would be correct;
7. Tricky, vaguely written test items do not measure pupil achievement. These kinds of items definitely should be omitted in teacher developed tests;
8. In evaluating responses to essay items, ideas written by pupils are more important than the mechanics of writing, such as spelling, handwriting, capitalization, and punctuation. The mechanics of writing then may be separated from written content in assessing learner achievement.

Hopkins and Stanley wrote:

"Tests provide objective measurements on which educational decisions are based. From the standpoint of instruction, tests provide for feedback, motivation, and overlearning. From that of administration, they facilitate 'quality control', programme evaluation and research, classification and placement, selection, accreditation, mastery, and certification. From that of guidance, they serve to diagnose special aptitudes or abilities.

Rating Scales and Checklists

Rating scales and checklists may also be used to evaluate pupil achievement. In using the rating scale, the teacher must determine relevant behaviours of pupils to assess. The following is a model rating scale:

Name of pupil ______________ Date ______________

	Good	Average	Needs improving
Can write topic sentence well	______	______	______

Has unity of content within a paragraph	______	______	______
Displays appropriate sequence in paragraphs	______	______	______

In using a rating scale device to assess achievement, the teacher must evaluate each student in terms of what can be expected considering capacity and past achievement of the involved pupil. The teacher may forget individual pupil achievement unless selected observations are recorded.

The teacher must write relevant behaviours on a checklist when using this device to assess learner achievement. The following is an example of a checklist:

Name of pupil ______________ Date ______________

(Check the area or areas pupils need guidance in.)

1. The pupils speaks clearly when participating in discussions;
2. The learner respects ideas presented by others;
3. The pupil interacts with the thinking of others in a discussion.

The following criteria and considerations should be followed by teachers when developing and using scales and checklists to assess pupil achievement:

1. Only relevant behaviours should be written;
2. Behaviours should be specific and clearly stated;
3. Pupils should be involved in assessing their own achievement;
4. Feelings of the teacher will vary in making judgements when pupils are assessed at selected intervals;
5. Results from the assessment need to be used to improve the curriculum for each pupil.

Conferences and Assessing Achievement of Learners

Teacher-pupil conferences may be an excellent approach to use in assessing learner achievement. The following criteria should be emphasized in the conferences:

1. Mutual respect should be exhibited toward participants in the conference setting;
2. The thinking of the teacher and pupil must be respected;
3. Problem areas and possible solutions should be discussed in the conference;
4. Positive attitudes toward these conferences need to be developed and maintained.

Possible problem areas that can be identified through conferences could be the following:

1. the child's feeling toward reading content from library books;
2. specific difficulties that the pupil experiences in writing, such as agreement of subject and predicate, recognizing sentence pattern, reading content orally with voice inflection, and writing paragraphs using appropriate sequence;
3. the learner using appropriate stress, pitch, and juncture when presenting content orally;
4. specific problems that a child may have in speaking such as difficulties in articulation, voice control, or rate of speaking;
5. difficulties learner may experience in handwriting such as writing legibly, using correct letter formation, and aligning letters and words properly.

Parent-Teacher Conferences

Parents certainly must be involved in ongoing programmes of assessing pupil achievement. The child spends much time with parents or guardians. Thus, parents can have tremendous influence over their offspring. Relevant criteria must be adhered to in parent-teacher conference:

1. There must be a relaxed environment in assessing pupil achievement;
2. Respect for contributions made in a conference is a necessity;

3. Anger and hostility toward others definitely must not be a part of any conference;
4. Problem identification and possible solutions to these problems are key concepts to emphasize in parent-teacher conferences;
5. Results of any conference should not be used as a negative lever against pupils;
6. The teacher needs to be well prepared for the conference in having possible relevant items to discuss;
7. The major purpose of conducting parent-teacher conferences is to identify important problem areas and work in the direction of having an improved curriculum for each learner;
8. Notes should be written by the teacher for future reference when additional conferences are held.

Topics for consideration in a parent-teacher conference should be carefully selected. The support of parents must be enlisted in attempting to provide for each child in the class setting. The following are examples of areas to discuss in parent-teacher conferences:

1. guiding pupils in developing a desire to engage in creative writing in the home;
2. listening to the child read orally to parents in the home;
3. having an adequate number of library books for pupils in the home setting;
4. taking pupils on trips to nearby museums, libraries, and places of interest;
5. reading library books orally to preschool pupils containing interesting and meaningful content;
6. discussing ideas with children in the home setting to encourage listening and speaking skills.

Much information pertaining to a child can be obtained from parent-teacher conferences:

1. How parents feel toward their offspring?
2. What aspirations or goals parents have for their children?
3. How parents help their children in school work?
4. Concern shown by parents toward the child's achievement in school;
5. Willingness on the part of parents to cooperate with the teacher in developing an improved curriculum for pupils.

The teacher must be a good listener in a parent-teacher conference. This would be important for the following reasons:

1. to identify relevant problems with parents which need solving in order than an improved curriculum may be implemented for each learner;
2. to gather data pertaining to parental acceptance of each child.

The above obtained data must only be used to improve the curriculum for each individual learner.

Diaries, Logs, and Pupil Evaluation

Diaries and logs may be utilized effectively in appraising achievement. Learners reveal previous learnings obtained by writing diary entries and logs. Diary entries are written on a day to day basis by one child or by a committee on a rotation schedule. Logs are summaries written by a committee of pupils at selected intervals. All peoples in a class should have ample opportunities to experience the writing of diary or log entries.

The following is written as an example pertaining to diary entries in a unit of study pertaining to the Middle East:

September 1 (Monday). We studied about the Dead Sea which is about 1300 feet below sea level. There is no outlet from the Dead Sea; thus, the water has about 28 per cent mineral content. This makes it easy for anyone to float in the Dead Sea with no knowledge of swimming.

September 2 (Tuesday). Jericho is one of the oldest continuously inhabited cities on the face of the earth. It is a beautiful garden spot surrounded by desert land. Dates, oranges, bananas, grapefruit, figs, and pomegranates are grown here. Irrigation provides an adequate supply of water to grow crops.

September 3 (Wednesday). The Judean Hills located between Jerusalem and Jerricho look like mounds of sand dumped at different points. Jericho is about 700 feet below sea level while Jerusalem is about 2500 feet about sea level. The Judean Hills start to green in January and look very dry by September—the reason being that rain falls in Palestine only from November to April. There is no rain from April to November.

September 4 (Thursday). Old Jerusalem has a wall which surrounds it. The present wall around old Jerusalem was completed in 1542 by the Turks. There are very few cars driven inside the walls of Old Jerusalem; this is due to very narrow streets.

September 5 (Friday). The church of the Holy Sepulchre was built by the Crusaders in 1099 A.D. This church was built over the place where Crusaders believed Christ had been crucified and entombed.

Logs may be written at selected intervals by pupils to summarize previous learnings. Thus, in a unit on magnetism and electricity, the following summary statements may be written by pupils:

There are many different kinds of magnets such as bar, horseshoe, and electromagnets. Magnets have a north pole and a south pole. Poles of magnets can be determined in that opposite poles of magnets attract whereas like poles repel.

There are many advantages in having pupils individually or in committees write diary entries and log items:

1. Pupils reveal what has been learned previously;
2. Learners determine what is relevant to record;

3. Pupils can be creative in expressing ideas obtained;
4. Learners may select which committee they wish to participate in;
5. The mechanics of writing may also be assessed.

Standardized Tests

At selected intervals, it can be good procedure to use standardized tests to asses pupil achievement in areas such as *(a)* reading comprehension, *(b)* vocabulary growth, *(c)* purposes in reading, *(d)* capitalization, *(e)* spelling, *(f)* punctuation, *(g)* usage, and *(h)* grammar.

Results from standardized tests may be used to guide pupils in the following ways:

1. to diagnose pupils difficulties in different facets of the language arts;
2. to utilize data in developing a relevant language arts curriculum;
3. to select learning activities which aid pupils in achieving important objectives.

Results of standardized tests should not be utilized in the following negative ways:

1. As a 'lever' against a child to work up to grade level achievement pertaining to the present grade level the child is in;
2. A uniform curriculum in terms of scope and sequence for all learners;
3. Teachers teach learnings contained in the tests to pupils.

Sociometric Devices

Very frequently committee work is used in ongoing units of study in the language arts. All educators would agree that social development of pupils is of utmost importance. Thus, there are many reasons for emphasizing committee work:

1. to help pupils develop increased proficiency in getting along well with others;

2. to guide learners to gain relevant information as a result of having worked in committees;
3. to aid pupils in emotional adjustment through satisfying experiences in committee work.

In Summary

There are many techniques available to evaluate each pupil's achievement. Many approaches need to be used to assess learner achievement. Results obtained must be used to improve the curriculum.

Mehrens and Lehmann wrote the following summary statements, among others, on evaluation in education:

1. Measurement and evaluation are essential to sound educational decision making;
2. The term test often suggests presenting a standard set of questions to be answered;
3. The concept of measurement is broader than that of testing. We can measure characteristics in ways other than by giving tests;
4. Evaluation is the process of delineating, obtaining, and providing useful information for judging decision alternatives;
5. Every person must at some time make educational decisions;
6. A good decision is one that is based on relevant and accurate information. The responsibility of gathering and imparting that information belongs to the educator.

REFERENCES

Calder, Clarence R., Jr. and Eleanor M. Antan. *Techniques and Activities to Stimulate Verbal Learning New York:* The Macmillan Company, 1970.

Ediger, Marlow and Digumarti Bhaskara Rao, *Teaching Social Studies Successfully*, New Delhi, India: Discovery Publishing House, 2000.

Hopkins, Kenneth D., and Julian C. Stanley. Educational and Psychological Measurement and Evaluation. Sixth edition. Englewood Cliffs, New Jersey: Prentice Hall, Inc., 1981.

Langacker, Ronald W. *Language and Structure*. New York: Harcourt, Brace, and World, Inc., 1968.

Manning, Duane. *Toward A Humanistic Curriculum*. New York: Harper and Row, Publishers, 1971.

Mehrens, William A., and Irvin J. Lehmann. *Measurement and Evaluation in Education and Psychology*. Third edition. New York: Holt, Rinehart and Winston, 1984.

Newman, Harold (Ed.). *Effective Language Arts Practices in the Elementary School*. New York: John Wiley and Sons, Inc., 1972.

Ober, Richard, et. al. *Systematic Observation of Teaching*. Englewood Cliffs: Prentice-Hall, Inc., 1971.

Ragan, William B., and Gene D., Shepherd. *Modern Elementary Curriculum*. Sixth edition. New York: Host, Rinehart, and Winston, Inc., 1982. Chapter three.

Raths, James, et. al. (Eds.) *Studying Teaching*. Second edition. Englewood Cliffs: Prentice-Hall, Inc., 1971.

Remmers, H.H., et. al. *A Practical Introduction to Measurement and Evaluation*. New York: Harper and Row, Publishers, 1960.

Taylor, Ronald L. *Assessment of Exceptional Students*. Englewood Cliffs, New Jersey: Prentice-Hall, Inc., 1984.

Walsh, Bruce W., and Nancy E. Betz. *Tests and Assessments*. Englewood Cliffs, New Jersey: Prentice-Hall, Inc., 1985.

19

The Structure of the English Language

The structure of the English language is important for pupils to know about. Knowing structural ideas can assist learners in getting the feeling of what comes next sequentially in oral or silent reading. Having objectives to achieve pertaining to these structural ideas can be quite abstract and difficult. We have observed in classrooms at different grade levels how learning key ideas and these structural ideas can be interesting and useful in reading. During the 1960s and 1970s, the structure of each academic disciplines became major objectives for pupil attainment. However, educators must say that careful selection of what to teach is always important. The structure of knowledge emphasizes the selection of what is relevant and important to teach. It is ridiculous to think that the structure of knowledge movement was stressed only in the 1960s and 1970s. Determining key ideas and main ideas to teach is always important. Determining the structure of the English language, and any language for that matter, is very important. Much wasting of time occurs if teachers teach what is irrelevant and unimportant. The structure of knowledge movement also emphasized that pupils learn these ideas inductively. Inductive learning today is very important. Pupils like to discover rather than receive knowledge through lecture or heavy use of explanations. When pupils engage in problem solving, they are learning inductively. Thus, a problem is determined by pupils with teacher guidance in an ongoing lesson or unit of study. The problem is contextual and not outside the present learning activity being pursued. The problem indicates feelings of perplexity and uncertainty as to a course of action. The problem needs to be clear and unambiguous.

Pupils may then obtain information in answer to the problem. A variety of learning opportunities may be involved here when securing needed information or data. Sometimes, much time is needed in the solving of problems. At other times, instant decisions need to be made. Little time is then available to gather information. The information secured is used to develop an answer or hypothesis. The hypothesis is evaluated in a real life situation. Inductive learning then is used in problem solving, be it in literature or any curriculum area. Problem solving is always important in school and in society due to individuals facing problems in many facets of life.

Learning structural ideas can be quite complicated and lack purpose such as application. However, we have come to believe, after observing many student and cooperating teachers in the public schools, that enjoyable ways can be found to have pupils achieve key, major ideas in English as it relates to reading instruction. Listening, speaking, and writing are also involved here.

To emphasize the structure of knowledge approach in teaching, the teacher should:

1. have an excellent knowledge of major generalisations in sentence patterns since these key ideas become objectives for learner attainment;
2. sequence learning opportunities in that individuals experience the enactive (objects and items), the iconic (semi-concrete materials of instruction), and the symbolic (abstract ideas);
3. appraise pupils to ascertain how many of these structural ideas are being attained by pupils in a spiral curriculum. With a spiral curriculum, pupils meet up

again and again at increasing levels of complexity the structural ideas which serve as objectives of instruction;

4. ask quality questions of pupils so that they may truly learn in an inductive manner. Inductive teaching then assist pupils to achieve the structural ideas;
5. use enactive, iconic and symbolic materials in inductive approaches in learning (Ediger, 1997).

Sentence Patterns

There are five sentence patterns, in particular, that pupils should have knowledge about in order to become more proficient in reading. These five patterns will come up again and again in oral or silent reading. Enjoyable, yet scholarly methods may be used to guide pupil achievement in attaining these five sentence patterns. The first pattern is the subject/predicate pattern. The reading teacher may take sentences from the basal reader or a library book read by children to illustrate sentence pattern. Sentence pattern number one—Boys swim. There are just two words here to express a complete thought or idea. Pupils in class can be asked for another word which would replace 'Boys'. There are numerous correct responses here. One word is 'girls'. A brain-storming approach can be very interesting for pupils to see how many words would fit in. The sentence pattern stays the same and yet the subject changed from 'Boys' to 'Girls'.

Pupils may wish to do journal writing on different sentence patterns discussed in class. It is good too if learners reflect upon what has been written. Reflecting stresses thinking about diverse sentence patterns and using these win writing sentences in journal writing. Application of what has been learned emphasizes review, practice and use of sentence patterns in a multitude of ways. Pupils may wish to bring pictures to class which illustrate what is shown in an illustration. These illustrations are also good to indicate concepts stressed in sentence patterns, such as 'Fish swim' for sentence pattern number one above.

A next sequential question could call for words that replace the predicate part 'swim'. Responses to be given by pupils might include the most obvious word 'swam'. Learners need to experiment with different words to take to place of 'swims', such as using a singular subject with a singular predicate. Here, pupils could dramatize or use pantomime to illustrate a verb in a sentence. When verbs show action, it is relatively easy to dramatize/pantomime the contents.

A second sentence pattern for pupils to study and experience is the subject/predicate/direct object pattern, such as Bill hit the ball. Here again, pupils may suggest an endless number of words to substitute for the subject 'Bill'. Substitutions could also be made for the predicate 'hit', as well as for the direct object 'ball'. Substitutions for each of these three words could be the following, as an example—Carl, caught and fish. Most pupils enjoy working with sentence patterns in this way. They also notice how the English language works, even with changes being made.

A third sentence pattern involves the subject/linking verb, predicate adjective pattern, such as 'Flowers are beautiful'. This sentence pattern brought on diversity of responses from a class of fourth graders when they noticed the many words that may be substituted and yet the sentence pattern stays the same. One pupil brought a vase of flowers to school, a concrete experience, to show the third sentence pattern mentioned. After the class discussed the vase with flowers, pupils added another learning activity not previously mentioned above. The activity emphasized using concrete materials in the classroom to show sentence pattern number three—Flowers are beautiful. What did pupils come up with? The following materials were used to show this sentence pattern:

1. The eraser was dusty. This sentence stressed what was observed at the chalkboard.
2. The food was delicious. This sentence came from eating in the school lunchroom.
3. The desk was dirty. A pupil observed his own desk in the classroom.

A fourth sentence pattern is represented by the subject/predicate/indirect object/direct object pattern such as, 'Sally, gave Sue a present. Sally gave 'what'? The answer is 'present'. 'Present' is the direct object whereas to whom was the present given? The answer is 'Sue'. 'Sue' is the indirect object.

At this point, pupils may be ready to experiment with what makes for a subject of a sentence. The subject will tend to be a noun or pronoun. A noun is a word that can be changed from singular to plural, such a girl/girls and woman/women. Singular refers to one whereas plural indicates two or more of something. This is relatively easy for pupils to access. Pupils may also experiment with the subject doing the acting, such as 'caught' the ball. The subject may also receive the action such as the package was wrapped by Alice. Thus, something was done to the object of the sentence which was 'package'.

In their journals, pupils listed nouns and checked these with the teacher. Pupils in committees drew pictures of nouns representing those which are singular as compared to those which are plural. Active and passive voice of subjects was dramatizes such as—The boy was revived by two classmates. Here, a pupil lay motionless on the floor with two classmates. Applying artificial respiration! Pupils do like to dramatize and be creative in the language arts involving the study of sentence patterns.

A fifth sentence pattern is the subject/predicate/predicate nominative pattern, such as 'Alice is a singer'. Alice equals singer in this sentence. It names the same person. 'Alice' is singular and needs a singular verb such as 'is'. 'Alice is also the name of a person and thus comes under the traditional definition of what a noun is, such as a person place, or thing. The word 'singer' is a noun too since it refers to a person. 'Singer' is singular and when comparing that word with 'singers' where more than one person is in evidence.

Pupils can provide many responses as to substitutions that can be made for the words—Alice, is, singer; the sentence pattern of subject/predicate/predicate nominative would stay the same, e.g. Bob was a swimmer (Ediger, 1988).

In studying these five sentence patterns, pupils do not need to memorize content. In fact, when brain-storming, many correct responses are given by learners and they can experience much success inductively. Open-ended answers are given by pupils are these usually harmonize with the many possibilities that are necessary in terms of responses given. Pupils need to be successful learners so that they are increasingly more motivate. Pupils tend to develop knowledge and feelings pertaining to the structure of the English language which assist then to read in a more confident manner. For example, the subject/predicate sentence pattern indicates there are certain words that would fit into this pattern. Pupils then receive cues and clues as to which words should follow in sequence (Ediger, 1997).

Higher levels of cognition might well be an end result when pupils engage in thinking about different sentence patterns. Sternberg (1997) has developed an excellent model for the teachers to use when teaching and pupils are assisted to think at a higher cognitive level.

Memory: Remember what a gerund is or what the name of Tom Sawyer's aunt was.

Analysis: Compare the functions of a gerund to that of a participate, or compare the personality of Tom Sawyer to that of Huckleberry Finn.

Creativity: Invent a sentence that effectively uses a gerund, or write a very short story with Tom Sawyer as a character.

Practicality: Find gerunds in newspapers or magazine articles are describe how they are used or say what general lesson about persuasion can be learned from Tom Sawyer's way of persuading his friends to whitewash Aunt Polly's fence.

Let's consider sentence pattern number one—The subject/predicate pattern—'Boys swim'. Using the Strenberg model, the lowest level of thinking would be memory. Here, pupils could recall 'the subject/predicate sentence pattern. They might also recall what a noun is and what verb is. For *analysis*, pupils may be asked to explain the difference between the noun and the verb. The stress *creativity*, the pupils may be asked to write a sentence containing a noun and a verb. For *practically*, pupils might locate nouns and verbs in a very short story.

The Thornberg model provides guidance to teachers in having pupils move upward to higher levels of thought with four levels, namely memory, analysis, creativity and practicality in studying grammar as well as in the structure of the English language.

Expanding Sentences

Pupils with teacher guidance enjoy making sentences longer or expanding them. For each of the five sentence patterns discussed above, the sentence can be expanded. If we take the first sentence pattern of subject/predicate—Alice is a singer, the word 'Alice' does lend itself to expansion with single words, but it does better with phrases and clauses. One could say 'Brave Alice is a singer'. The single word 'brave' describes 'Alice'. If a noun 'girl' is substituted for 'Alice'. Then an endless number of single words may be given to describe 'girl'. The following are provided as examples: small, tall, young, bashful, aggressive and hostile among others. There are many predicate nominatives that can take the place of 'singer' such as older, younger, experienced, amateur, beautiful and tall among others.

Phrases are another way to expanding sentences. Generally, pupils rather easily that phrases contain more than one word and yet do not contain a subject and predicate. The following are phrases which modify 'girl':

1. with a red sweater, such as "The girl with a red sweater was a singer";
2. feeling well, such as "Feeling well, the girl was a singer";
3. On the pond, such as "The girl on the pond was a singer".

Later on, in sequence and when readiness is in evidence, pupils may study and learn if a phrase is adjective and modifies a noun or is adverb and modifies a verb, adjective or another adverb.

A clause can do much to clarify meanings in a sentence and at the same time the concept of expansion is being emphasized:

The girl *who has black hair* is a singer.

The dependent clause is underlined and contains a subject 'who' and a direct object 'hair'. A clause has a subject and a predicate, but does not express a complete thought.

Pupils, may provide words which take the place of the subject 'girl' and the predicate nominative 'singer'. They may also give words that replace the direct object of the dependent clause 'hair'. Pupils should notice that a dependent clause does not make sense by itself, *e.g.* "who has black hair'. The verb or predicate of the dependent clause 'has' may also be changed to 'had' and yet the pattern of sentence is the same. The teacher should make lessons interesting and meaningful on sentence patterns and no go beyond what pupils can possibly understand. The goal inherent in sentence patterns is for pupils to feel and understand similarities in a sentence pattern. Pupils will become better readers as a result. Pupils will know that the English language has unique routines which are predictable, such as each of the five sentence patterns. They will understand how to expand sentences and why this is done. When pupils read, they will notice these same patterns of expansion, such as single word adjectives and adverbs; adjective and adverb phrases and adjective, adverb and noun clauses. At the beginning in sequence, pupils will learn about single words modifying the subject and predicate pattern; subject, predicate, direct object pattern; subject, linking verb, predicate nominative pattern; subject linking verb, predicate adjective pattern; and subject predicate, indirect object, direct object pattern.

What about pupils using technical terminology such as 'predicate nominative'? We would say the teacher may use these and other complex terms, but not require pupils to memorize them. Meaning, however, is very important for pupils as to what a predicate nominative is when sequencing learning opportunities (Ediger, 1996).

Evaluation of Pupil Achievement

There are numerous procedures to use in evaluating pupil achievement pertaining to knowledge and skills in the structure or patterns of sentences. Teacher observation can be an excellent approach, providing quality standards are used. With teacher observation, the philosophy of constructivism is in evidence. Thus, within context, pupils are applying what has been learned about sentence patterns. Within the framework of every day lessons, pupils are indicating progress in contextual situations.

Standardized and norm referenced tests may be used to ascertain pupil achievement. However, pupils are showing here how well they have achieved outside the context of learning. Tests, no doubt, will always be with us and we can use results from these tests to indicate where pupils specifically need help. Diagnosis and remediation would then be involved.

Howard Gardner's (1993) theory of multiple intelligence has much to offer in terms of how to evaluate pupil achievement. As the name indicates, pupils have numerous intelligences, not just one only. Pupils individually may possess one or more of these intelligences:

1. verbal/linguistic such as reading and writing well;
2. logical/mathematical such as in strengths of the left brain hemisphere with its logical thinking as well as the other component parts in mathematical proficiency;
3. visual/spatial such as pupils excelling in art work, geometry and architecture;
4. musical intelligence such as in composing, singing and playing musical instruments;
5. bodily/kinesthetic such as in athletics, dance and pantomime;
6. interpersonal such as pupils doing well when working harmoniously in group settings;

7. intrapersonal whereby pupils achieved well on an individual basis;
8. scientific in which pupils use methods of objectivity in scientific knowledge obtained;
9. the human experience such as in coping well with the everyday problems that come about.

How then does the Theory of Multiple intelligences relate to pupil learning and evaluation in the structure of knowledge in reading and writing?

First, the heart of knowing about and using sentence patterns emphasizes verbal/linguistic intelligence. Here, pupils reveal their strengths through oral use of and written work in sentence patterns. Using these patterns in oral and silent reading also stresses use of the structure of language. We must remember, pupils with other intelligences may not reveal what has been learned through verbal/linguistic intelligence, although this must always be stressed in ongoing lessons and units of study. With logical intelligence, the pupil, needs to realize, for example, that substitutions made for the subject/predicate/direct objective pattern of sentence need to be logical. We have noticed pupils who make illogical substitutions such as Bill (subject) caught (predicate) the 'if'. The word 'if' does not fit in logically.

Bodily/kinesthetic intelligence may be used frequently since pupils can dramatize content in a sentence pattern and attach meaning in so doing. Interpersonal or intrapersonal intelligence may be used in that the former stresses pupils working in committees where the latter emphasizes learners working individual on sentence patterns. We should add musical intelligence here since pupils individually who are talented in music may wish to put sentence patterns to an appropriate rhythm. A pupil even invented a dance to go along with syllabication related to a musical accompaniment. There are many possibilities here when stressing using multiple intelligences. Pupils individually may be able to reveal learning better through multiple intelligences as compared to using verbal/linguistic approaches only/largely when studying structure in the English language.

Conclusion

Pupils having knowledge and skill pertaining to the structure of the English language should become better readers and writers. There are sentence patterns which hold true again and again. There are ways of expanding sentences which are also very consistent. Learners need to enjoy learning opportunities emphasizing structure in the English language. It certainly need not be boring or dull and dry. Rather there are learning opportunities which fascinate pupils and motivate toward greater achievement.

As pupils study the structure of the English language, they should be better able to predict what will come in sequence in reading as well as in writing. Vocabulary growth and development should also be in the offing since pupils experiment with sentences, words, phrases and clauses. There should be much journal writing on the part of pupils when reading and writing are stressed as being interrelated. When pupils hypothesize as to which words might take the place of others in a sentence, individual differences are provided for and all may be successful learners because each pupil can present possible words in context.

The interests of pupils need to be focused upon structural ideas and their component parts. The teacher needs to be certain that pupils are attaching meaning to these structural ideas. There are not be memorized for purposes of passing a test, but rather to use what has been learned in reading and writing. Thus, the level of application is very important since structural ideas have much use. We believe that teachers need to spend time in having pupils perceive how learning the structure of language is practical in reading and writing across the curriculum.

REFERENCES

Ediger, Marlow (1997), *Teaching Mathematics in the Elementary School*, Kirksville, Missouri: Simpson Publishing Company, 28.

Ediger, Marlow (1988), *Language Arts Curriculum in the Elementary School*. Kirksville, Missouri: Simpson Publishing Company, 8-18.

Ediger, Marlow (1997), *The Modern School*. Kirksville, Missouri: Simpson Publishing Company, 199.

Ediger, Marlow (1996), *Elementary Education*. Kirksville, Missouri: Simpson Publishing Company, 38-39.

Gardner, Howard (1993), *Multiple Intelligences: The Theory in Practice*. New York: The Basic Books.

Lakshmi, Bhagya L. and Bhaskara Rao, Digumarti (1999). *Reading and Comprehension*. New Delhi: Discovery Publishing House.

Thornberg, Robert J. (1997), "What Does it Means to be Smart?" *Educational Leadership*, 54 (6), 20-24.

20

The Literature Curriculum

What can the teacher do to encourage pupils to read library books in the classroom setting? Chambers recommends the following:

> *"First, and above all, is our attitude about the role of reading—real reading—in the classroom. If we help students understand that the purpose of developmental reading and the acquisition of reading skills is to give them the key to the world of literature and all its wonders, we have moved forward, indeed. The library, or the library corner, should not be a place for free activity alone, or an extracurricular activity. Instead, it should be an interesting place to which children can go often, expecting to find an exciting, changing collection of good books. It should be a place of adventure and delight where children are encouraged to hunt, browse, and explore. It should be a place where he can choose books that will give him answers or provide delight. Weekly book talks can attest to our attitude about books. By our attention to a good trade book in the book talk, we indicate the worthwhileness of children's literature. Children are affected by our attitudes toward things. That is part of the way then learn. The way we view the role of children's literature as part of their lives does a great deal in teaching them the value of reading that literature.*
>
> *Special and adequate time for reading is vital in helping children become readers of books. Recreational reading is not to be considered a haphazard, spotty activity, or suitable only for out-of-school reading. We can assign regular times during the school week to trade book reading. Often two regular reading periods can be given to recreational reading, leaving the other three days of that period to*

> *basal devices and skill building. These periods of recreational reading can be part of the class routine—to be expected with the regularity of arithmetic, spelling, and social studies."*

Pupils need to experience a quality literature curriculum. Thus, the reading curriculum needs to go beyond goals of having learners identify new words as well as developing skills pertaining to diverse types of comprehension. There are numerous reasons for emphasizing a quality literature curriculum.

First of all, pupils cannot experience all facets of living directly. They can learn, however, from vicarious experiences, *e.g.* reading what others have done, achieved, acquired, and experienced. There are, of course, selected experiences that none of us would wish to live through. Thus, a reader can learn much from others' deeds, thoughts, and acts. A reader might then be able to formulate his/her own goals in life more adequately through reading what others have experienced. There are groups in society who wish to censor diverse selections from the literature curriculum. The censored selections appear much more so on the senior high school level than the elementary school level. The literature curriculum, however, must assist pupils to formulate their own goals and purposes in life.

Values can be dictated to pupils by parents, teachers, and others in society. Too frequently, dictation of values to the young has been effective. Also, the dictated values may not be appropriate in a changing society. Conservative values then might not be applicable in the coming years. There are values, however, that have endured in space and time, such as doing unto others that which we would want done to us. Even then, in changing times and situations, the Golden Rule needs reinterpretations and modified implementations. From a study of literature, pupils can evaluate and adopt selected desired values. Donoghue wrote:

> *While the children's first exposure to literature is Mother Goose and other rhymes and stories. children should gradually experience every type and form of literature in a school programme that is*

comprehensive and sequentially plotted throughout the elementary grades. Such a programme not only strengthens the developmental reading curriculum but contributes in a significant way to the attainment of several other objectives of elementary education as listed below:

- *The school aims to meet the needs of individual pupils—and literature is widely diversified;*
- *The school aims to provide a learning program which will utilize the natural interests of its pupils—and literature appeals to all age groups;*
- *The school aims to provide socially satisfying experiences for its children and to develop in its pupils a wider social understanding—and good stories and pleasing verse are enjoyed more when they are shared with others;*
- *The school aims to give each child self-insight—and books introduced in childhood can sometimes bring about a profound change in one's outlook on life;*
- *The school aims to give each pupil in knowledge and appreciation of his cultural heritage—and literature is the means whereby much of that heritage is preserved and perpetuated;*
- *The school aims to stimulate and foster creative expression—and book experiences are an exciting springboard to art, drama, and other expressionistic activities.*

Secondly, reading quality literature can provide relaxation for the reader. Much is spoken and written about means of coping with stress. Individuals in society need to cope with many unwanted situations. The involved person needs to find ways of dealing with stress. Reading can be a good way of restoring equilibrium. One can forget about stressful situations when reading. The reader can become so thoroughly engrossed in reading ideas that little or no time in inherently available for worrying, regretting, or fearing.

The teacher and parents must be actively involved in assisting pupils to become proficient in reading. The teacher alone cannot perform this vital responsibility for the pupil. Parents must also like reading and support a quality reading curriculum in the school/class setting. The pupil must assume major responsibility in wanting to learn to read. Otherwise, how can a pupil learn to read in order to achieve goals pertaining to relaxing the self?

Thirdly, literature for pupils can provide a guidance resource. There are learners who experience grave personal and social problems. Difficulties are involved when identifying problems and attempting to assist pupils in overcoming these difficulties. No doubt, an adequate number of good counsellors are lacking in the school setting. Children's literature can provide assistance to pupils in attempting to cope with personal and social problems. What kinds of problems do pupils experience? These might well include poverty, shyness, aggressiveness, hostility, ill health, obesity, excessiveness tallness or shortness, and loneliness. The teacher needs to guide pupils individually to choose library books which assist in coping with problematic situations.

Fourthly, each pupil may receive assistance from reading literature in becoming knowledgeable about diverse kinds of careers. Too frequently, workers in society have drifted into a job or occupation. The 'drifting' into the world of work has made for feelings of dissatisfaction in the occupational/vocational arena. Certainly, a quality career education programme an provide pupils with selected understandings, skills, and attitudes needed to be successful ultimately in the world of work. Each person needs to achieve optimally in the career arena. Working at jobs/occupations that are not personally rewarding can make for feelings of futility. Literature on careers written for learners on different achievement levels can provide necessary subject matter for pupils contemplating the world of work.

The centralized/classroom library needs library books and other reading materials on diverse levels of achievement pertaining to many relevant careers. The teacher needs to introduce learners to reading materials on careers. With appropriate readiness experiences, learners can be guided to read content pertaining to the world of work.

Fifthly, skills in reading can be developed when literature is being read by children. Too frequently, basal textbooks are read by learners. Basal materials may not meet the reading needs of selected pupils. Then too, library books generally are chosen by the involved learner; the subject matter in these books is usually not assigned to pupils, unless a specific purpose is involved. Teachers may feel that too many pupils are turned off in reading when basal materials are utilized in the reading curriculum. Library books chosen by the involved pupil may provide the needed spark to encourage reading.

Sixthly, pupils can learn much subject matter related to different curriculum areas when engaged in the reading of library books. There are library books written on diverse levels of achievement pertaining to many nations on the face of the earth. Thus, pupil achievement in diverse social studies units can be aided when selected library books are read. In other curriculum areas—science, mathematics, health, art, music, and physical education—related library books are in evidence which learners may read.

Montebello listed the following criteria for teacher self-evaluation suggestions, as well as pupil evaluation suggestions:

Teacher Self-Evaluation Suggestions

1. Do I have a planned literature programme as part of an integrated language arts curriculum?
2. Does my classroom reflect a well-planned, thoughtfully organized body of literature experiences?
3. Do I focus on literature as literature as well as use tradebooks to enhance and enrich studies in other curriculum areas?
4. Is 'pleasure' present in my literature programme?
5. Is there a balanced programme between instruction and the encouragement of individual free reading?
6. Is time for independent reading scheduled and provided?
7. Is time available regularly?
8. Do I guide youngsters into the delights of reading for enjoyment as well as for information?
9. Do I read aloud to the youngsters as a way of introducing them to the best in literature?
10. Does the reading aloud occur in intermediate grades as well as in primary grades?

11. Do I go beyond literature stories in the readers?
12. Are enough tradebooks sufficiently accessible to youngesters in my classroom?
13. Do those tradebooks reflect the diversity of interest, tastes, and abilities present in my classroom?
14. Are my feelings for books reflected in the behaviours I exhibit toward and about books?
15. Am I enthusiastic for and about literature?
16. Do I give literature a respected place in the school programme?
17. How many new tradebooks have I read this year?

Pupil Evaluation Suggestions

1. Does he read?
2. Does his attitude reflect a desire to read?
3. Is he 'catching' an appreciation for good books?
4. Does he read widely?
5. Does he choose to read for enjoyment?
6. Does he read for personal purposes as well?
7. How much does he read?
8. What does he read?
9. How does he interpret his reading achievement? Is it limited to skill development, or does progress in reading include appreciational and recreational reading?
10. When he evaluates his success in reading, does he include personal reading and appreciation as part of achievement?
11. Does he apply what he read to his life?

Quality Literature in the Curriculum

Most basal reading programmes tend to emphasize pupils' mastering diverse word recognition techniques, such as using configuration clues, phonetic analysis, syllabication, structural analysis, context clues, and picture clues. The ultimate goal in word recognition for pupils should be the recognize words immediately as sight words. In addition to word recognition techniques, basal reading approach emphasizes learners achieving comprehension skills such as reading to acquire facts, directions a sequence of ideas, main ideas, and generalization, as well as reading critically, reading creatively, and reading to solve problems. However, there are additional ingredients that need to become a part of a relevant literature curriculum for children.

Setting of the Story

The language arts teacher needs to guide pupils to understand and attach meaning to the setting of a story or library book. Where did the events take place? Pupils need to understand if events took place in a rural, urban or suburban area. Also, learners need to attach meaning to which city, state, or nation one or more events took place. Certainly, human behaviour differs when events in literature take place in a rural, as compared to suburban or urban region. Behaviour of human beings, of course, differs much among individuals within a rural, or a suburban, or an urban region.

In dealing with the setting of a story, pupils also need to understand *when* an event (or events) took place. Time is a significant factor to consider when the reader attempts to attach meaning to content in children's literature. Historical fiction, for example, pertains to a study of selected events in the past. Types of transportation, clothing, homes, schools, communication, recreational endeavours, and foods eaten might well depend upon the period of time being studied in history. Thus, a pupil needs to consider time elements, as well as geographical regions when attaching meaning to children's literature.

The specifics or details of the setting may either be suggested or stated directly. The setting of a story might also reveal characterization, as well as sequential ensuing events in the story.

Characterization

In addition to the setting of a story, professional writers of novels also spend considerable time in describing the involved characters. What kind of a person (or persons) are specific individuals within a story? Do the individuals remain stable in terms of traits possessed, or are growth and change inherent? There certainly are numerous character traits that any one individual may possess. A person might then be shy but friendly, intelligent, hard working, and achievement oriented. The same person may also posses traits of being altruistic.

A different person might be aggressive, hostile, irresponsible, and handsome. The person may possess traits of being intelligent but not utilizing talents and abilities possessed. Thus, each learner should be guided to describe character traits of human beings in a story. Inferences must also be developed. Writers, of course, do not always state factually the kinds of characters within a story. To be able to attach meaning to content read, pupils need to understand the concept of *characterization* as it relates to actual human beings in a story or novel.

There are diverse means used by authors to describe personality and character of human beings. Thus, a writer may discuss the effect of one character on others. The feelings and thoughts within each character might be described. Also, the physical appearance, deeds, and speech of any character need adequate consideration within a story. Reasons for each character behaving as he/she did should be analyzed by pupils.

Plot in the Literature Curriculum

Language arts teachers need to assist learners, inductively and/or deductively, to discover the plot in a given literary selection. Thus, the pupil is guided to ascertain *what* happened in a story. Too frequently, pupils have completed reading a library book without understanding what truly happened in the selection. Diverse kinds of comprehension skills need to be developed within learner in order to understand the concept of plot. Two previous concepts discussed, related to a quality literature curriculum, involved *setting* and *characterization*. These concept in any literary selection need understanding so that comprehensive meaning is attached to a sequence of happenings involving *plot*. If pupils do not understand what actually happened in a given selection, they have not understood the plot of a library book or story. Essential ingredients in a quality literature curriculum must be emphasized by the language arts teachers. Thus, the *plot* of a selection needs to be understood by learners; otherwise, comprehension and meaning are being omitted in the ongoing literature curriculum.

A quality literature curriculum involves pupils utilizing diverse word recognition techniques. Also, an adequate number of purposes in comprehension needs emphasis in ongoing lessons and units. In addition to mastering word recognition techniques and developing comprehension proficiency, learners need to attach meaning to literary concepts, such as *setting*, *characterization*, and *plot*.

Tiedt and Tiedt wrote:

> *Literature has seldom been part of the reading programme in the elementary school, for reading has been dominated by the basal reading series. What are the advantages of a literature-reading programme over the traditional controlled-vocabulary anthology? The use of literature in a reading programme for elementary school students offers quality content to a course of study which has concentrated solely on the teaching of skills. It is time that we acknowledge the value of provocative material in exciting the student about reading. Until we have this excitement present in the reading lesson, we will not develop a nation of readers.*
>
> *Many titles from children's literature can be, and are being, used as reading text material. The advantages of Pippi Longstocking, a Wrinkle in Time, and Johnny Tremain over the familiar basal reader are overwhelming:*
>
> 1. *Excellent writing-imagery, use of words, storytelling ability.*
> 2. *Continuity of a longer story—plot development, characterization;*
> 3. *Greater interest value—intrigue, atmosphere, entertainment,*
> 4. *Integration of literature, language, and composition studies.*

Point of View

In analyzing subject matter in a quality literature curriculum, pupils also need to be guided to understand who, in particular, is telling the story. Thus, from whose point of view are the events are incidents being told? Pupils need to notice if and when characters in a story actually speak, or is a narrative account being presented? In the first, second, or third person (noun or pronoun) actually presenting ideas, rather than sequential descriptions being utilized in presenting ideas?

Meanings attached to reading a story, novel, or library book may vary much depending upon *who* is presenting sequential content. Professional writers of novels pay much attention to point of view in developing literary works.

If the author or a character in the story tells sequential content, the story is delimited to the thoughts, experiences, perceptions, and expressions of that person relating ordered events in the literature being read. The narrator is the person telling the story. If the author tells the story, he/she generally, remains anonymous and makes few or no references to the personal self. Generally, if a character in the story is narrating content, he/she refers to the self as 'I'.

Theme in Literature

What is the main idea in the story, library book, or novel? Thus, pupils need to consider the concept of *theme. Theme* involves the author's idea or ideas pertaining to situations in life. The writer may directly state the involved theme. The theme might also be implied. Ordinarily, *theme* as a concept does not involve moral standards, or rules to live by. In reading a literary selection, the reader needs to ask what the consumable content says about nature, about people, and about life itself.

Irony of the Situation

Each learner needs readiness experience to achieve objectives in the literature curriculum. Never should teachers emphasize selected goals unless pupils can be successful in achieving the stated objectives. Pupils, as well as the teacher, become frustrated if the former are not ready to attain new ends. Feelings of failure hinder pupils in developing an adequate self-concept. Feelings of adequacy are necessary in order to achieve relevant goals. Thus, pupils need to be ready to understand the concept of *irony of the situation*, or it should not be emphasized in the literature curriculum.

What is *irony of the situation*? Events turn out differently for any one character, as compared to what the involved reader anticipated. Supposing, a character is portrayed as having experienced a noble, undefiled background. As a surprise tactic, the writer reveals, directly or indirectly, that the character was involved in a series of thefts and robberies. Or, a person having grown up in highly unfortunate settings becomes a quality leader in the community. As a further example, a person in combat files numerous successful bombing missions over enemy territory. The same character arrives home safely, only to die in an automobile accident involving travel to a routine destination.

In the concept of *irony* in literature, the author tries to hide his true feelings, pertaining to an incident, event, or deed. The character's deeds may not be consistent with stated beliefs.

Satire in Literature

Selected writers in literature emphasize *satire* as a means of evaluating people and society. The purpose involved in satire is to expose ill, evils, or follies in order to promote an improved society. Humour may be used to expose weaknesses in society. Sometimes, caustic bitterness is also utilized by selected writers of satire.

Supposing that satire is used in literature, the writer may state rational, worthwhile listed goals in a school that learners are to achieve. Students, however, are uninspired and bored in school. The absentee rate is high and tardy students are quite apparent when the school day starts.

As a second example of *satire*, the writer may quote teachers saying to pupils how important it is to read good library books and to read whenever it is possible to do so. In reality the teacher is poorly prepared for each day of teaching and views television, uncritically, each spare moment of time devoted to recreational endeavours. Thus, in actual life the teacher does little or no reading.

Learning Activities in the Literature Curriculum

Which kinds of experiences might learners pursue as a result of their endeavours in reading quality literature?

Pupils individually with teacher guidance may discuss content read. The language arts teacher needs to be knowledgeable about the content of many library books written for children. Thus, the teacher may ask selected questions involving comprehension of content in the chosen book completed by the learner. Questions discussed should stimulate, not minimize, reading of children's literature on the part of the learner.

A pupil may pencil sketch a favourite setting, plot, or character contained in a library book. Comprehension may well be revealed by the involved learner in the completed pencil sketch. The drawing must reveal comprehension, and not the work of a professional artist. To be sure, quality art work needs to be emphasized by the individual learner in terms of optimal progress.

A learner may write a letter to the author of the library book read. Hopefully, the pupil will receive an actual response from the writer. The pupil may wish to express appreciation for content in the book. Also, the pupil may wish to write specifically what was of interest in the completed library book.

A diorama may be made be a learner containing a three dimensional scene of major generalizations achieved, as a result of reading. The goal of diorama development is to portray scenes and situations as neatly and accurately as possible. Hopefully, the art activity will stimulate pupil interest in reading.

Additional learning activities for pupils involving children's literature include:

1. writing and advertisement to encourage other learners to read the same library book;
2. presenting an advertisement orally indicating the merits of the completed library book;

3. giving a critical analysis indicating strengths and weaknesses of a book read in children's literature;
4. role playing the writer of a library book to indicate purposes in its writings;
5. writing a different setting or plot;
6. reading a different book by the same author or a book containing a similar title;
7. writing a play based on the contents of the library book;
8. engaging in a pantomime or in a creative dramatics presentation involving selected content read;
9. developing sequential illustrations pertaining to ideas read;
10. presenting an oral report to the class, following desired standards, involving salient ideas in the completed library book;
11. participating in a seminar involving depth discussion with other learners who have read the same literary work;
12. outlining interesting content from a story or library book;
13. writing a summary containing significant subject matter;
14. developing a bookmark or book jacket for a chosen library book;
15. writing creative content, such as what if the setting of the library book had taken place in *(indicate a geographical region)*, rather than its actual setting. Or, what if the main character had not been a part of the story, how would the ending have differed?

Fisher and Terry summarized research from four studies made in the area of children's literature. They wrote the following implications from the involved studies:

1. *A literature based language arts programme should begin in kindergarten and continue through the elementary grades;*

2. *A variety of rich... reading materials should be provided for children;*
3. *It is important that teacher consistently read books aloud to their children. Oral language activities—such as discussions of the story, role playing, or puppetry—should frequently be used as follow-ups to reading aloud;*
4. *Children should be encouraged and motivated to increase their independent reading.*

In Summary

Literature is a significant part of the total school curriculum. Each pupil needs to experience a quality children's literature curriculum. The reading curriculum needs to incorporate pupils developing proficiency in diverse word recognition skills, as well as in a variety of purposes involving comprehension. Also, quality literature needs adequate emphasis. Thus, concepts such as the *setting of the story, characterization, plot, point of view, theme, irony of the situation*, as well as *satire* need to be inherent in literature. Each pupil, however, needs to be ready to understand these concepts prior to their implementation in the literature curriculum. Learners individually need to attach interest, meaning, and purpose in ongoing activities and experiences.

REFERENCES

American Library Association. *A Multimedia Approach to Children's Literature*. Chicago: American Library Association. 1972.

Anderson, Paul S. *Language Skills in Elementary Education*. Second Edition. New York: Macmillan, 1972.

Boyd, Gertrude. *Teaching Communication Skills in the Elementary School*. New York: Van Nostrand Reinhold, 1970.

Boyd, Gertrude. *Teaching Poetry in the Elementary Schools*. Columbus, Ohio: Merrill, 1973.

Burrows, Alvina T., Diane L. Monson, and Russell G. Stauffer. *New Horizons in the Language Arts*. New York: Harpot & Row, 1972.

Chambers, Dewey W. *Children's Literature in the Curriculum*. Chicago: Rand McNally and Company, 1971.

Cohen, Monroe D., ed. *Literature with Children*. Washington, D.C.: Association for Childhood Education International, 1972.

Coody, Betty. *Using Literature with Young Children*. Dubuque, Iowa: William C. Brown, 1973.

Corcoran, Gertrude B. *Language Arts in Elementary School: A Modern Linguistic Approach*. New York: Ronald, 1970.

Donoghue, Mildred R. *The Child and the English Language Arts*. Second Edition. Dubuque, Iowa: Wm. C. Brown Publishers, 1975.

Fisher, Carol J., and C. Ann Terry. *Children's Language and the Language Arts*. Second Edition. New York: McGraw-Hill Book Company, 1982.

Greene, Harry A., and Walter T. Petty. *Developing Language Skills in the Elementary Schools*. Fourth Edition. Boston: Allyn in Bacon, 1971.

Haviland, Virginia, ed. *Children's Book of International Interest*. Chicago: American Library Association, 1972.

Hensing, Esther D., ed. *Good and Inexpensive Books for Children*. Washington, D.C.: Association for Childhood Education International, 1972.

Hurlimann, Bettina. *Three Centuries of Children's Book in Europe*. Cleveland: World Publishing, 1968.

Johnson, Edna, et. al. *Anthology of Children's Literature*. Boston: Houghton Mifflin, 1970.

Lamb, Pose, ed. *Literature for Children Series*. Dubuque, Iowa: William C. Brown, 1970.

Lansdale, Bernard J., and Helen K. Mackintosh. *Children Experience Literature*. New York: Random, 1972.

Montebello, Mary S. *Literature for Children: Children's Literature in the Curriculum*. Edited by Pose Lamb. Dubuque, Iowa: William C. Brown, 1972.

Smith, James A. *Adventures is Communication: Language Arts Methods*. Boston: Allyn and Bacon, 1972.

Smith, James Steel. *A Critical Approach to Children's Literature*. New York: McGraw, 1967.

Sutherland, Zena, and May Hill Arbuthnot. *Children and Books*. Seventh edition. Glenview, Illinois: Scott Foresman and Company, 1986.

Tiedt, Tris M., and Sidney W. Tiedt. *Contemporary English in the Elementary School*. Second Edition. Englewood Cliffs, New Jersey: Prentice-Hall, Inc., 1975.

Whitehead, Robert. *Children's Literature: Strategies of Teaching*. Englwood Cliffs, N.J.: Prentice-Hall, 1968.

21

Teaching Additional Languages

Teaching additional languages means teaching a second, third or further language within students' countries of origin or in countries to which they have migrated. Because there are so many languages in the world and so many reasons why students should learn them, the teaching of additional languages is a great challenge and opportunity for educators.

Introduction

For several reasons, we have chosen the last two words in this chapter titled 'Teaching additional language' rather than commonly used terms 'second languages' or 'foreign languages'. Students may actually be learning not a second but a third or fourth language. 'Additional' applies to all, except, of course, the first language learned. An additional language, moreover, may not be foreign since many people in their country may ordinarily speak it. The term 'foreign' can, moreover, suggest strange, exotic or, perhaps, alien—all undesirable connotations. Our choice of the term 'additional' underscores our belief that additional languages are not necessarily inferior nor superior nor a replacement for a student's first language.

Our view is that students should be taught how to use an additional language clearly, accurately and effectively for *genuine* communication. They should read and listen to live language; they should speak and write it in ways that can be understood by native and non-native speakers. Learners, moreover, should eventually be able to produce and comprehend additional languages independently without the aid of a teacher.

We begin by presenting some key general principles of such 'communicative language' teaching and follow with principles about particular kinds of teaching. In each case, we briefly summarize the research, and then discuss classroom practices that follow from it.

Comprehensible Input

Comprehensible input refers to meaningful oral and written language somewhat above the learners' current level of mastery. Such input allows for the acquisition of grammar and vocabulary, which, in turn, makes exposure to additional input more comprehensible. Mere exposure to language is insufficient. Learners must take notice of key features in order for comprehensible input to be beneficial. Although such input is necessary, it is insufficient, as discussed in the next section on opportunities for interaction.

Several classroom-teaching strategies derive from the idea of comprehensible input:

- Teachers should expose their students to listening and reading materials that are somewhat above their current language proficiency levels;
- Students should be asked to understand the material, not merely to reproduce it;
- Teachers should focus the students' attention on key grammar and vocabulary items;
- Students should be asked to guess the meaning of the input based on their prior knowledge of the topic, and on other known words and concepts within the text;
- Teachers should try to create situations within and outside the classroom that expose students to sources of comprehensible input.

Language Opportunities

Learners need opportunities to practice language with one another. Conversations are important since they require attentiveness and involvement on the part of learners. By conversing, they can practise adapting vocabulary and grammar to a particular situation and making their own contributions to the conversation comprehensible.

The best conversations for such learning exchange real information, ideas and feelings among the participations. By engaging in such activities, learners have opportunities to try to make themselves understood. They receive immediate feedback as to whether they were successful and where alternative language is needed. As they engage in such exchanges, learners also receive additional comprehensible input, which further aids language acquisition.

Several classroom-teaching strategies derive from these research findings:

- Teachers should go beyond simple language drills to create opportunities for meaningful interaction in the classroom by using activities in which students employ natural language examples in real language situations;
- Students should be encouraged to work in pairs or small groups, with the teacher serving as an occasionally helpful observer rather than a controlling force;
- Teachers should employ activities in which students have to solve problems in which each party must contribute information that others do not possess and which challenges students' minds;
- When feasible, the tasks should relate to students' needs and interests so as to motivate them;
- Teachers should usually avoid intervening in these activities while they are occurring, but should provide feedback after they conclude.

Language Practice

Communicative-language teaching employs activities that prepare students for natural, appropriate additional-language use outside the classroom. Language is viewed as more than grammar drills and word memorization. The goal is to train students in language skills that enable them to function easily by themselves without their teachers. Students need to learn with language is effective and culturally appropriate in natural discourse. Errors in additional-language learning are a natural part of learning, but they should be detected and corrected early. Supervised by their teachers, students can practice with one another and detect and correct each other's errors.

The teacher's role is not to control and dominate the classroom. Instead, the teacher can present real-language models to the students (comprehensible input), provide information and focus to the language forms being studied, use a limited amount of controlled exercises so that students gain confidence, and then allow students to interact with each other by using language for natural communicative functions. Thus, the classroom should be neither completely learner-centered nor completely teacher-controlled; rather both contribute the learning. In addition to the general classroom implications below, we have included more specific teaching strategies in the sections that follow.

Teachers should not only use traditional language drills in the classroom; they should also:

- Employ freer, open-ended activities (with more than one possible solution) that allow students to experiment with language to develop oral and written fluency;
- Use materials that represent real, natural language, not artificially, constructed textbook language that presents patterns that no speaker would ever use in natural situations. The learning tasks presented by the instructor should mirror real-life language use;
- Provide meaningful feedback to students on how they performed the communicative activities and provide

suggestions for improvement. Feedback should first focus on how well the students did on the communicative aspects of the task and then on the forms used by the student.

Learning Strategies

Classes cannot allow enough time to teach everything about additional languages. If students are taught how to learn on their own, they can acquire vocabulary and language skills by themselves without their teachers. Successful strategies include taking a slow breath to reduce anxiety, raising pertinent questions about difficult points, and being sensitive to the difficulties of others. Other strategies are tricks to memorize words, guessing and then checking meanings, and maximizing opportunities for language practice.

Teachers can employ several techniques for encouraging language-learning strategies:

- Observe students to see which learning strategies lead to better learning;
- Instruct students in strategies that can help them successfully learn and which allow them to become independent;
- Be aware of learners' emotions and use techniques to reduce their anxiety;
- Encourage students to share successful strategies with each other;
- Teach students strategies that can help them compensate when they do not understand or cannot think of a word or phrase.

Listening

Students need to comprehend natural spoken language— in lectures, the media (radio, cinema and television), and in face-to-face conversations. Many students have a greater need to understand than to speak an additional language. Listening is crucial for language acquisition because it provides 'comprehensible input' (previously discussed).

How do we comprehend spoken language? One model is called 'bottom-up' processing. According to this view, we piece together a message by first understanding the smallest units of language—sounds. Then, we connect the sounds together to form words. Our knowledge of words enables us to understand phrases, then sentences, and finally entire passages. An alternative view is known as a 'top-down' approach. In this model, based on our knowledge of the topic and situation, we can figure out the specific meaning of a passage; and sentences, phrases and words that form the message.

Current theory suggests an 'interactive' model, in which listeners simultaneously use both top-down and bottom-up strategies. One strategy compensates for gaps in the other,until the entire messages is understood.

There are many types of listening. Sometimes we listen for the general meaning of a message, sometimes for specific information. At times listening is a one-way process (*e.g.* a lecture or a movie), and at other times it is two-way and involves both listening and speaking as in a conversation. Some listening entails mainly information exchange; other listening may be more social and emotional in which feelings are more prominent.

For listening comprehension, the following teaching strategies can be recommended:

- Before listening to a passage, ask students what they know about the topic in order to remind them of their prior knowledge. A teacher may also preview difficult vocabulary and ideas prior to listening;
- Following the listening, ask students about the general points of the passage;
- In details are to be recalled, allow students to take notes;
- Use natural language for listening passages. It is better to use short pieces of real language at the beginning levels than artificial teacher-made language;

- Use a variety of different listening activities such as one-way and two-way, and informational and emotional.

Speaking

Additional language instruction formerly consisted of students' memorizing dialogues and practising grammar drills. Current research supports a model known as 'communicative competence'. Although students must learn the grammar and vocabulary, these alone do not lead to fluency. Since natural language is unpredictable and speakers arrive at meaning through active communication, students must be taught how to manage real conversation—how to start and end conversations, how to respond appropriately, and how to express their beliefs, opinions and feelings. Students need to learn what is culturally appropriate and how language varies depending on the situations; they may need to learn about people involved, their moods, and other social and cultural factors. A fluent speaker needs to know how to link utterances together to create clear and effective discourse.

Students must also learn how to manage conversations when there are communication breakdowns. These modern views caused changes in the teaching of speaking. Students should engage in 'unscripted' or spontaneous language since that is the nature of usual speaking practices. The teacher's role is to provide language patterns that are needed, guide students in how to form natural language, and then to create opportunities for practice. Teachers must provide judicious coaching and encouragement so that students will actively practice speaking.

When teaching speaking, the following instructional strategies are recommended:

- Present to students the linguistic and vocabulary patterns and make sure they understand how they are formed, when they are used, and their cultural implications;
- Teach students speech acts (to agree/disagree, apologize, make excuses, etc.), forms to manage

conversations (openings, interruptions, closings, etc.), and strategies for round-about speaking when they don't know a specific word;

- Provide controlled practice so students can feel comfortable with the patterns;
- Have students use the patterns in natural language situations that are relevant to their speaking needs. Pretending they are asking for directions or requesting a hotel room are examples;
- Allow the students to make errors, but also provide feedback on what is successful and unsuccessful.

Reading

The ability to read ordinary texts in an additional language is a crucial skill that students should master. Reading, like listening, is an interactive process. Students need to master bottom-up skills: recognizing letters, understanding words and phrases, and comprehending sentences. At the same time, top-down knowledge is important in reading comprehension. Background knowledge enables readers to understand a passage, and to make a sensible guess when a word or phrase is not understood. Efficient readers make use of both top-down and bottom-up strategies; they use one to compensate for lack of knowledge of the other. Therefore, teachers need to provide instruction in both types of strategies in a comprehensive reading programme.

Skilled readers can also adapt their speed to their purpose and the text. Sometimes they read an entire passage carefully and slowly seeking the main ideas, detailed information, the inferences and implications. Sometimes they quickly scan a text to find out the major points or to answer a single question. Such tasks need to be taught. To acquire them, students need to read a wide variety of naturally occurring texts: both literary and non-literary, academic and non-academic, formal and informal. Thus, a reading programme should not only use traditional reading passages, but also contain such things as maps, schedules menus and signs. Finally, a course in reading should include both intensive reading, which is done in classroom situations and emphasizes specific reading skills, and more extensive reading done by students outside of class, which provides additional reading opportunities.

Following from these research findings are several general teaching strategies:

- Teach bottom-up reading skills, such as rapidly processing common words and phrases, and call attention to rhetorical markers such as 'however' and 'therefore';
- Refresh background knowledge before reading a passage;
- Use natural language texts and select material that corresponds to the various types of readings that students will encounter;
- Teach appropriate reading strategies that correspond to the texts and real-life tasks: reading for general meaning, recalling specific information, understanding inferences and implications, skimming, scanning, etc.;
- Provide numerous opportunities for reading, both inside and outside of classes.

Writing

Two major approaches to the teaching of writing have been under discussion for some time. The first, known as the 'product approach', focuses on the final outcome of writing, which is a logical, error-free essay. Students are given a model text, which they study, analysis and then reproduce. Different models are presented for different types of writing.

In contrast is the 'process approach' to writing, which emphasizes the steps a writer goes through when creating a well-written text. Among the stages taught are: *brainstorming* or writing down many ideas that may come to an individual's mind; *outlining*, which organises the ideas into a logical sequence; *drafting*, in which the writer concentrates on the content on the message rather than the form; *revisions* in response to the writer's second thoughts or feedback provided by peers or teachers; *proof-reading* with an emphasis on form; and the *final draft*. All of the processes should be explained, taught and practised by the students.

Some recent research suggests the value of focusing on various writing 'genres' in an effort to identify, compare and contrast writings in different fields, such as science and literature. Rather than three incompatible approaches, a writing programme should integrate product, process and genre writing into a coherent whole. In addition, many students may need special practice in non-academic materials—letters, forms, resumés, lists, etc. These, too, might be appropriately include in writing classes.

The following are some suggestions for teaching writing:

- Teach students the stages necessary to writing: brainstorming, writing a first draft, revising, editing, etc.;
- Provide models of successful writing samples and discuss the features that make them effective;
- Discuss audience expectations of acceptable writing and how different genres use different writing styles;
- Select writing topics that are of interest to the students and represent tasks that students will need to master in future writing;
- Teach students real-life writing tasks like filling out forms, letters, charts, etc.

Grammar

In traditional additional languages courses, teachers spent much time concentrating on formal grammar. Yet, mere presentation of grammatical forms in isolation, followed by drills may not lead to correct use and students may continue making grammatical errors when trying to communicate. Current research suggests that language teaching needs to be more than grammar instruction. Learners need to understand the meaning of the form, as well as the discourse in which the form appears. Students, moreover, may need to practise and master some vocabulary before they can appreciate and benefit from explicit instruction in grammar. It is then, after an error occurs, that the teacher's corrective feedback may be most beneficial.

The following are basic procedures for teaching a grammatical pattern:

- Present the grammar form in natural discourse, explaining how the form is made, any irregular forms, and any spelling or pronunciation issues;
- Provide numerous examples of natural language in which the form can be studied and provide any contextual information on how to use the form appropriately;
- Make sure the students can recognize the form and its functions, before asking the students to produce the form;
- Provide activities that allow students to use the form in natural communicative ways, not just in simple drills;
- If efforts occur, provide meaningful feedback on what forms should be used and why, but remember it often takes time for students to master a form completely.

Comprehensible Pronunciation

Researchers have debated whether it is possible for older additional-language learners to obtain a native-like accent. Most agree that few such students can achieve a native-like accent. For most communication purposes, it is generally unimportant to do so. Students need to develop the ability to be understood by other speakers, not to sound like a native. Pronunciation must be comprehensible and not detract from the understanding of a message. Thus, teachers must work on the pronunciation of individual sounds, both vowels and consonants and on the various sound combinations.

Of equal importance is teaching the intonation, stress and rhyme patterns of the additional language, which often block effective communication. Inability in these areas causes more communication problems than the inaccurate pronunciation of individual sounds.

In teaching pronunciation, students need practice in natural contexts. Feedback is an essential part of pronunciation instruction, since students may not be able to evaluate how successful they are in creating the pattern. When selecting a pronunciation feature, the instructor should illustrate how native language patterns may facilitate or hinder communication in the additional language.

Several teaching strategies should be helpful in teaching pronunciation:

- Teach students to listen carefully to pronunciation. Often contrasting it with another pattern will enable them to recognize the important differences;
- Encourage students to use the pattern in isolation and then in natural sentence contexts;
- Students should also use the pattern in sentences of their own making;
- Teach students to produce correct intonation, stress and rhythm;
- Learning pronunciation is difficult and takes time. Difficult patterns may need re-teaching.

Conclusion

In closing this brief account of effective additional language teaching, three points deserve emphasis:

- The various language skills discussed above should be integrated in realistic language situations. In preparing a report, for example, students may need to read and write. They may also need to discuss their ideas with their peers, which entails listening and speaking. Imagining particular language situations may make it clear how to integrate the various language skills;

- Since useful language facility requires comprehension and fluency in ordinary, non-academic settings, paper-and-pencil tests will ordinarily be insufficient by themselves. A broader approach would include assessment of students' comprehension of a variety of naturally spoken language passages and ability to respond fluently in conversations;
- In designing and teaching courses for additional languages, educators should assess students' prior language abilities and cultural experience, their specific language needs, the situations in which they will use the additional language, and the proficiency level expected. From this assessment, they can select appropriate course material and activities that are authentic, motivating and challenging.

REFERENCES

Aebersold, J.; Field, M. 1997. *From Reader to Reading: Issues and Strategies in Second Language Classrooms*. Cambridge, United Kingdom, Cambridge University Press.

Anderson, N. 1999. *Second-Language Reading: Issues and Strategies*. Boston, MA, Heinle and Heinle.

Br[illegible]n, B. 1992. *Listening to Spoken Language*. 2nd ed. London, Longman.

Brow[illegible] [illegible].; Yule, G. 1983. *Teaching the Spoken Language*. Cambridge, United Kingdom, Cambridge University Press.

Brumfit, C. 1984. *Communicative Methodology in Language Teaching*. Cambridge, United Kingdom, Cambridge University Press.

Bygate, M. 1987. *Speaking*. Oxford, United Kingdom, Oxford University Press.

Campbell, C. 1999. *Teaching Second-Language Writing: Interacting with Text*. Boston, MA, Heinle and Heinle.

Celce-Murcia, M. 1991. *Teaching English as a Second or Foreign Language*. 2nd ed. New York,. Newbury House.

—. 1991. Grammar Pedagogy in Second- and Foreign-Language Teaching. *TESOL Quarterly* (Alexandria, VA), No. 25, p. 459-80.

Celce-Murica, M.; Brinton D.; Goodwin, J. 1996. *Teaching Pronunciation: A Reference for Teaching of English to Speakers of Other Languages*. Cambridge, United Kingdom, Cambridge University Press.

Celce-Murcia, M.; Larsen-Freeman, D. 1999. *The Grammar Book: An ESL/EFL Teacher's Guide*. 2nd ed. Boston, MA, Heinle and Heinle.

Day, R.; Bamford J. 1988. *Extensive Reading in the Second-language Classroom*. Cambridge, United Kingdom, Cambridge University Press.

Doughty, C.; Pica T. 1986. 'Information Gap' Tasks: Do They Facilitate Second-Language Acquisition? *TESOL Quarterly* (Alexandria, VA), No. 20. p. 305-25.

Ellis, R. 1988. *Classroom Second-Language Development*. London, Prentice-Hall.

— 1990. *Instructed Language Acquisition*. London, Blackwell.

Ferris, D.; Hedgcock, J. 1998. *Teaching ESL Composition: Purpose, Process and Practice*. Hillsdale, NJ, Erlbaum.

Hadley, A. 1993. *Teaching Language in Context*. Boston, MA, Heinle and Heinle.

Kenworthy, J. 1987. *Teaching English Pronunciation*. London, Longman.

Krashen, S. 1982. *Principles and Practices in Second-Language Acquisition*. Oxford, Pergamon.

Lightbown, P.; Spade, N. 1993. *How Languages are Learned*. Oxford United Kingdom, Oxford University Press.

Long, M.; Porter, P. 1985. Group Work, Interlanguage Tasks and Second-Language Acquisition. *TESOL Quarterly* (Alexandria, VA), No. 19, p. 207-27.

McCarthy, M.; Carter, R. 1994. *Language as Discourse: Perspectives for Language Teachers*. London, Longman.

Mendelsohn, D. 1994. *Learning to Listen*. San Diego, CA, Domine Press.

Morley, J. 1994. *Pronunciation Pedagogy and Theory: New Views, New Dimensions*. Alexandria, VA, TESOL.

Nunan, D. 1991. *Language Teaching Methodology*. London, Prentice-Hall.

—. 1999. *Second Language Teaching and Learning*. Boston, MA, Heinle and Heinle.

O'Malley, J.; Chamot, A. 1990. *Learning Strategies in Second-Language Acquisition*. Cambridge, United Kingdom, Cambridge University Press.

Oxford, R. 1990. *Language Learning Strategies: What Every Teacher Should Know*. New York, Newbury House/Harper and Row.

Reid, J. 1993. *Teaching ESL Writing*. Englewood Cliffs, NJ, Prentice-Hall/Regents.

Rust, M. 1990. *Listening in language Learning*. London, Longman.

Savignon, S. 1991. Communicative Language Teaching: State of the Art. *TESOL Quarterly* (Alexandria, VA), No. 25, p. 261-77.

Wendon, A. 1991. *Learner Strategies for Learner Autonomy*. Englewood Cliffs, NJ, Prentice-Hall.

Williams, J. 1995. Focus on Form in Communicative Language Teaching: Research Findings and he Classroom Teacher. *TESOL Journal* (Alexandria, VA), Vol. 4, No. 4, p. 12-16.

Authors' Addresses

Prof. Elliot L. Judd, University of Illinois of Chicago, U.S.A.

Prof. Lihua Tan, Guizhou, University of Technology, China.

Prof. Herbert J. Walberg, University of Illinois at Chicago, USA.

Courtesy: International Academy of Education, Brussels, Belgium and UNESCO's International Bureau of Education, Geneva, Switzerland.

Bibliography

Reference Books for Additional Reading

Bhaskara Rao, Digumarti (1994). *Scientific Aptitude*. New Delhi: Ashish Publishing House. pp: 100.

Bhaskara Rao, Digumarti (1995). *Animal Kingdom*. New Delhi: Discovery Publishing House.

Bhaskara Rao, Digumarti (1995). *Batracology*. New Delhi: Discovery Publishing House.

Bhaskara Rao, Digumarti (1996). *Scientific Attitude vis-a-vis Scientific Aptitude*. New Delhi: Discovery Publishing House.

Bhaskara Rao, Digumarti, ed. (1996). *Encyclopaedia of Education For All*. 5 Vols. New Delhi: APH Publishing Corporation.

Vol. I Education For All: The World Conference.

Vol. II Education For All: The EPA-9 Summit.

Vol. III Education For All: Quality Education For All.

Vol. IV Education For All: Planning and Monitoring.

Vol. V Education For All: The Indian Scenario.

Bhaskara Rao, Digumarti, ed. (1996). *Global Perceptions on Peace Education*, 3 Vols. New Delhi: Discovery Publishing House.

Bhaskara Rao, Digumarti, ed. (1996). *National Policy on Education*, 2 Vols. New Delhi: Anmol Publications Pvt. Ltd.

Bhaskara Rao, Digumarti, ed. (1997). *Care the Child*, 2 Vols. New Delhi: Discovery Publishing House.

Bhaskara Rao, Digumarti, ed. (1997). *Education for the 21st Century*. New Delhi: Discovery Publishing House.

Bhaskara Rao, Digumarti, ed. (1997). *Reflections on Scientific Attitude*. New Delhi: Discovery Publishing House.

Bhaskara Rao, Digumarti (1997). *Scientific Attitude*. New Delhi: Discovery Publishing House.

Bhaskara Rao, Digumarti, ed. (1997). *Success Story of a Primary Education Project*. New Delhi: APH Publishing Corporation.

Bhaskara Rao, Digumarti, ed. (1997). *World Food Summit*. New Delhi: Discovery Publishing House.

Bhaskara Rao, Digumarti, ed. (1998). *Adolescence Education*. New Delhi: Discovery Publishing House.

Bhaskara Rao, Digumarti, ed. (1998). *Community and School Nutrition Education*. New Delhi: Discovery Publishing House.

Bhaskara Rao, Digumarti, ed. (1998). *District Primary Education Programme*. New Delhi: Discovery Publishing House.

Bhaskara Rao, Digumarti, ed. (1998). *Earth Summit*, 2 Vols. New Delhi: Discovery Publishing House.

Bhaskara Rao, Digumarti, ed. (1998). *National Policy on Education: Towards an Enlightened and Humane Society*. New Delhi: Discovery Publishing House.

Bhaskara Rao, Digumarti, ed. (1998). *Reforming School Education*. New Delhi: Discovery Publishing House.

Bhaskara Rao, Digumarti, ed. (1998). *Teacher Education in India*. New Delhi: Discovery Publishing House.

Bhaskara Rao, Digumarti, ed. (1998). *World Summit for Social Development*. New Delhi: Discovery Publishing House.

Bhaskara Rao, Digumarti, ed. (2000). *Education For All: Achieving the Goal*. 3 Vols. New Delhi: APH Publishing Corporation.

Vol. I The Global Consensus.

Vol. II Mid-Decade Review Reports of Regional Seminars.

Vol. III Issues and Trends.

Bhaskara Rao, Digumarti, ed. (2000). *International Encyclopaedia of AIDS*, 11 Vols in 13 Parts. New Delhi: Discovery Publishing House.

Vol. 1 Introduction to HIV/AIDS.

Vol. 2 HIV/AIDS—Issues and Challenges, 2 Parts.

Vol. 3 HIV/AIDS—Socio Economic Realities.

Vol. 4 HIV/AIDS Law Ethics and Human Rights, 2 Parts.

Vol. 5 AIDS and NGOs.

Vol. 6 AIDS and Home Care.

Vol. 7 STD Case Management.

Vol. 8 HIV Prevention and Care—Teaching Modules for Nurses and Midwives.

Vol. 9 HIV/AIDS Prevention Education for Educational Institutions.

Vol. 10 Instructional Modules for AIDS Education.

Vol. 11 School Health Education to Prevent AIDS and STD—A Package for Curriculum Planners.

Bhaskara Rao, Digumarti, ed. (2000). *International Encyclopaedia of Science and Technology Education*. 11 Volumes. New Delhi: Discovery Publishing House.

Vol. 1 Science and Technology Education.

Vol. 2 Science Education in Developing Countries.

Vol. 3 Organisational Structure of Science.

Vol. 4 Science Education in Asia and the Pacific.

Vol. 5 Science and Technology Education for All.

Vol. 6 Values, Ethics, Talent and Girls in Science and Technology Education.

Vol. 7 Popularization of Science and Technology Education.

Vol. 8 Science, Power and Society.

Vol. 9 Information Technology.

Vol. 10 Teacher Training in Science and Technology Education.

Vol. 11 Science, Technology and Society: A Curriculum Framework.

Bhaskara Rao, Digumarti, ed. (2001). *Distance Education in Different Countries*. New Delhi: APH Publishing Corporation.

Bhaskara Rao, Digumarti, ed. (2001). *Decentralised Management of Education (Management of Education in Panchayati Raj and Municipal Bodies)*. New Delhi: Discovery Publishing House.

Bhaskara Rao, Digumarti, ed. (2001). *Electrochemistry for Environmental Protection*. New Delhi: Discovery Publishing House.

Bhaskara Rao, Digumarti, ed. (2001). *Global Educational Studies*. New Delhi: Discovery Publishing House.

Bhaskara Rao, Digumarti, ed. (2001). *Global Synthesis of Educational Assessment*. New Delhi: Discovery Publishing House.

Bhaskara Rao, Digumarti, ed. (2001). *International Encyclopaedia of Human Rights*, 7 Volumes in 13 Parts. New Delhi: Discovery Publishing House.

Vol. 1 International Instruments of Human Rights, 2 Parts.

Vol. 2 Regional Instruments of Human Rights.

Vol. 3 Human Rights and The United Nations, 2 Parts.

Vol. 4 Fact Files of Human Rights, 2 Parts

Vol. 5 Study Stories of Human Rights, 3 Parts

Vol. 6 International Meetings on Human Rights, 2 Parts.

Vol. 7 Professional Training in Human Rights.

Bhaskara Rao, Digumarti, ed. (2001). *Jomtein Decade of Education*. New Delhi: Discovery Publishing House.

Bhaskara Rao, Digumarti, ed. (2001). *Nuclear Materials: Issues and Concerns*, 2 Vols. New Delhi: Discovery Publishing House.

Bhaskara Rao, Digumarti, ed. (2001). *World Conference on Education for All*. New Delhi: APH Publishing Corporation.

Bhaskara Rao, Digumarti, ed. (2001) *World Conference on Higher Education*. New Delhi: Discovery Publishing House.

Bhaskara Rao, Digumarti, ed. (2001). *World Conference on Science*. New Delhi: Discovery Publishing House.

Bhaskara Rao, Digumarti, ed. (2003). *Chernobyl: Never Again*. New Delhi: Discovery Publishing House.

Bhaskara Rao, Digumarti, ed. (2003). *Habitat Agenda*. New Delhi: Discovery Publishing House.

Bhaskara Rao, Digumarti, ed. (2002). *Inspiring Experiences in Teacher Education*. New Delhi: Discovery Publishing House.

Bhaskara Rao, Digumarti, ed. (2002). *International Studies in Education*. New Delhi: Discovery Publishing House.

Bhaskara Rao, Digumarti, ed. (2002). *Military Conversion: Impact on Science and Technology*. New Delhi: Discovery Publishing House.

Bhaskara Rao, Digumarti, ed. (2003). *Virology and Immunology*. New Delhi: Discovery Publishing House.

Bhaskara Rao, Digumarti, ed. (2002). *United Nations Millennium Summit*. New Delhi: Discovery Publishing House.

Bhaskara Rao, Digumarti, ed, (2003). *World Assembly on Aging*. New Delhi: Discovery Publishing House.

Bhaskara Rao, Digumarti,'ed. (2003). *World Conference on Human Rights*. New Delhi: Discovery Publishing House.

Bhaskara Rao, Digumarti, ed. (2002). *World Education Forum*. New Delhi: Discovery Publishing House.

Bhaskara Rao, Digumarti, ed. (2003). *Education Employment and Human Resource Development*. New Delhi: Discovery Publishing House.

Bhaskara Rao, Digumarti, C.A.P. Swamy and B.S.V. Dutt (1997). *Self Evaluation in Student Teaching*. New Delhi: Discovery Publishing House.

Bhaskara Rao, Digumarti, C. Sridevi and K. Vijaya (1995). *Achievement in Social Studies*. New Delhi: Discovery Publishing House.

Bhaskara Rao, Digumarti and Digumarti Pushpa Latha (1994). *Achievement in Biology*. New Delhi: Discovery Publishing House.

Bhaskara Rao, Digumarti and Digumarti Pushpa Latha (1995). *Achievement in English*. New Delhi: Discovery Publishing Company.

Bhaskara Rao, Digumarti and Digumarti Pushpa Latha (1995). *Achievement in Science*. New Delhi: Discovery Publishing House.

Bhaskara Rao, Digumarti and Digumarti Pushpa Latha (1995). *Achievement in Mathematics*. New Delhi: Discovery Publishing House.

Bhaskara Rao, Digumarti and Digumarti Pushpa Latha, eds. (1998). *International Encyclopaedia of Women*, 5 Vols. New Delhi: Discovery Publishing House.

Vol. 1 Status of World's Women.

Vol. 2 Women, Education and Empowerment.

Vol. 3 Women Challenges and Advancement.

Vol. 4 Women and Family Health.

Vol. 5 Women and International Action.

Bhaskara Rao, Digumarti, Digumarti Pushpa Latha and Digumarti Harshitha. eds. (2001). *Biological Warfare*. New Delhi: Discovery Publishing House.

Bhaskara Rao, Digumarti, Digumatri Pushpa Latha and Digumarti Harshitha, eds. (2001). *Women as Educators*. New Delhi: Discovery Publishing House.

Bhaskara Rao, Digumarti and Digumarti Harshitha (2000). *Education in India*. New Delhi: APH Publishing Corporation.

Bhaskara Rao, Digumarti, and Digumarti Harshitha eds. (2001). *Assessing Learning Achievement*. New Delhi: Discovery Publishing House.

Bhaskara Rao, Digumarti and Digumarti Harshita, eds. (2001). *Energy Security*. New Delhi: Discovery Publishing House.

Bhaskara Rao, Digumarti, D. Harshitha and K.R.S.S. Rao, eds. (1999). *Advanced Biotechnology*. New Delhi: Discovery Publishing House.

Bhaskara Rao, Digumarti and D. Sridhar (2002). *Job Satisfaction of School Teachers*. New Delhi: Discovery Publishing House.

Bhaskara Rao, Digumarti and K.R.S. Sambasiva Rao, eds. (1996). *Current Trends in Indian Education*. New Delhi: Discovery Publishing House.

Bhaskara Rao, Digumarti and K. Vijaya (1995). *A Text Book Evaluation*. Ambala Cantt: The Associated Publishers.

Bhaskara Rao, Digumarti and N.V.M. Mohana Rao (2002). *Problems of Mentally Handicapped*. New Delhi: Discovery Publishing House.

Bhaskara Rao, Digumarti, V.V. Rao, V.V. Lakshmi and V.V. Krishna, eds. (2000). *Status and Advancement of Women*. New Delhi: APH Publishing Corporation.

Babu, P.C. and Digumarti Bhaskara Rao, ed. (2003). *Flowers of Wisdom*. New Delhi: Discovery Publishing House.

Bhagya Lakshmi, Lingineni and Digumarti Bhaskara Rao, ed. (2000). *Reading and Comprehension*. New Delhi: Discovery Publishing House.

Bhuvaneswara Lakshmi, G. and Digumarti Bhaskara Rao, ed. (2000). *Attitude Towards Science*. New Delhi: Discovery Publishing House.

Bhaskara Rao, Digumarti. (1996). *Dhrushya Sravana Bodhanapakaranamulu* (Audio Visual Teaching Aids). Guntur: Nagarjuna Publishers.

Bhaskara Rao, Digumarti (1993). *Jeevasashtra Bodhana* (Teaching of Biology. Guntur: Nagarjuna Publishers.

Bhaskara Rao, Digumarti (1995). *Vignanasasthra Bodhana*. (Teaching of Science). Guntur: Nagarjuna Publishers.

Bhaskara Rao, Digumarti (1997). *Vidya Manovignana Sashtram*. (Educational Psychology). Guntur: Creative Press.

Bhaskara Rao, Digumarti (1998). *DSC Study Material*. Guntur: Nagarjuna Publishers.

Bhaskara Rao, Digumarti (1998). *Upadhyayudu Vidya* (Teacher and Education). Guntur: Nagarjuna Publishers.

Bhaskara Rao, Digumarti (1998). *Vidya Dhrukpadhalu*. (Perspectives of Education). Guntur: Nagarjuna Publishers.

Bhaskara Rao, Digumarti (1999). *EdCET Teaching Aptitude*. Guntur Nagarjuna Publishers.

Bhaskara Rao, Digumarti (2001). *Bharata Samajamulo Upadhayayudu Vidya* (Teacher and Education in Emerging Indian Society). Guntur: Nagarjuna Publishers.

Bhaskara Rao, Digumarti (2001). *Bhoutika Sastra Bodhana Padhatulu* (Methods of Teaching Physical Science). Guntur Nagarjuna Publishers.

Bhaskara Rao, Digumarti (2001). *Jeeva Sastra Bodhana Padhatulu* (Methods of Teaching Biological Science). Guntur: Nagarjuna Publishers.

Bhaskara Rao, Digumarti (2001). *Vidya Manovignana Sastram* (Educational Psychology). Guntur: Nagarjuna Publishers.

Devraj, T.A.S. and Digumarti Bhaskara Rao, ed. (1997). *Trace Analysis of Uranium and Thorium*. New Delhi: Discovery Publishing House.

Durgani Rani, K. and Digumarti Bhaskara Rao, ed. (2000). *Educational Aspirations and Scientific Attitudes*. New Delhi: Discovery Publishing House.

Dutt, B.S.V. and Digumarti Bhaskara Rao (2001). *Empowering Primary Teachers*. New Delhi: Discovery Publishing House.

Ediger, Marlow and Digumarti Bhaskara Rao (1996). *Science Curriculum*. New Delhi: Discovery Publishing House.

Ediger, Marlow and Digumarti Bhaskara Rao (2000). *Teaching Mathematics Successfully*. New Delhi: Discovery Publishing House.

Ediger, Marlow and Digumarti Bhaskara Rao (2000). *Teaching Reading Successfully*. New Delhi: Discovery Publishing House.

Ediger, Marlow and Digumarti Bhaskara Rao (2001). *Teaching Science Successfully*. New Delhi: Discovery Publishing House.

Ediger, Marlow and Digumarti Bhaskara Rao (2001). *Teaching Social Studies Successfully*. New Delhi: Discovery Publishing House.

Ediger, Marlow and Digumarti Bhaskara Rao (2002). *Philosophy and Curriculum*. New Delhi: Discovery Publishing House.

Ediger, Marlow and Digumarti Bhaskara Rao (2002). *Improving School Administration*. New Delhi: Discovery Publishing House.

Ediger, Marlow and Digumarti Bhaskara Rao (2002). *Elementary Curriculum*. New Delhi: Discovery Publishing House.

Ediger, Marlow and Digumarti Bhaskara Rao (2002). *Language Arts Curriculum*. New Delhi: Discovery Publishing House.

Jayasree, Kandi and Digumarti Bhaskara Rao, ed. (1999). *Correlates of Socialisation*. New Delhi: Discovery Publishing House.

John Babu, Ch., T.J.R. Prasad, G.M. Madhukar and Digumarti Bhaskara Rao, eds. (2001). *Problem Solving in Mathematics*. New Delhi: APH Publishing Corporation.

Jyothi, Nirmala and Digumarti Bhaskara Rao, ed. (2002). *Non-Detention System in Education*. New Delhi: Discovery Publishing House.

Marja, Talvi and Digumarti Bhaskara Rao, eds. (1996). *Educational Leadership and Social Changes*. New Delhi: Discovery Publishing House.

Prabhakaram, K.S. and Digumarti Bhaskara Rao, ed. (1998). *Concept Attainment Model in Mathematics Teaching*. New Delhi: Discovery Publishing House.

Prasanth Kumar, J. and Digumarti Bhaskara Rao, ed. (1998). *Effectiveness of Distance Education System*. New Delhi: Discovery Publishing House.

Prasanth Kumar, J. and Digumarti Bhaskara Rao and G. Sundara Rao ed. (2000). *Open University Student Support Services*. New Delhi: Discovery Publishing House.

Ram Kumar, Ratnam and Digumarti Bhaskara Rao (2002). *Dukka: Suffering in Early Buddhism*. New Delhi: Discovery Publishing House.

Ramatulasamma K. and Digumarti Bhaskara Rao, ed. (2002). *Job Satisfaction of Teacher Educators*. New Delhi: Discovery Publishing House.

Rama Krishnaiah, D. and Digumarti Bhaskara Rao, ed. (1998). *Job Satisfaction of College Teachers*. New Delhi: Discovery Publishing House.

Ramesh, Ganta and Digumarti Bhaskara Rao, eds. (1998). *Environmental Education: Problems and Prospects*. New Delhi: Discovery Publishing House.

Rathaiah, L. and Digumarti Bhaskara Rao, eds. (1997). *International Innovations in Education*. New Delhi: Discovery Publishing House.

Rathaiah, Lavu, Digumarti Bhaskara Rao and Paturi Koteswara Rao. (1997) *Achievement Correlates*. New Delhi: Discovery Publishing House.

Reddy, Sudhakar and Digumarti Bhaskara Rao, ed. (2002). *Creativity in Adolescents*. New Delhi: Discovery Publishing House.

Sanjeeva Rao, P.C. and Digumarti Bhaskara Rao, ed. (1996). *A Text Book of Geology*. New Delhi: Discovery Publishing House.

Satya Narayana, V. and Digumarti Bhaskara Rao, ed. (2001). *Physical Education, Social Attitudes and Leadership Qualities*. New Delhi: Discovery Publishing House.

Srinivasulu Reddy, M., K R.S. Sambasiva Rao and Digumarti Bhaskara Rao, ed. (1999) *A Text Book of Agriculture*. New Delhi: Discovery Publishing House.

Vanaja, M. and Digumarti Bhaskara Rao, ed. (1999). *Inquiry Training Model*. New Delhi: Discovery Publishing House.

Valeri V. Koustiouk and Digumarti Bhaskara Rao, ed. (2002). *A Text Book of Cryogenics*. New Delhi: Discovery Publishing House.

Valeri V. Koustiouk and Digumarti Bhaskara Rao, ed. (2003). *Refrigiration and Environment*. New Delhi: Discovery Publishing House.

Veena Kumari, Balusu and Digumarti Bhaskara Rao (1996). *Operation Black Board*. New Delhi: APH Publishing Corporation.

Veena Kumari, B. and Digumarti Bhaskara Rao, ed. (2000). *Psycho-Social Correlates of Achievement*. New Delhi: Discovery Publishing House.

Venkata Rao, P. and Digumarti Bhaskara Rao (1989). *A Text Book of Zoology—Junior Intermediate*. Guntur: Vignan Publishers.

Venkata Rao, P. and Digumarti Bhaskara Rao (1989). *A Text Book of Zoology—Senior Intermediate*. Guntur: Vignan Publishers.

Venugopala Rao, K. and Digumarti Bhaskara Rao, ed. (2000). *Teacher Morale in Secondary School*, New Delhi: Discovery Publishing House.

Vidya, C. and Digumarti Bhaskara Rao, ed. (1996). *A Text Book of Nutrition*. New Delhi: Discovery Publishing House.

Vijaya Bharathi, D. and Digumarti Bhaskara Rao, ed. (2000). *Educational Philosophies of Swami Vivekanand and John Dewey*. New Delhi: APH Publishing Corporation.

Index